Glyphs of Uncertain Meaning

Tim Gaze

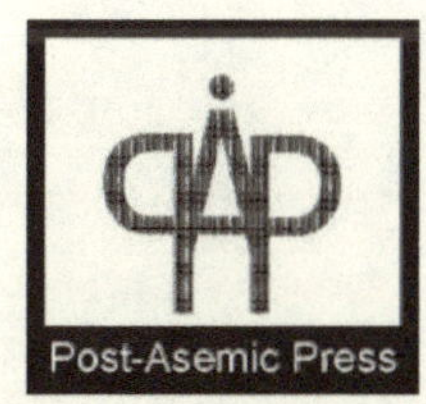

Post-Asemic Press 014

ISBN: 978-1-7348662-3-0

postasemicpress.wordpress.com

Contact: postasemicpress@gmail.com

Postasemicpress.blogspot.com

Cover art by Tim Gaze

Author’s preface by Tim Gaze

There is an art of writing which starts with letters rather than words, and explores ways they can be broken down, distorted and recombined. The letters, symbols and marks I use in my writing are best described as “glyphs”. Between 1998 and approximately 2008, I created many pages of improvised combinations of glyphs, some of them familiar and easily recognizable, and some not. A variety of writing tools was used: pens, pencils, marker pens, Chinese brush with bottled ink, and atomiser spray bottle with ink. Almost always, they were made on ordinary white A4 sized office paper.

The process of reading these glyphs is up to the reader. Regular reading of pages full of words is like walking on a level path with no obstacles, so that most readers travel at full steam ahead to get to the end of each page. In this collection, the idea isn't to read each page quickly and then turn the page. You are invited to ponder, even to find partial meanings or no meaning at all, at whatever speed works for you.

Some of these are well-balanced and are perhaps beautiful in the same way as calligraphy. Others are clumsy and perhaps ugly to many readers. I'm interested in the way meaning might be found in these glyphs, rather than whether or not they are conventionally beautiful. Instead of applying aesthetics, I hope you can find a sense of purposefulness, although the purpose might be mysterious and difficult to fathom. Different readers will come to different understandings of each of my glyph compositions.

If you need some sort of theory to justify this approach, the ideas of the linguist Roy Harris could be useful. To paraphrase him, every time we write is an act of improvisation, with the potential to produce something new, and every time we read is an act of improvisation, with the potential to find meanings not anticipated by the writer.

Henri Michaux is an obvious influence on my style. However, his work has been difficult to obtain in Australia. I first saw *Mouvements* around 1999, *Narration* and *Alphabets* a few years after that, and books such as *Saisir* a few years further on. So, I became familiar with Michaux while already exploring a similar area. International graffiti culture was also a big influence, especially the use of broad tip marker pens. My own limitations at neatly writing also shape what I do.

Over the time period in which these glyphs were created, I immersed myself in as much Chinese visual culture as I could lay hands on, especially cursive calligraphy and ancient pictographic signs. To a lesser extent, I explored Korean and Japanese visual culture. In the 20th century, Japanese calligraphers developed the controversial "single character" and "calligraphy of few characters" styles. My creations are similarly minimal compositions, without claiming to be calligraphy. If I'm approaching East Asian brush calligraphy traditions, it is as a baby ogre or barbarian child.

Some examples of concrete poetry and visual poetry from the 20th century use handwriting, although most include clearly legible words. In the 21st century, works similar to mine are published as visual poetry, although I wouldn't describe many of my glyph compositions as visual poems. I'll repeat what I said above, that there is another art of writing at a deeper level than words, which cannot comfortably be described as prose or poetry.

The term "asemic writing" is quite widely used for writing which isn't legible (or at least which doesn't contain legible words). My glyphs probably are asemic writing, although some of them are at least partly legible. If you get words out of my glyphs, then they're not asemic for you.

I'm an English-speaking Anglo-Celtic Australian man, attempting to transcend my origins, upbringing and geographical location to reach for a form of expression which can communicate across cultures, and speak to readers beyond the English language and Roman alphabet. My book could be seen as multicultural, or as part of a new, global culture.

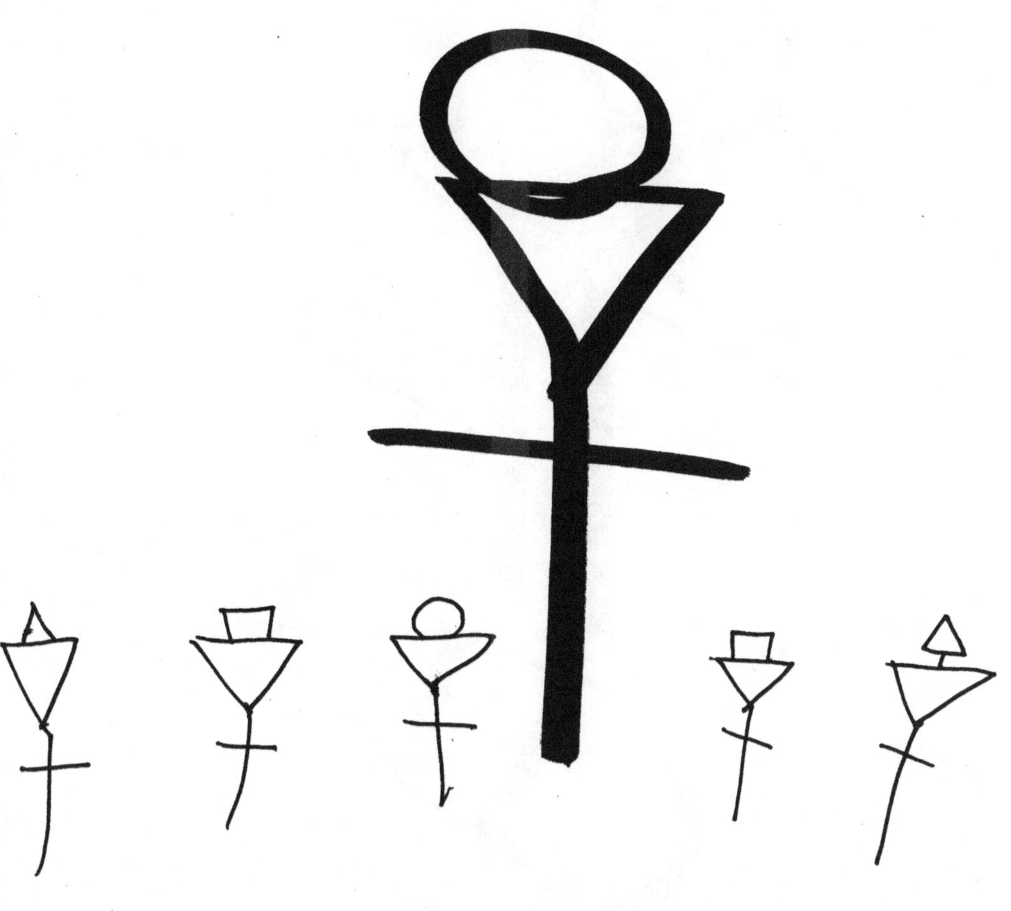

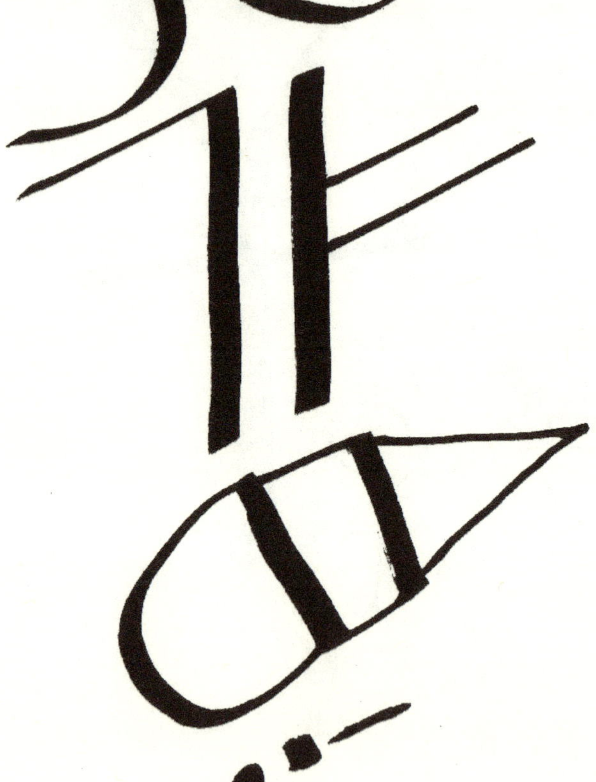

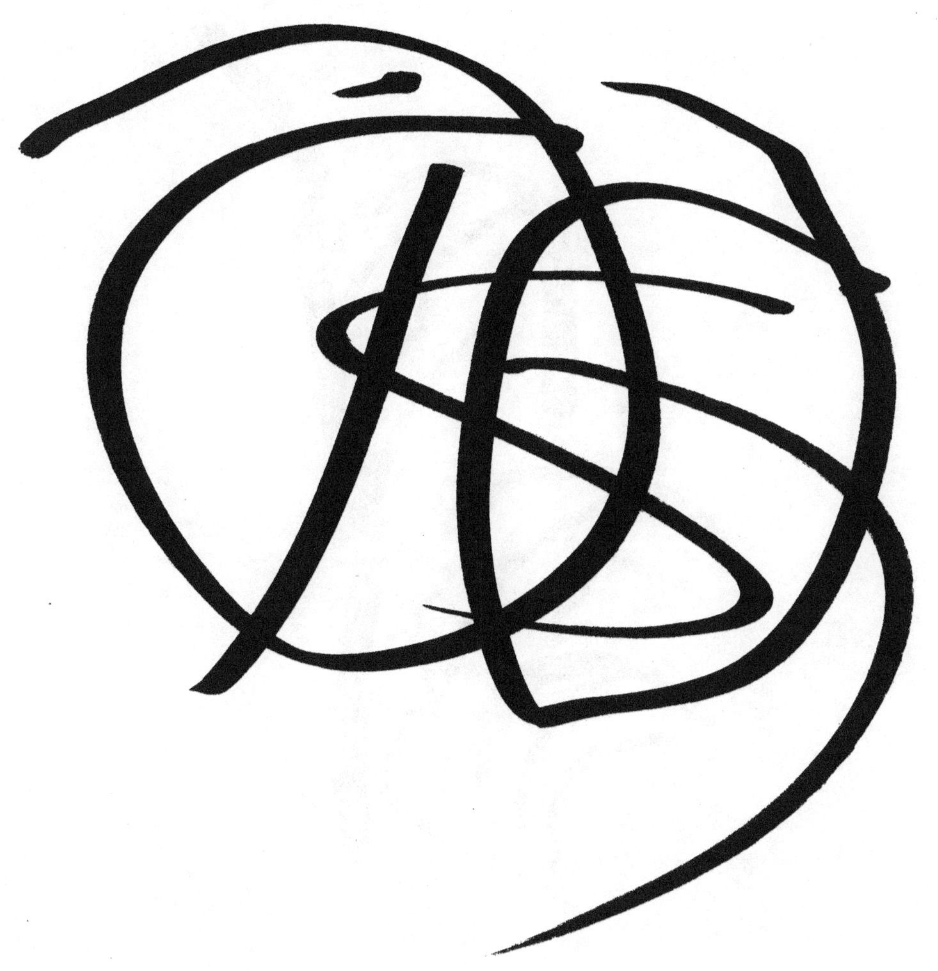

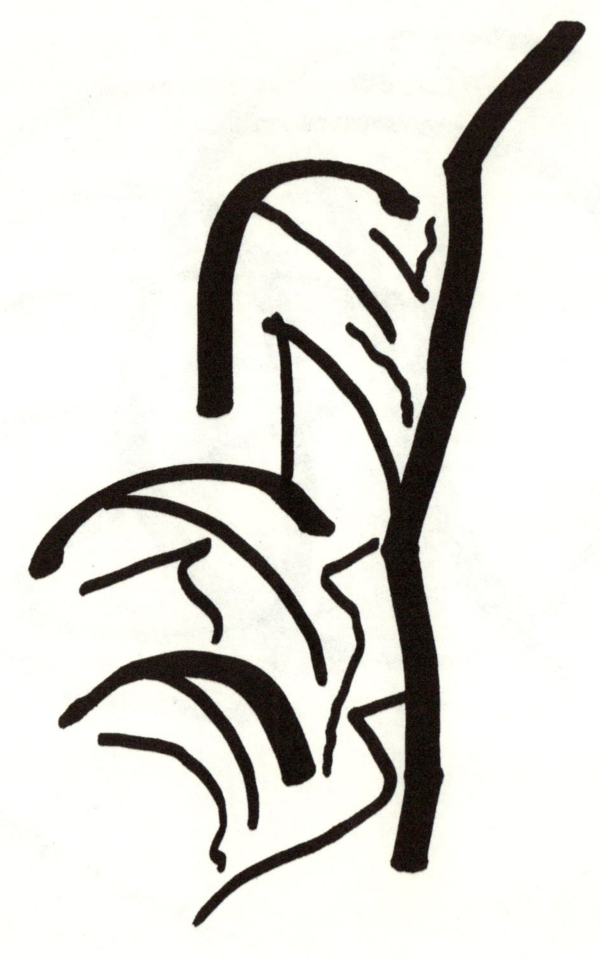

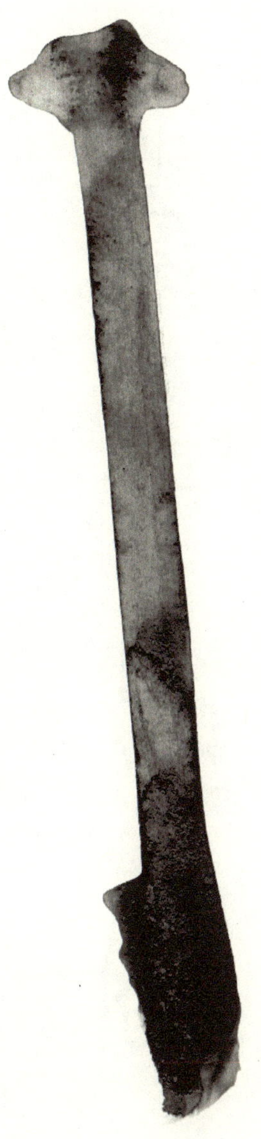

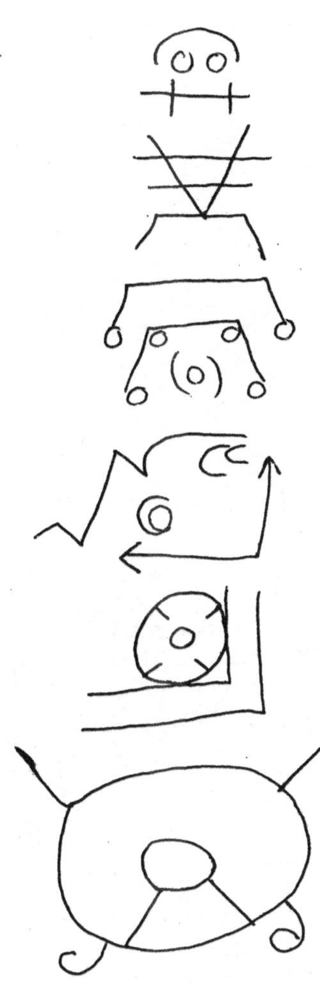

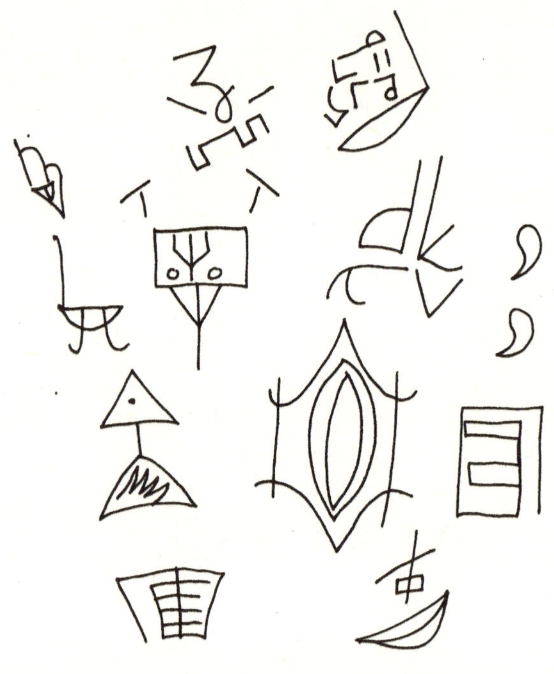

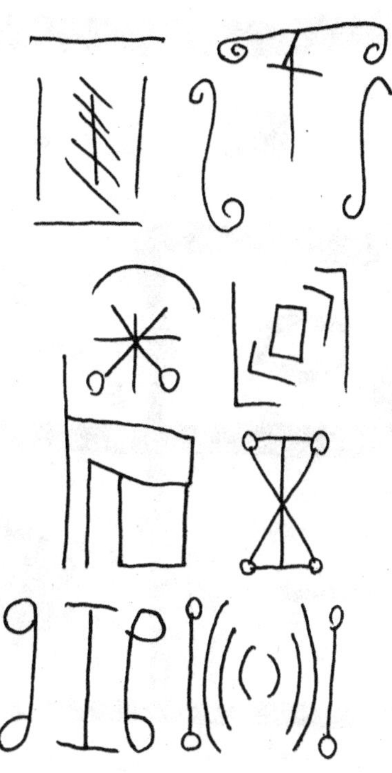

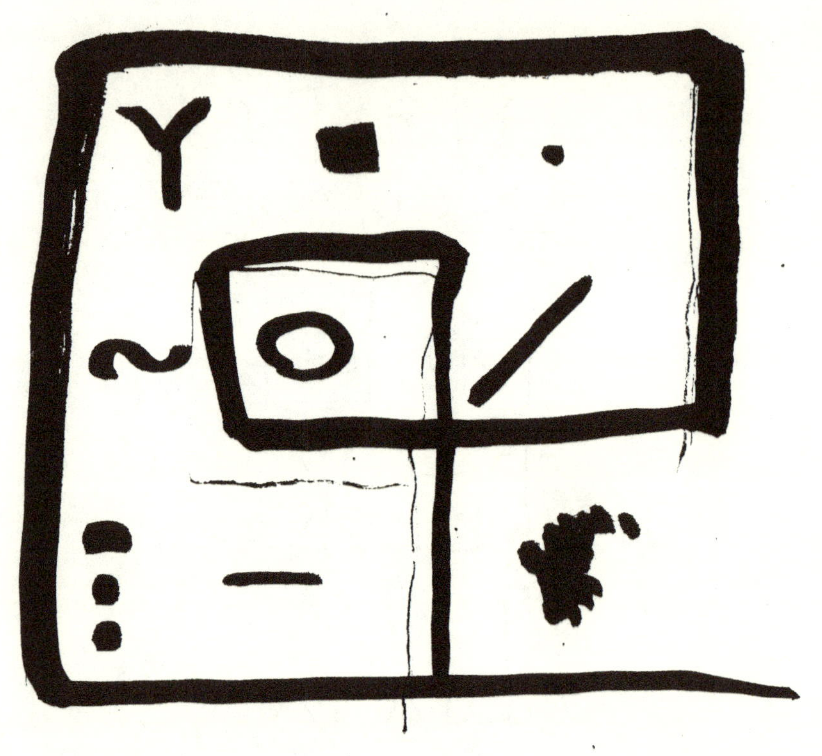

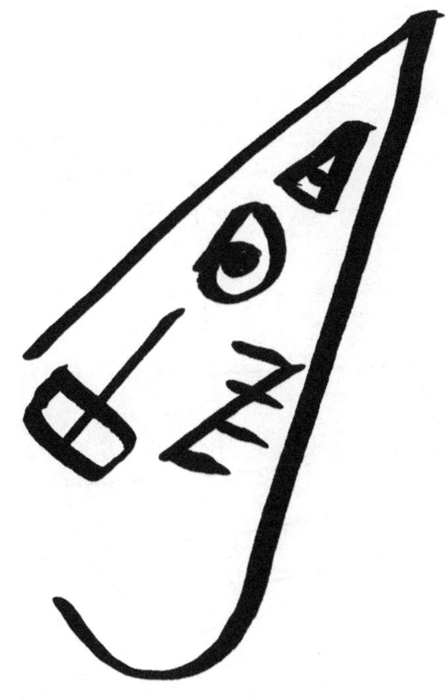

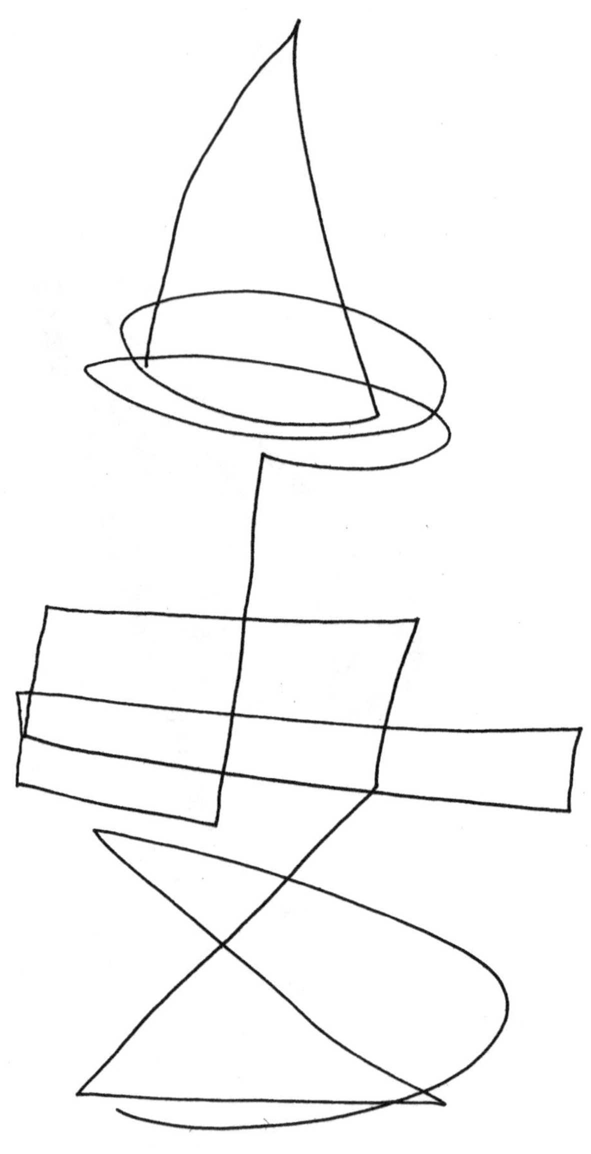

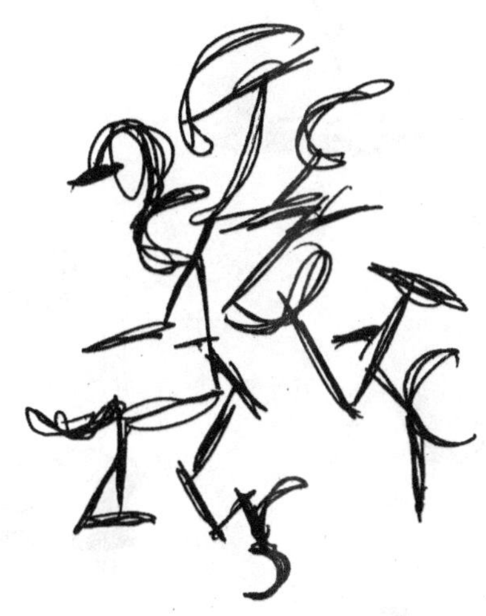

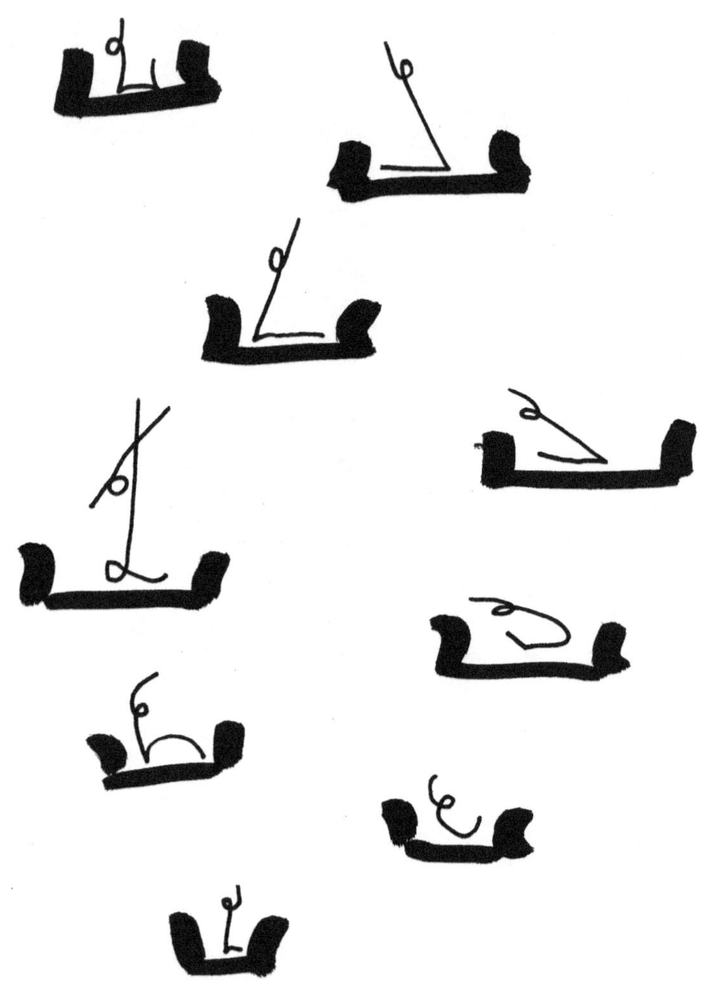

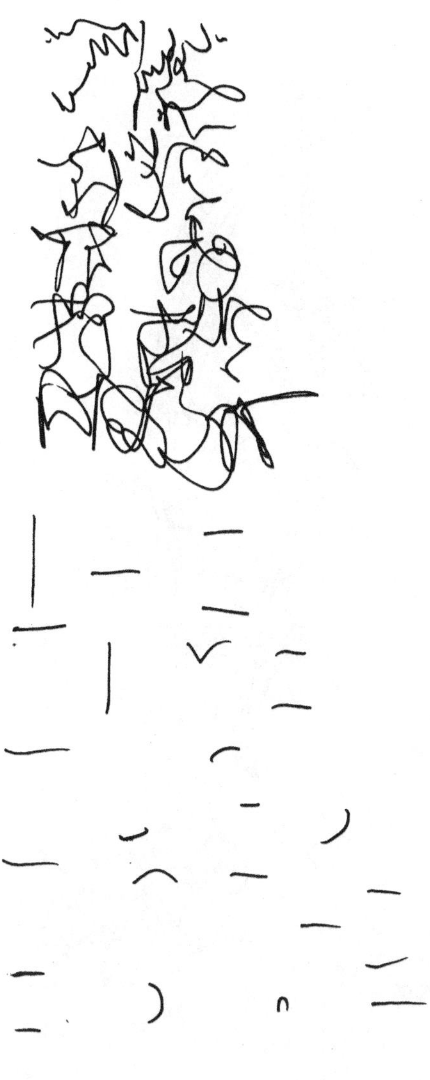

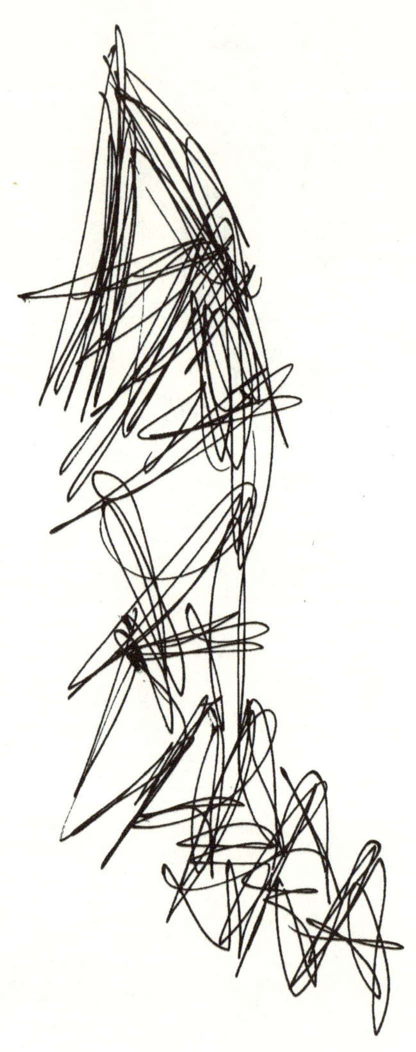

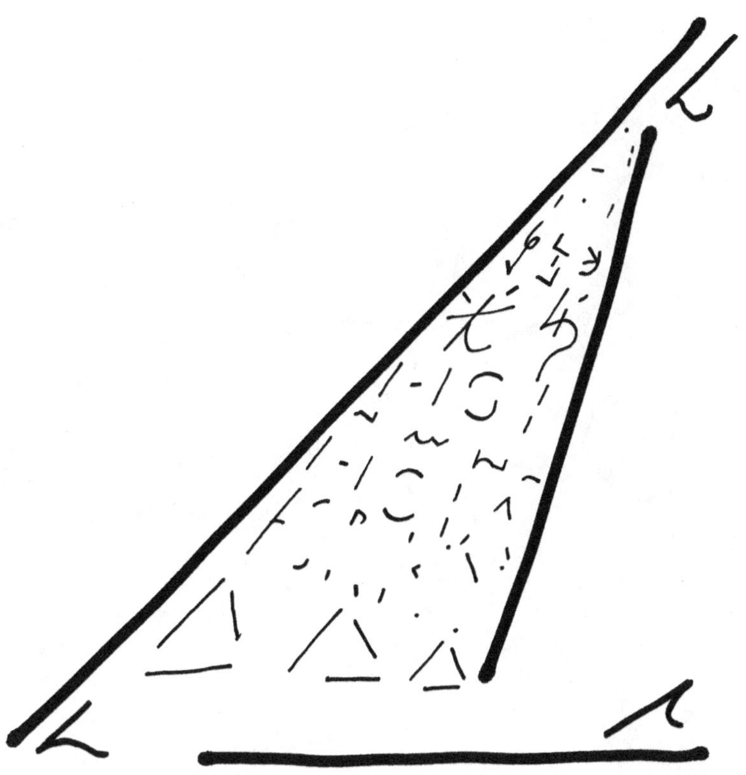

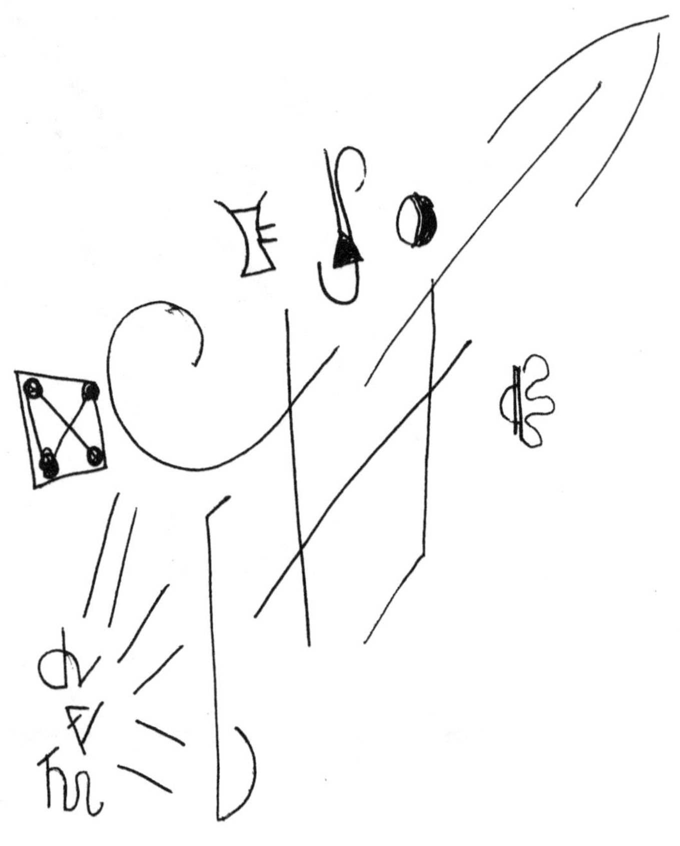

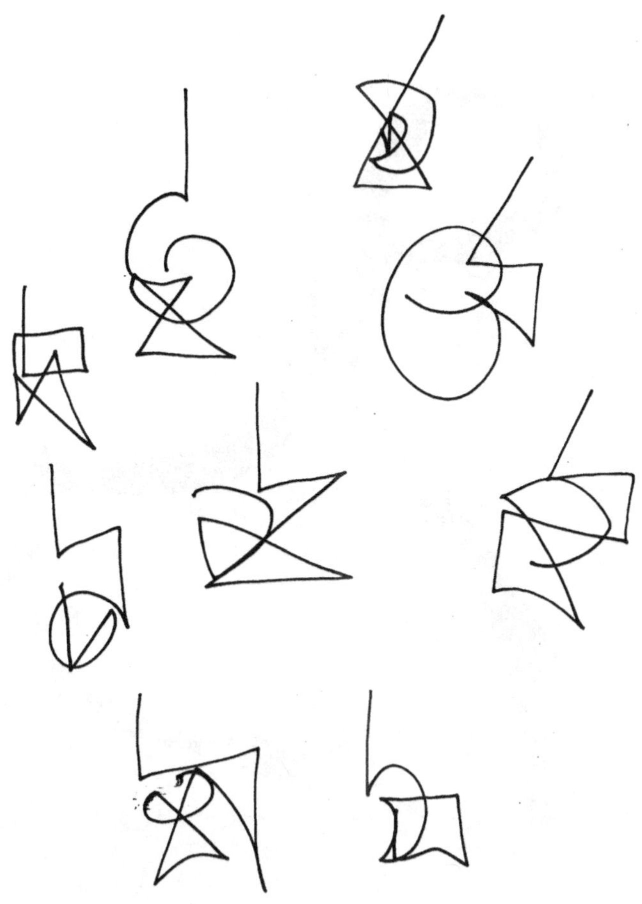

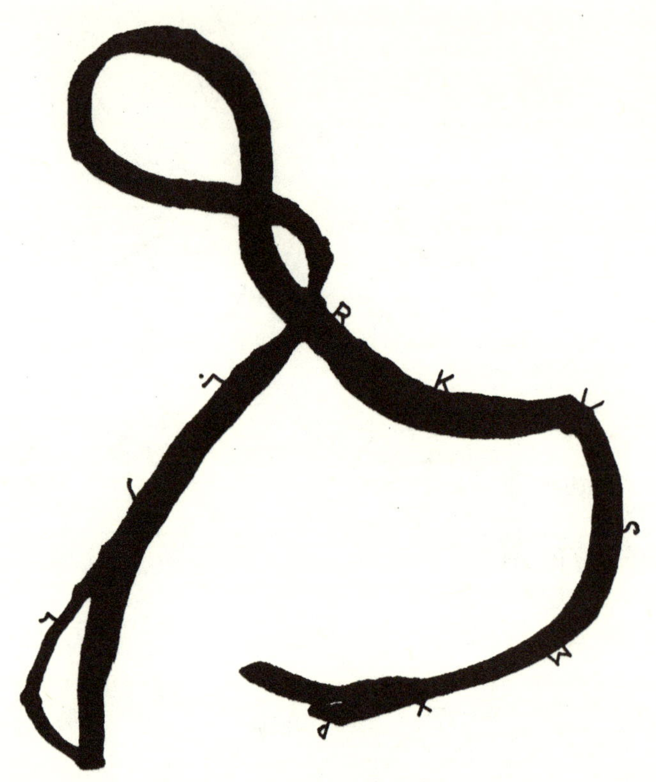

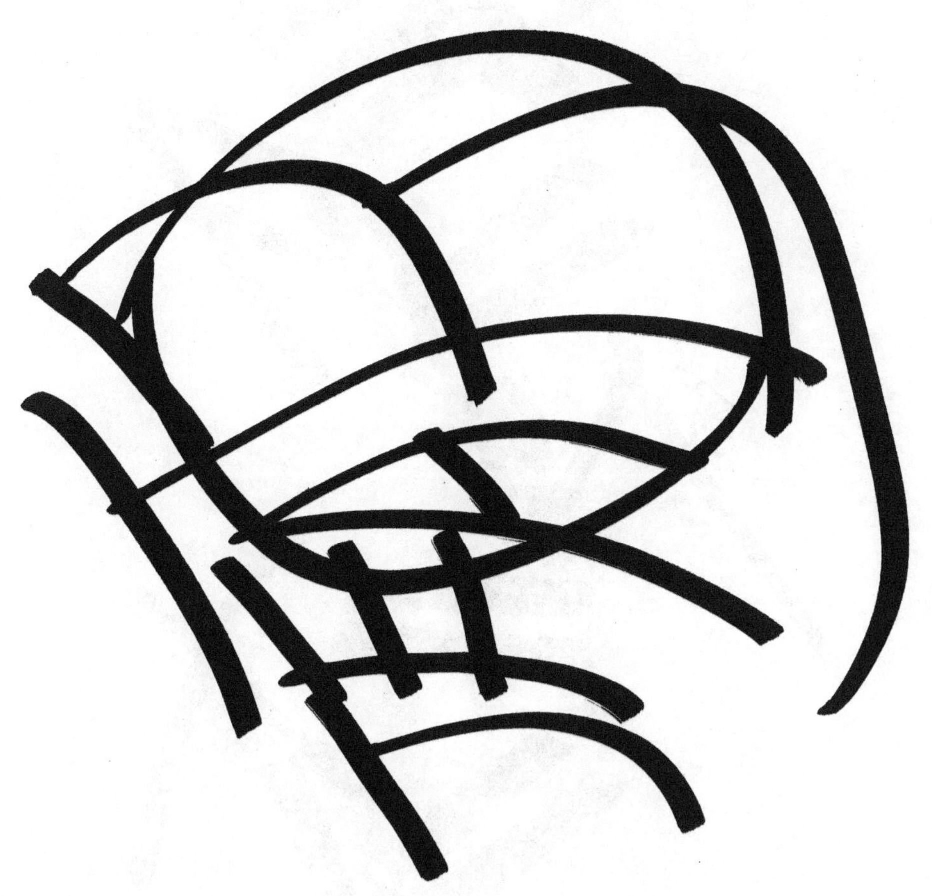

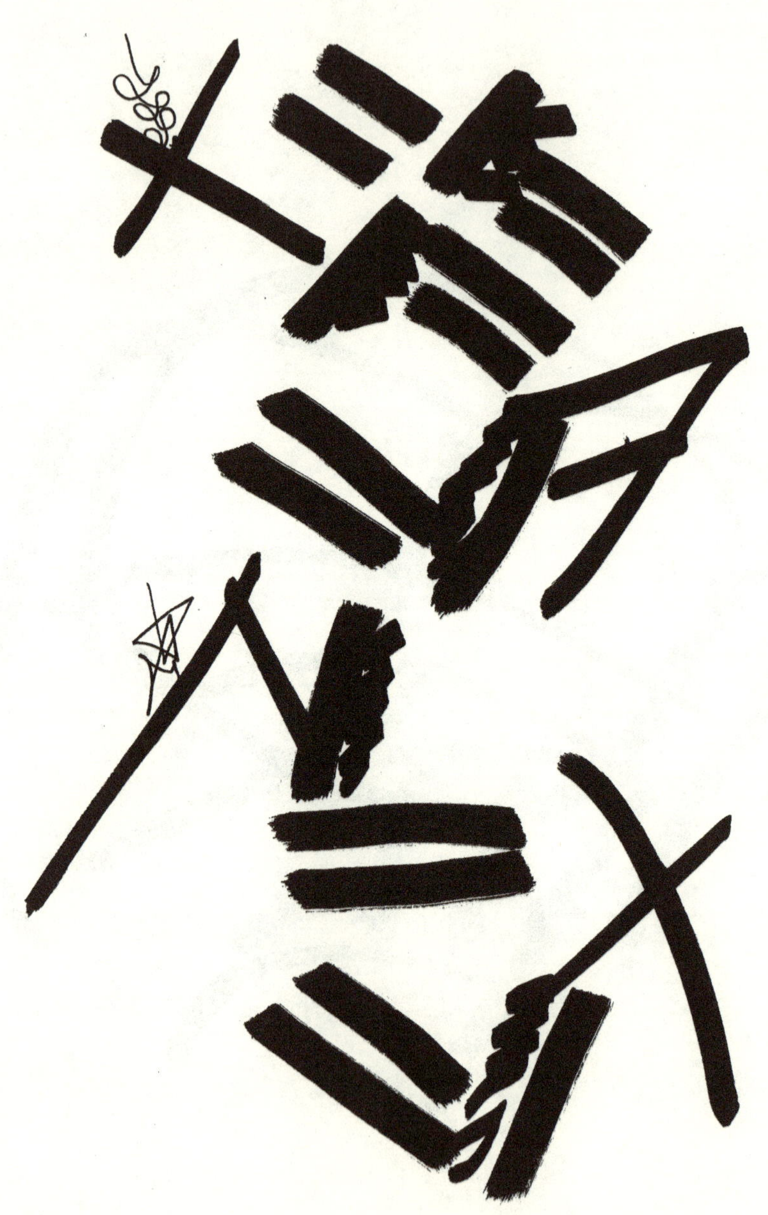

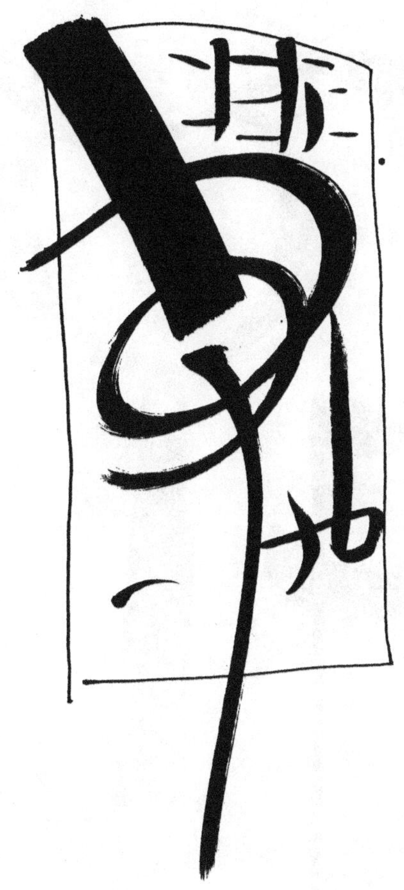

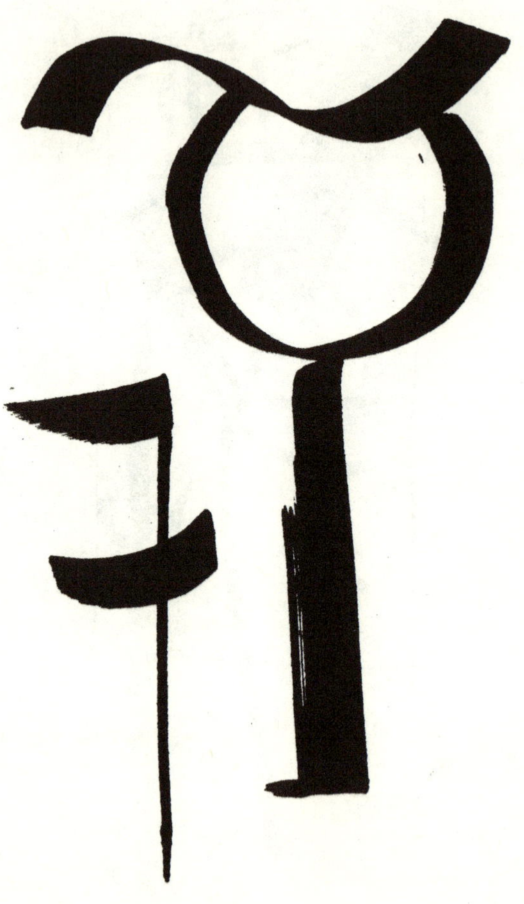

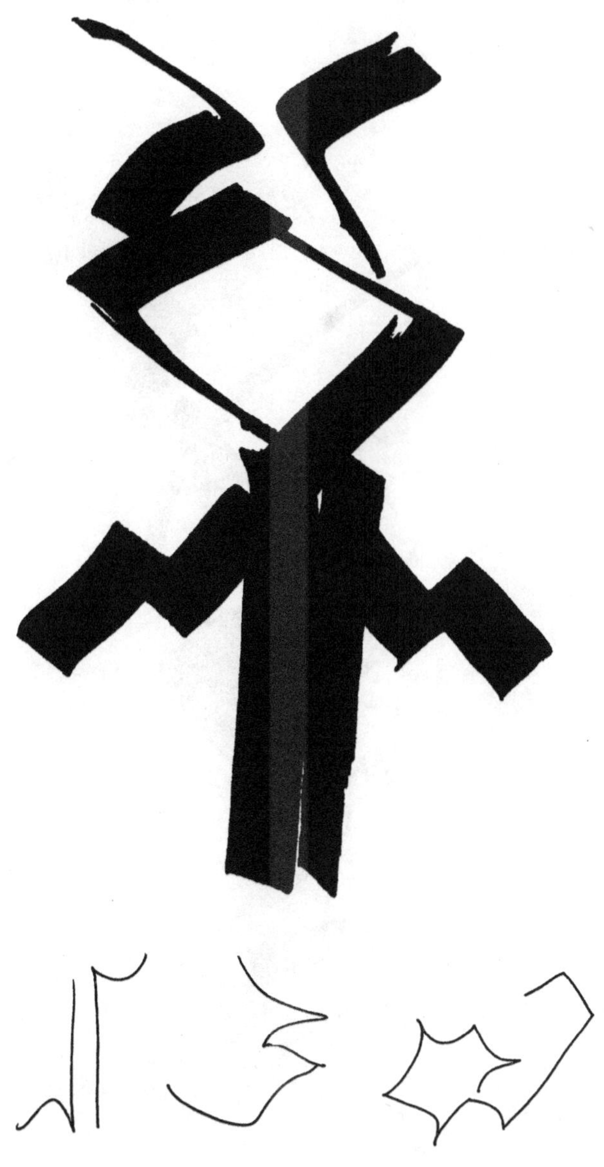

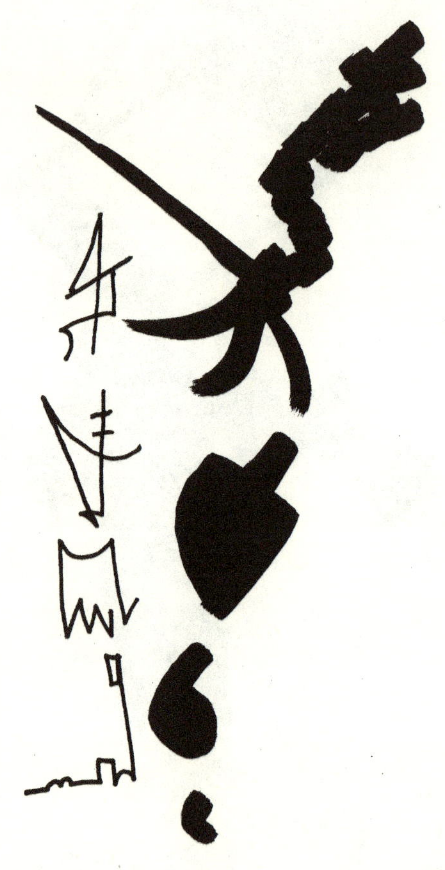

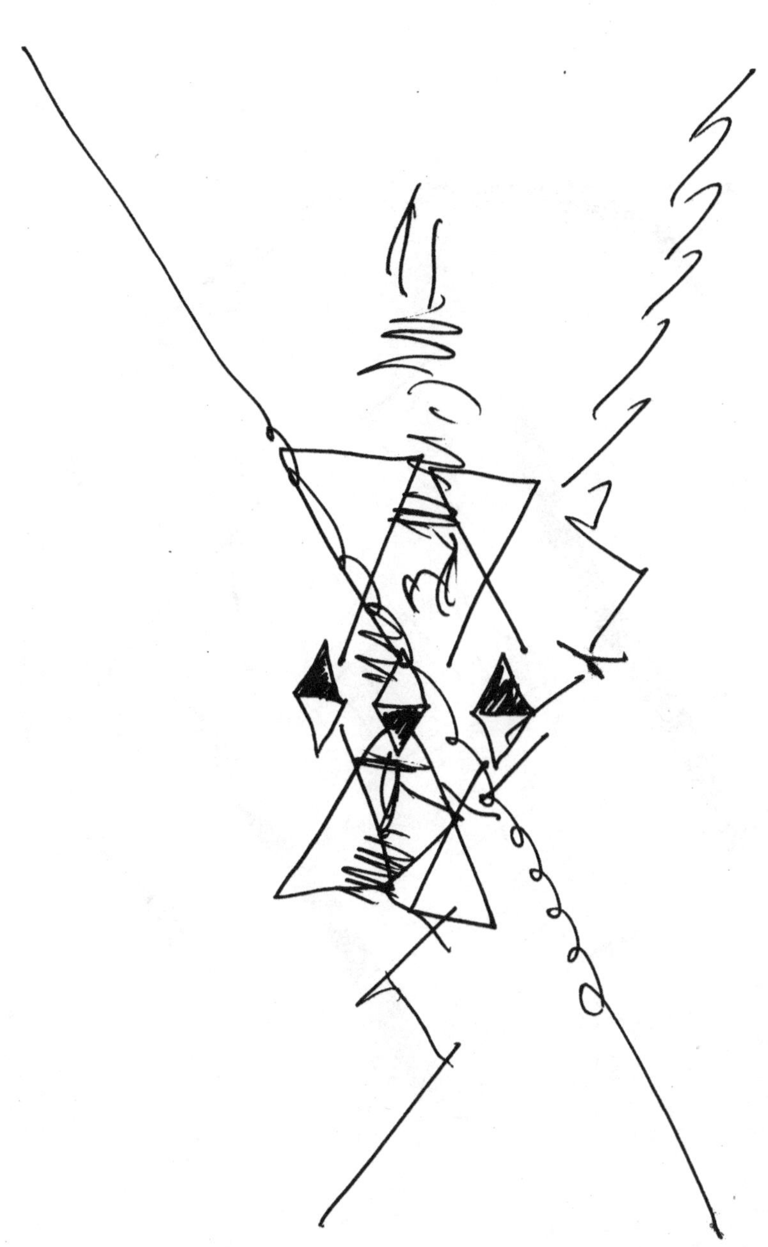

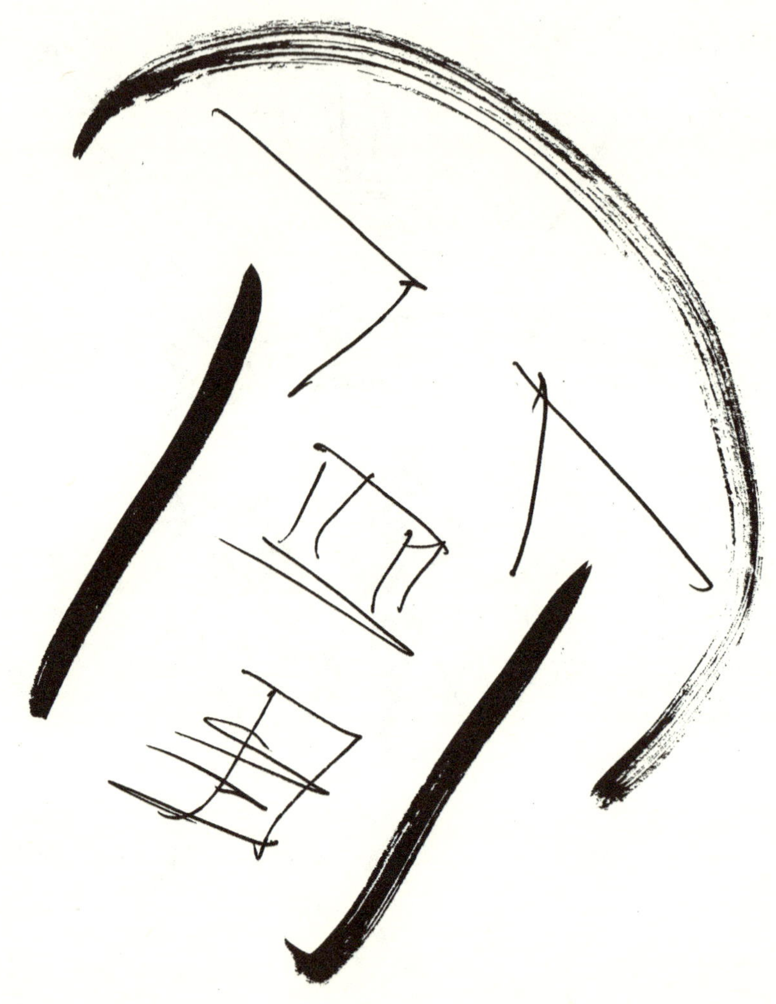

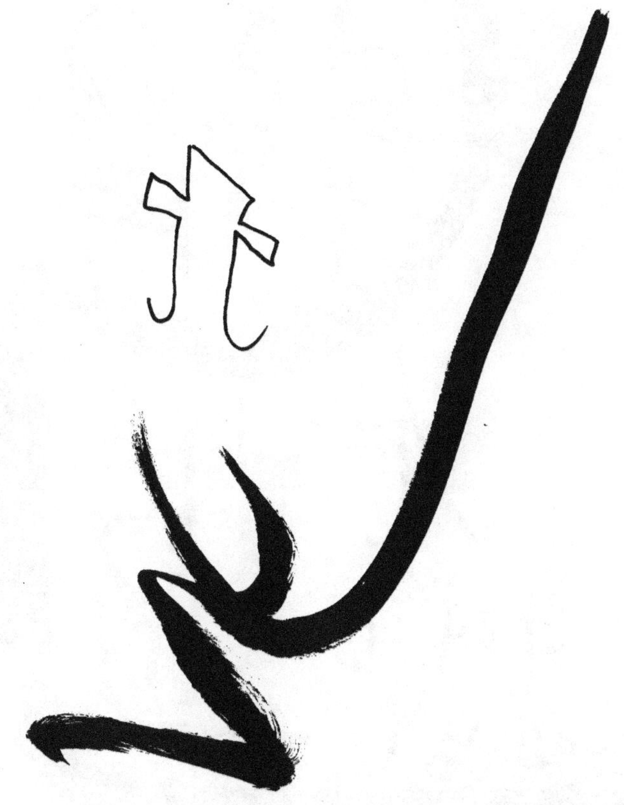

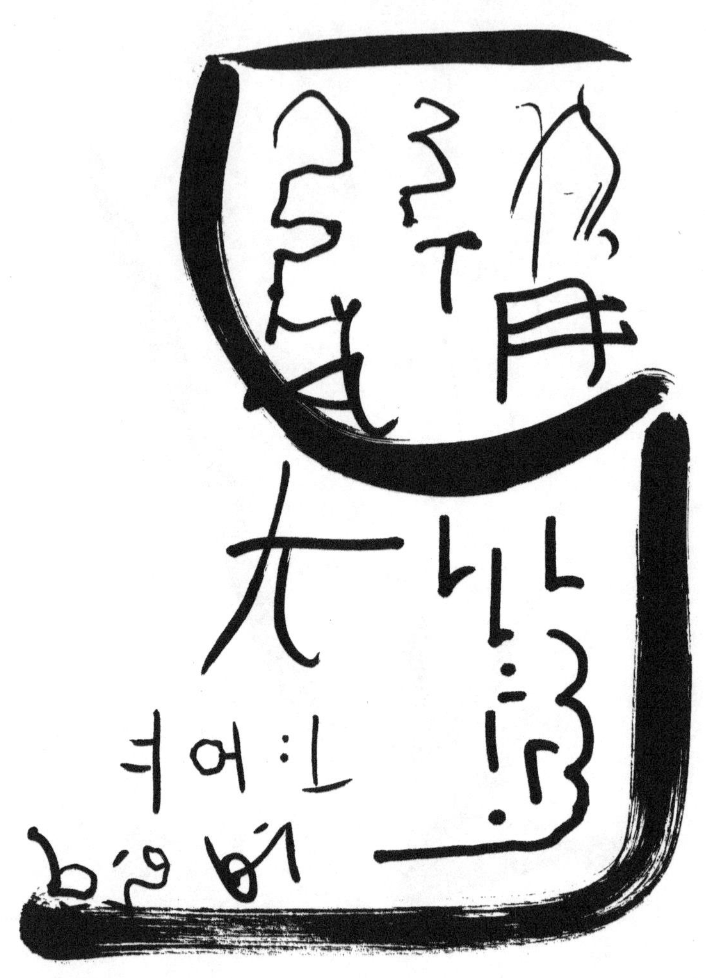

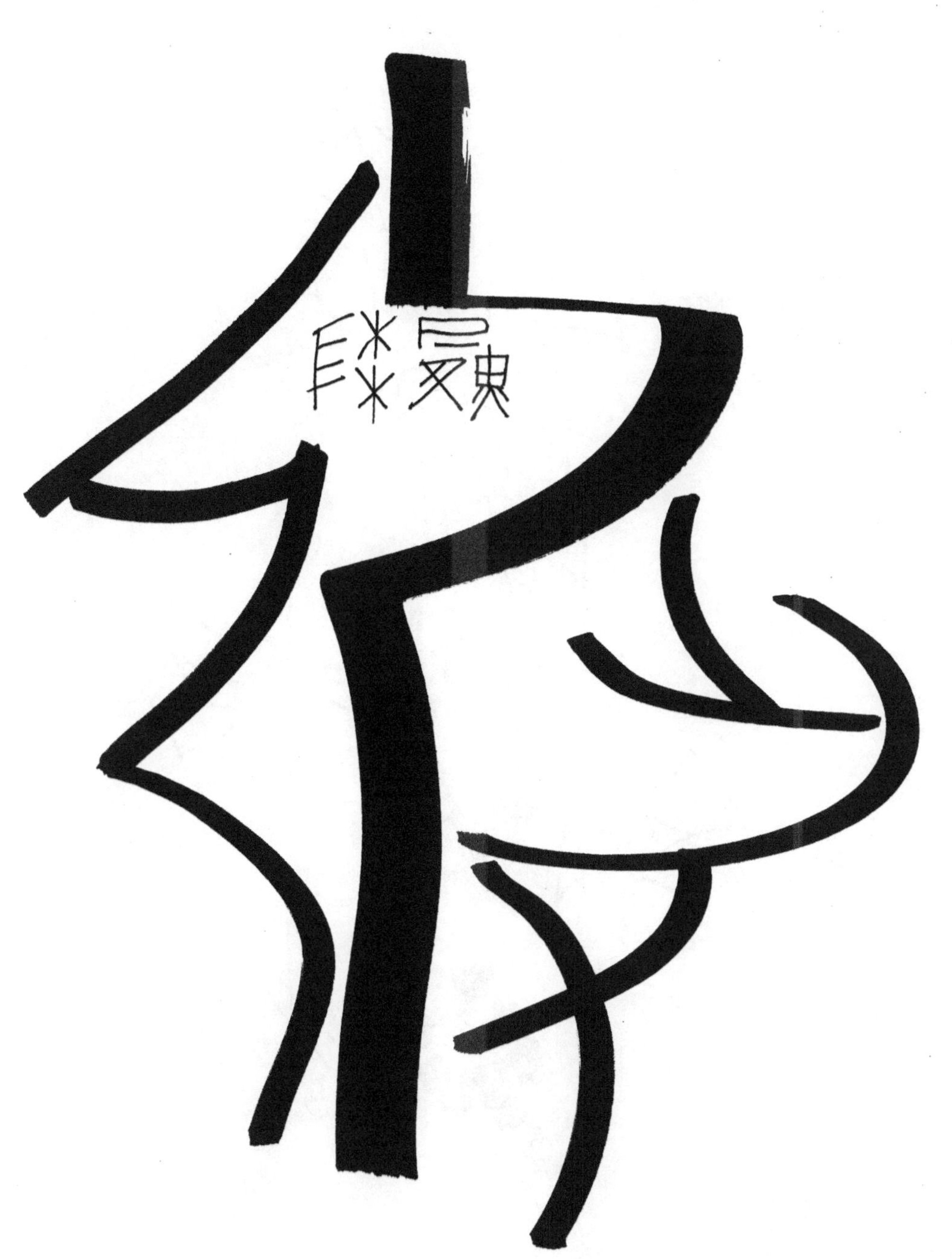

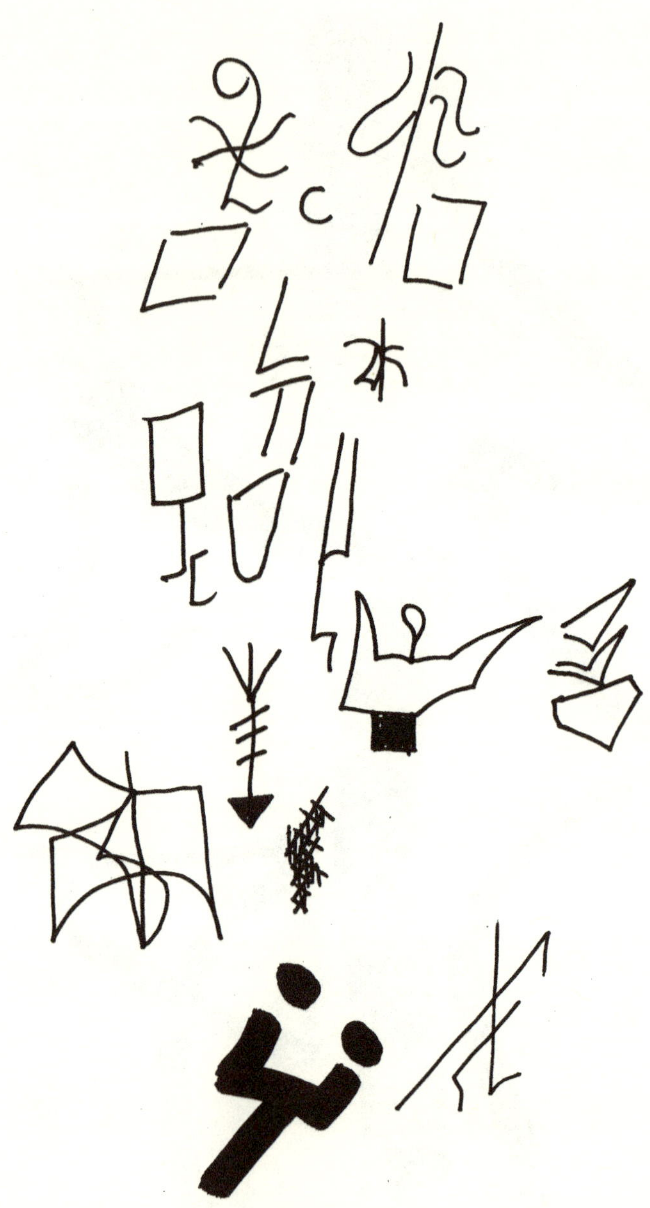

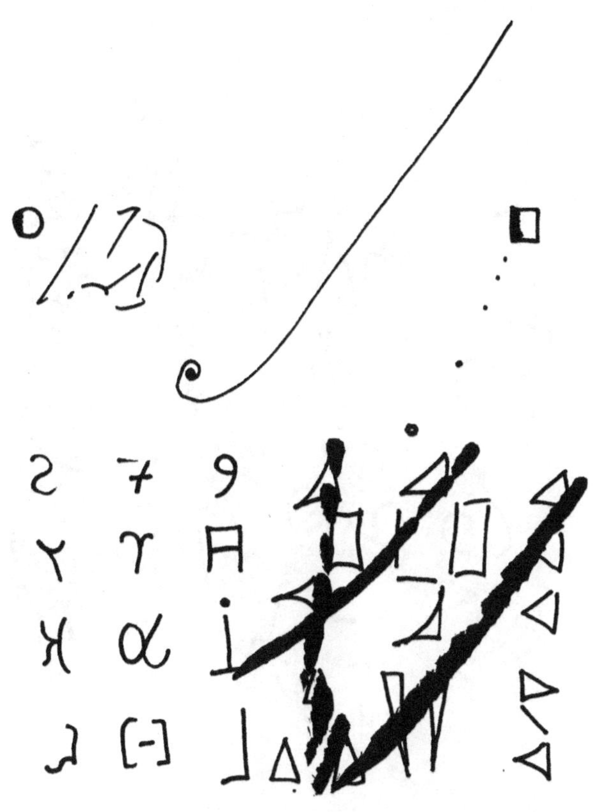

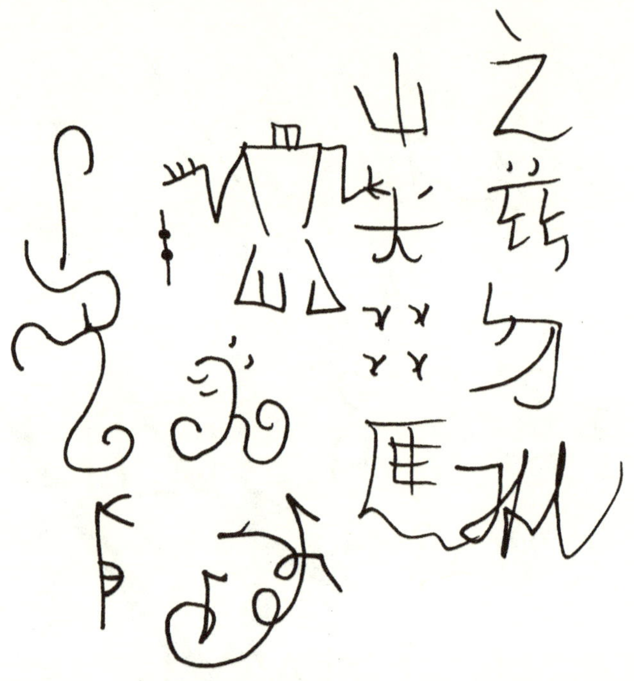

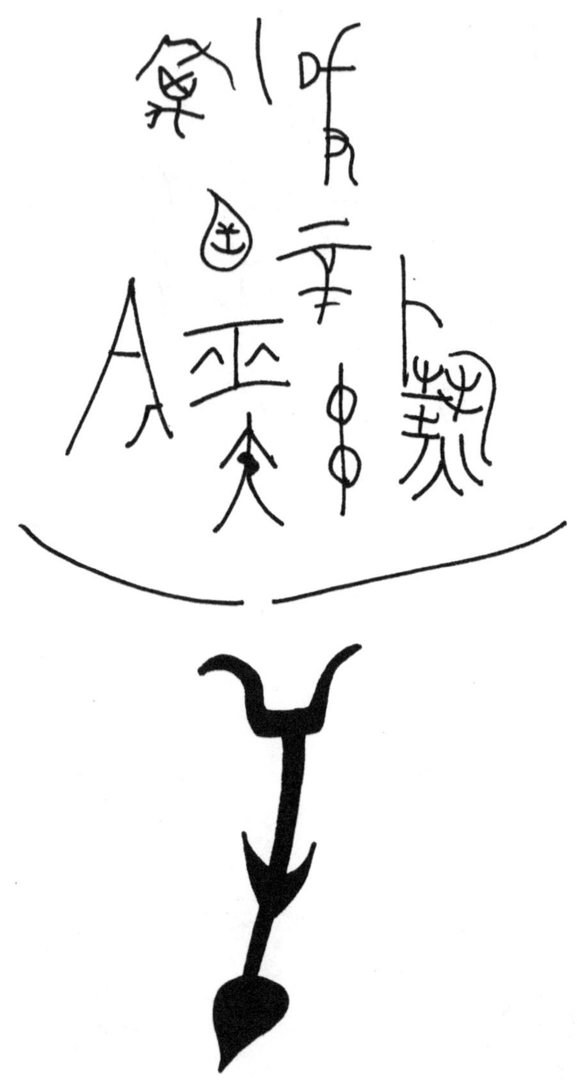

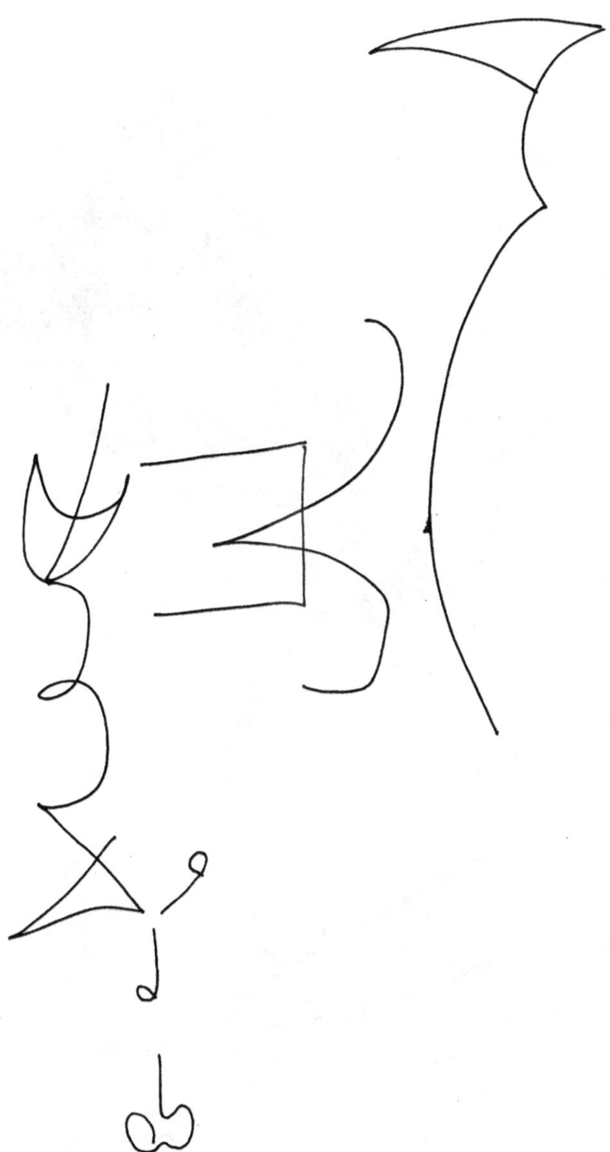

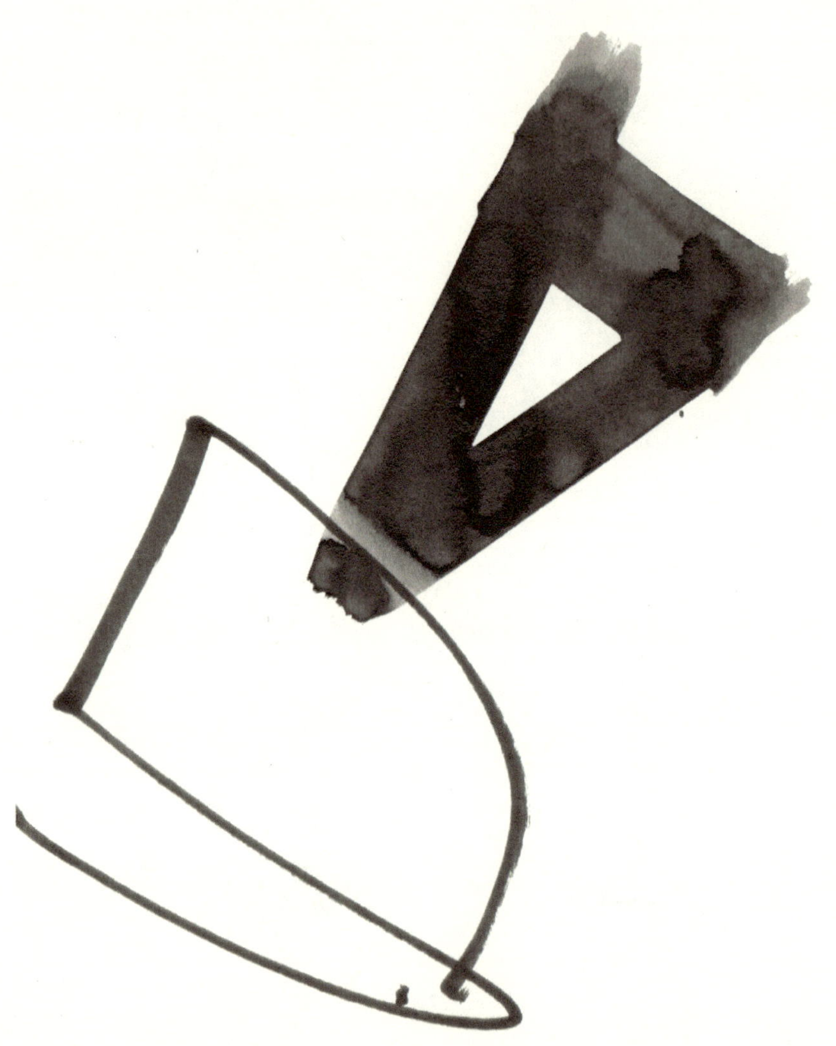

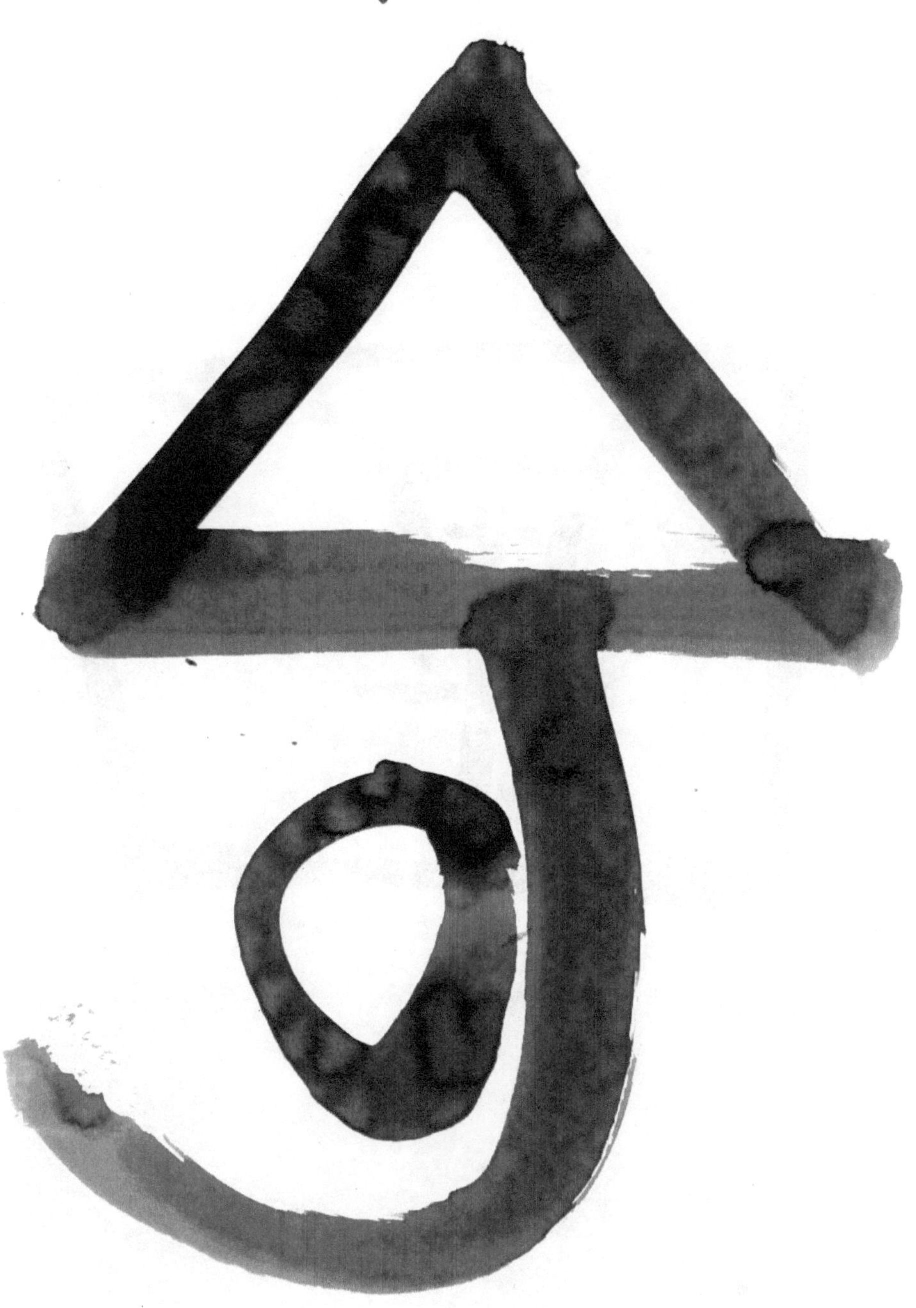

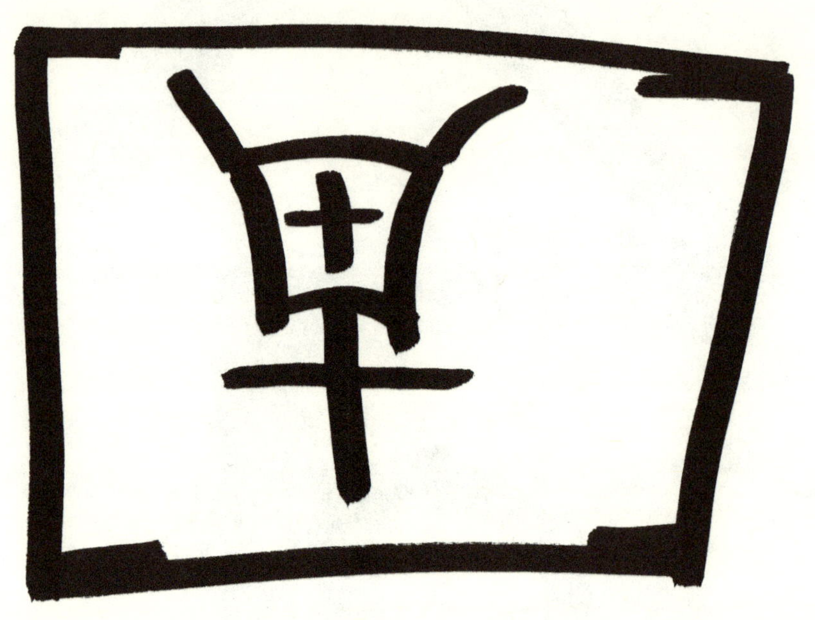

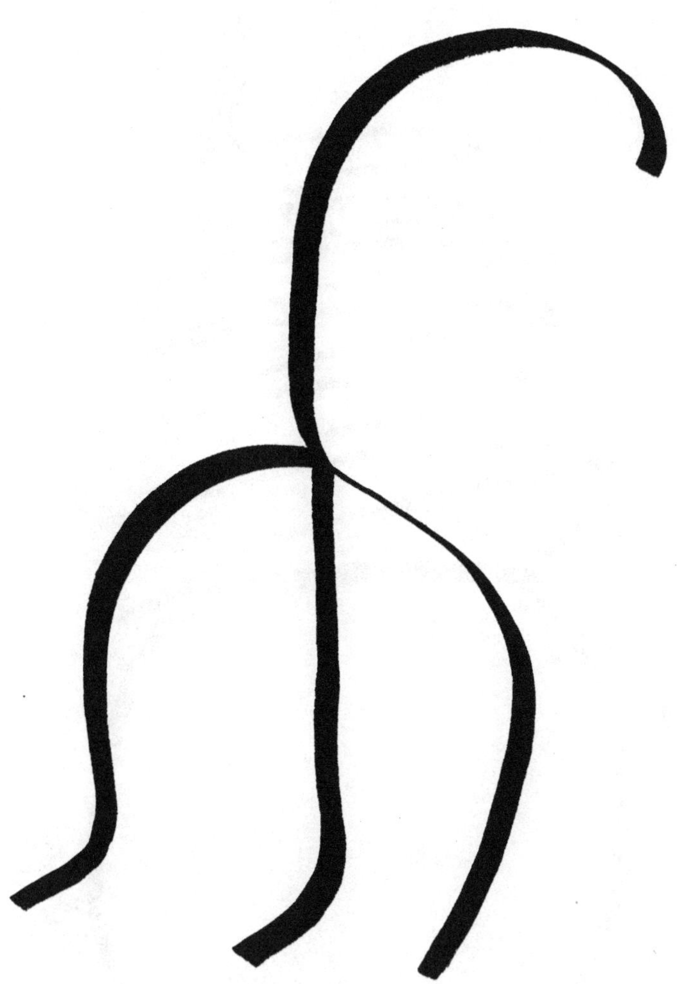

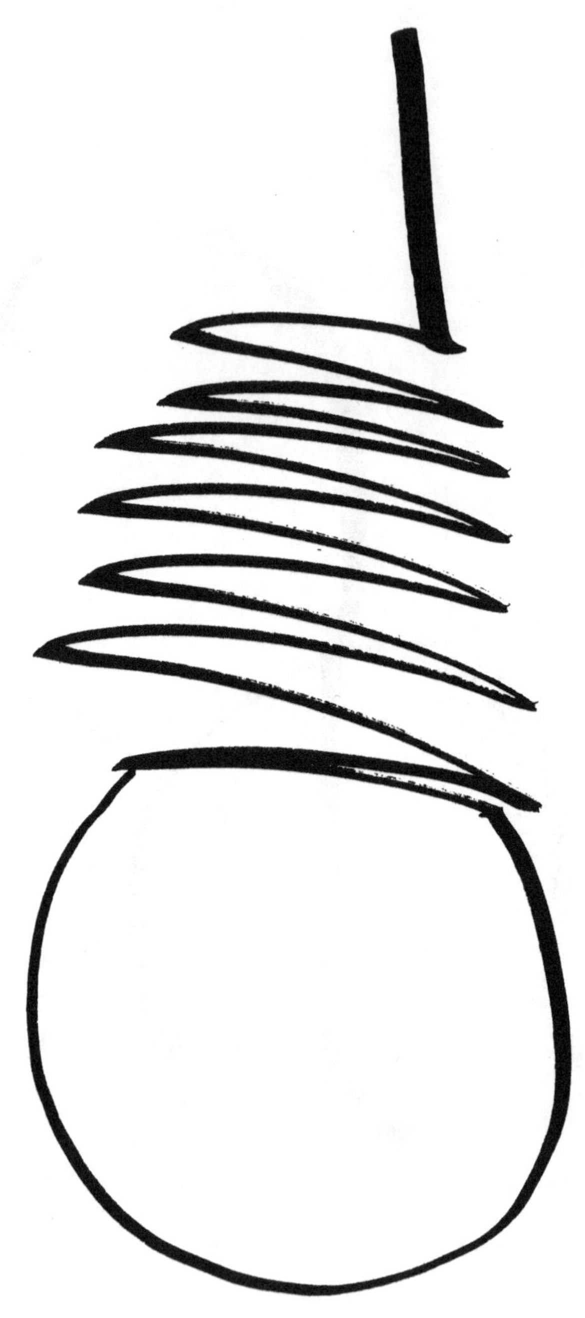

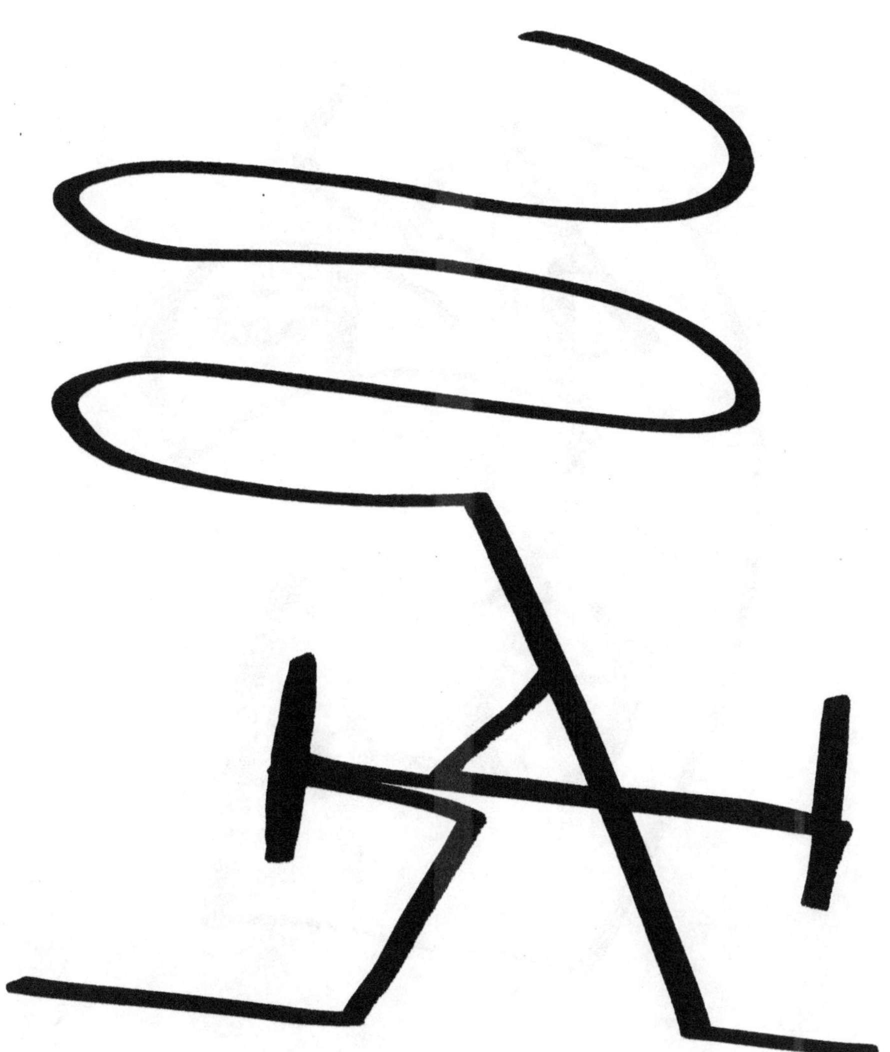

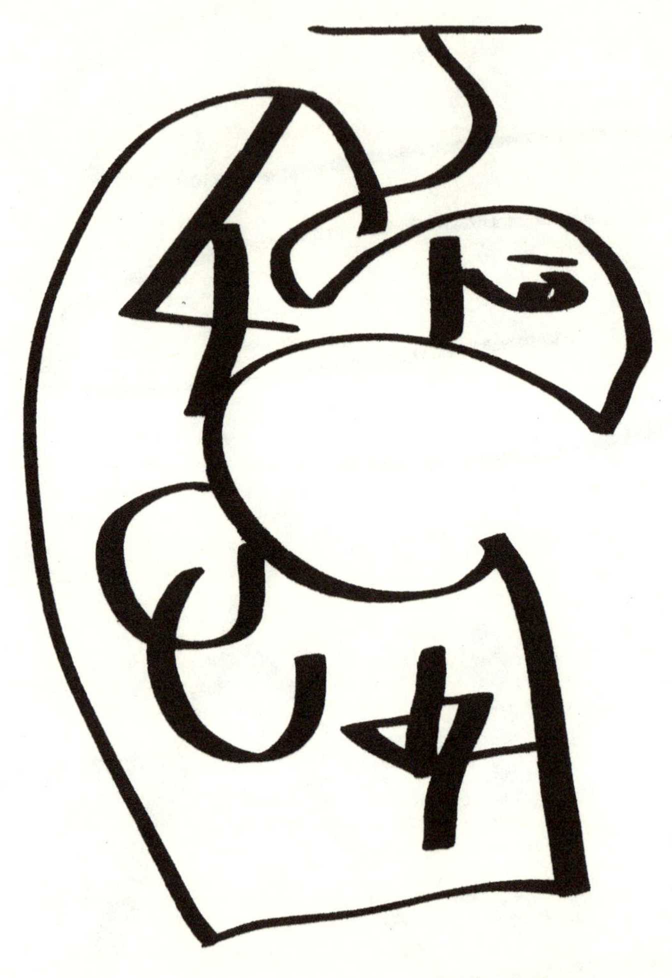

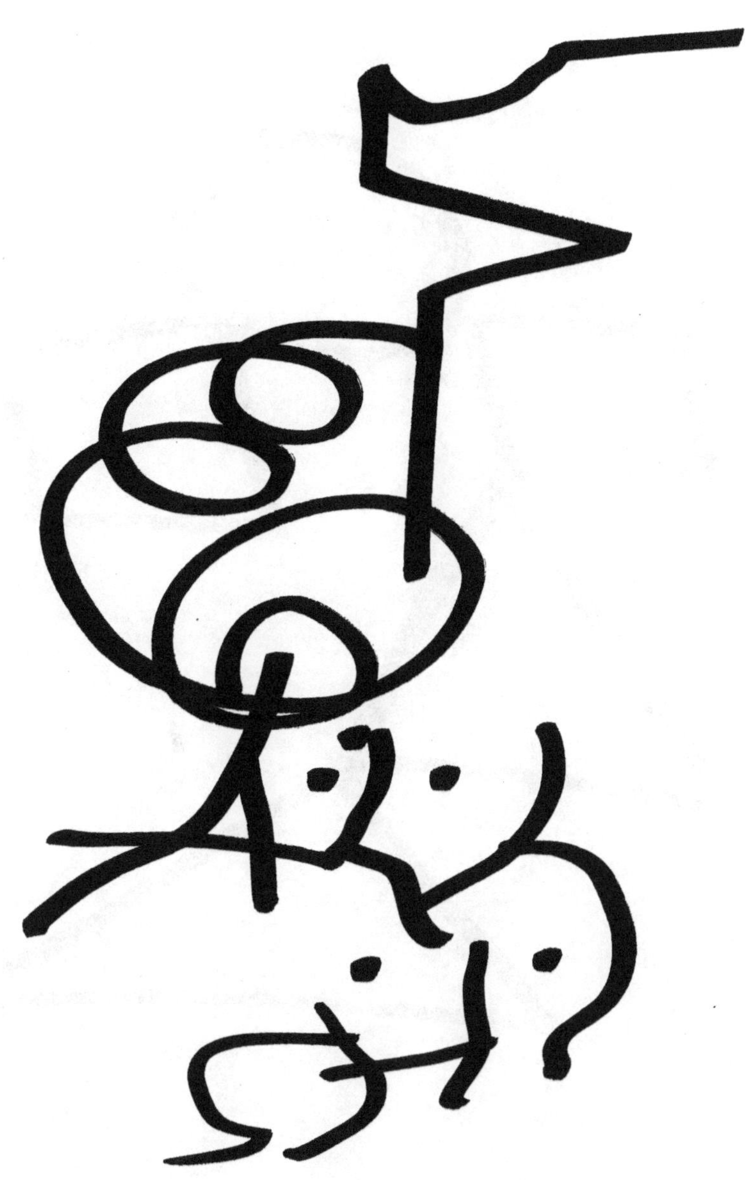

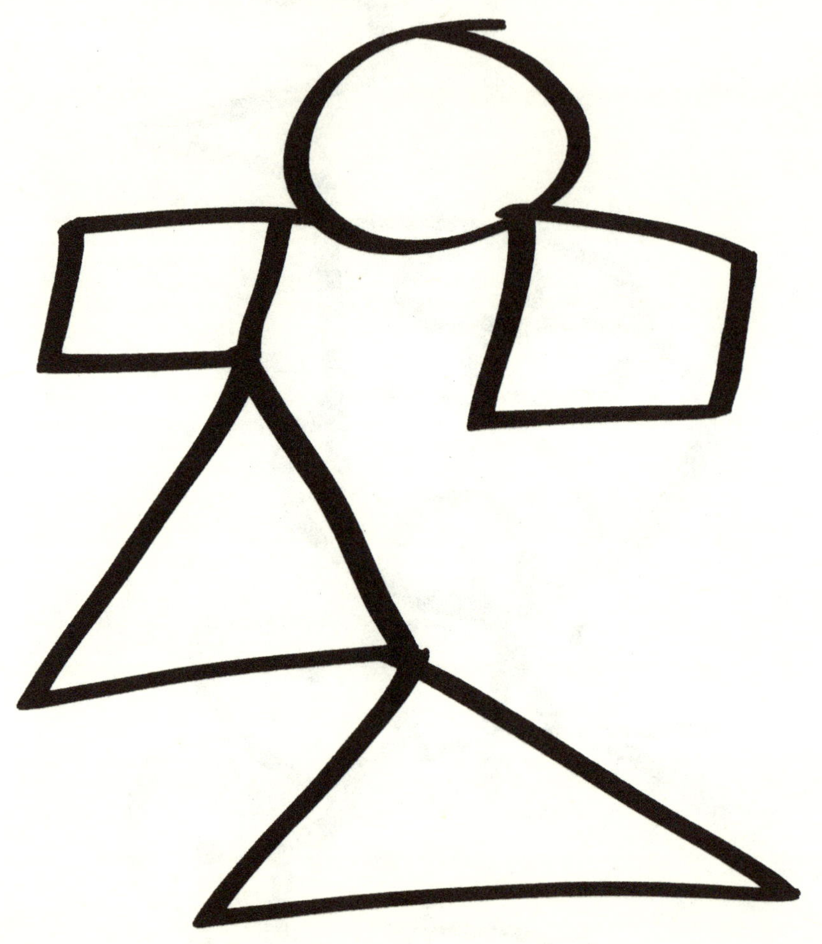

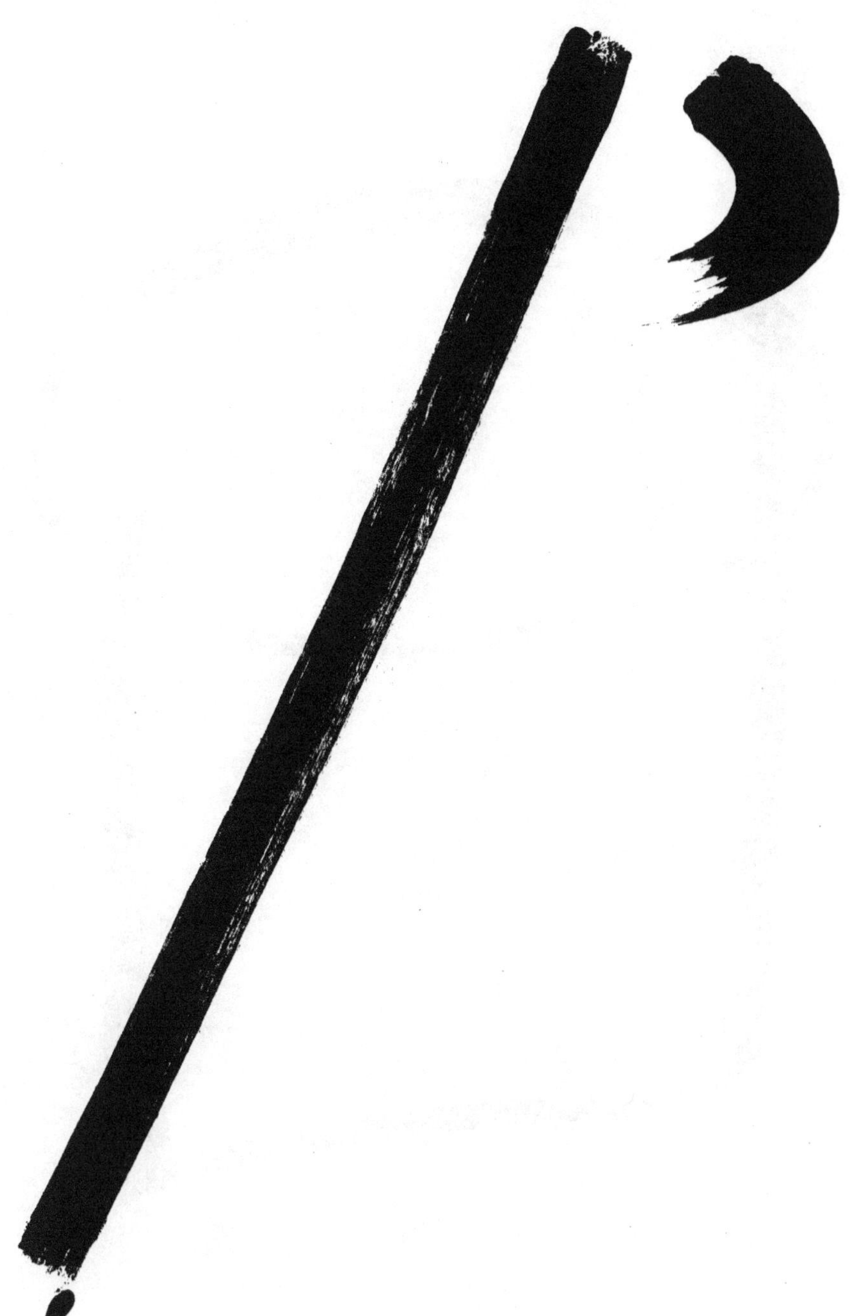

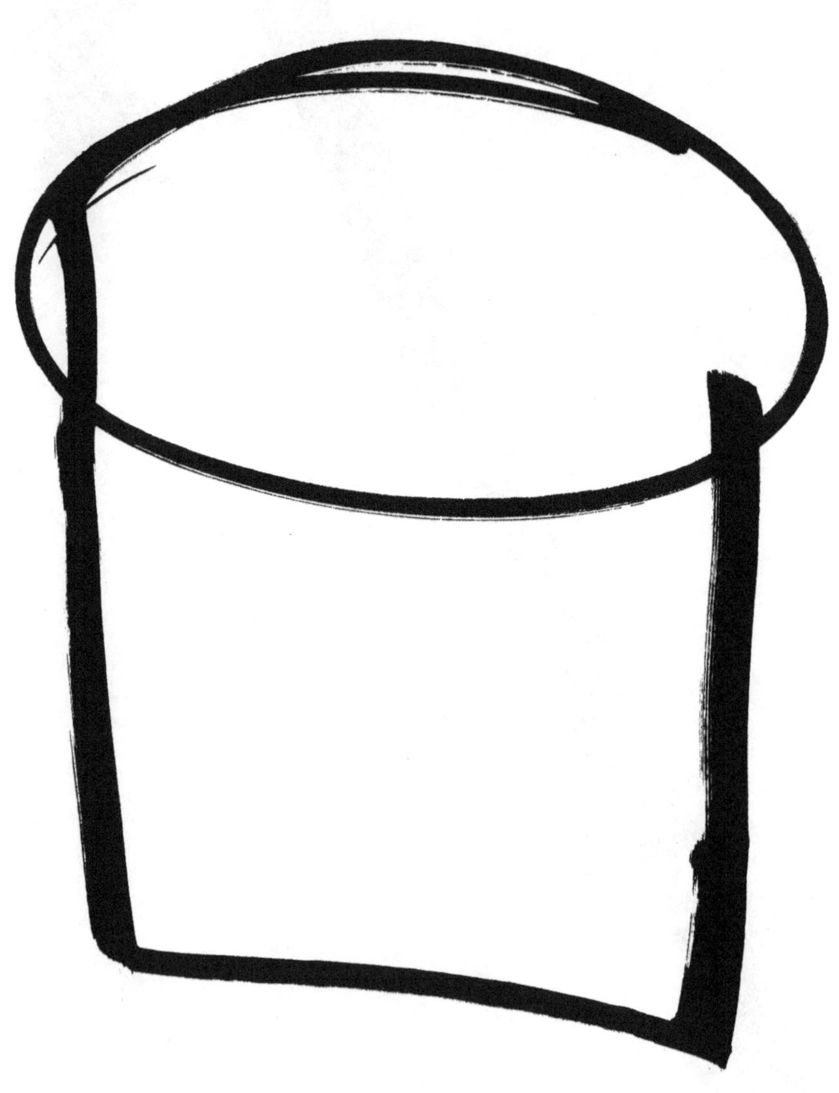

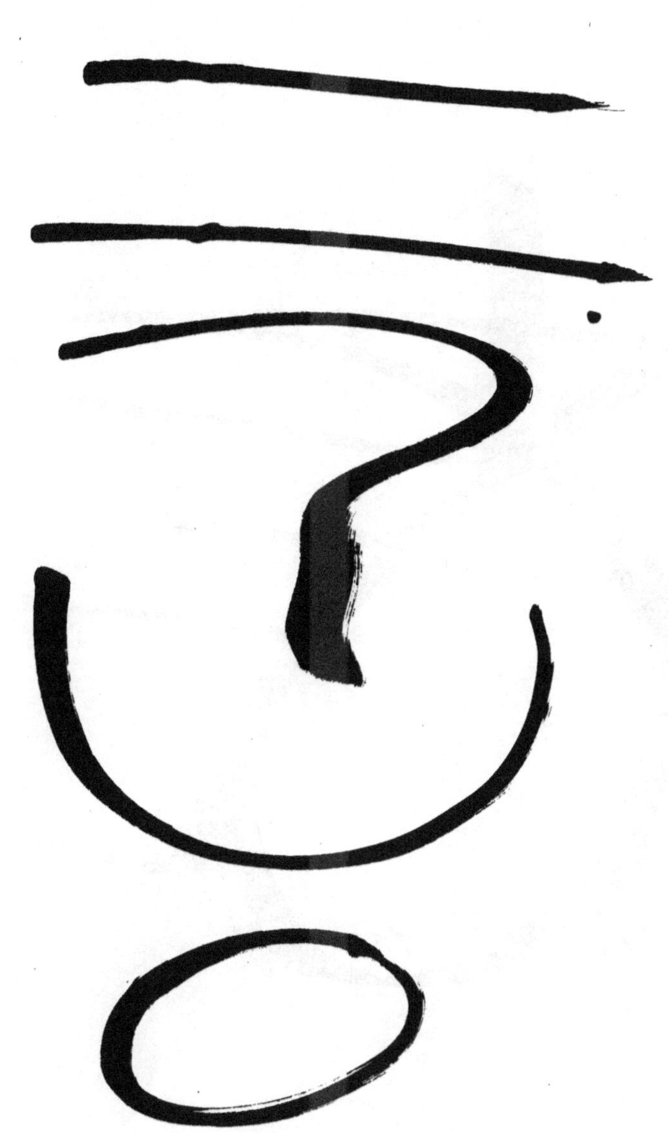

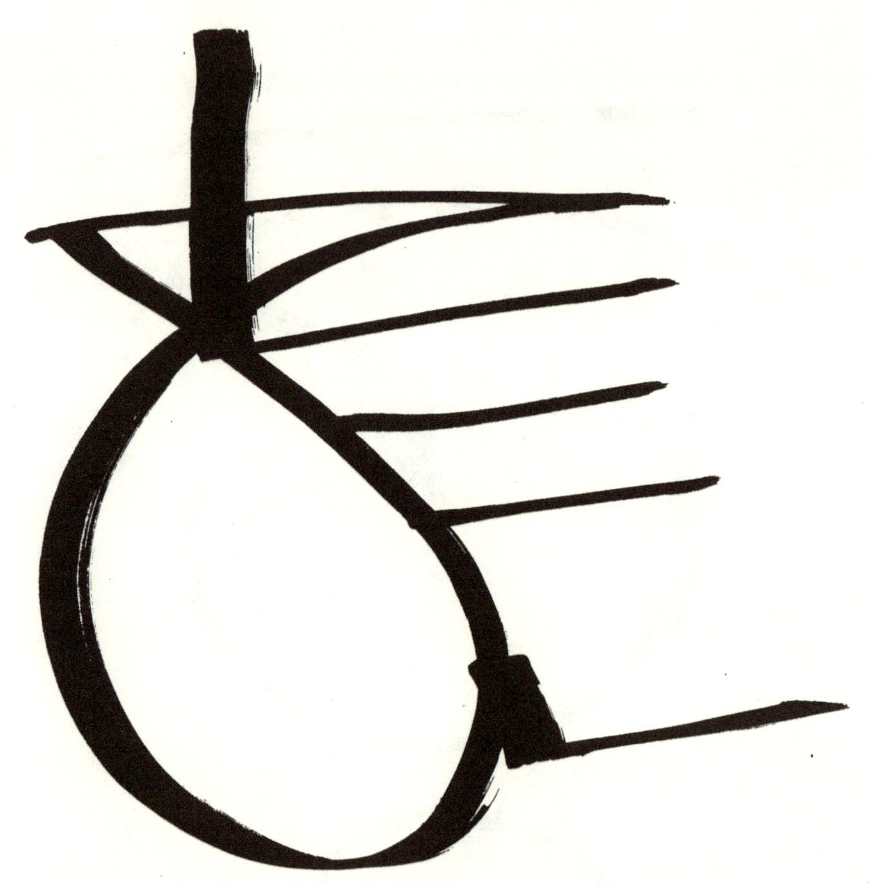

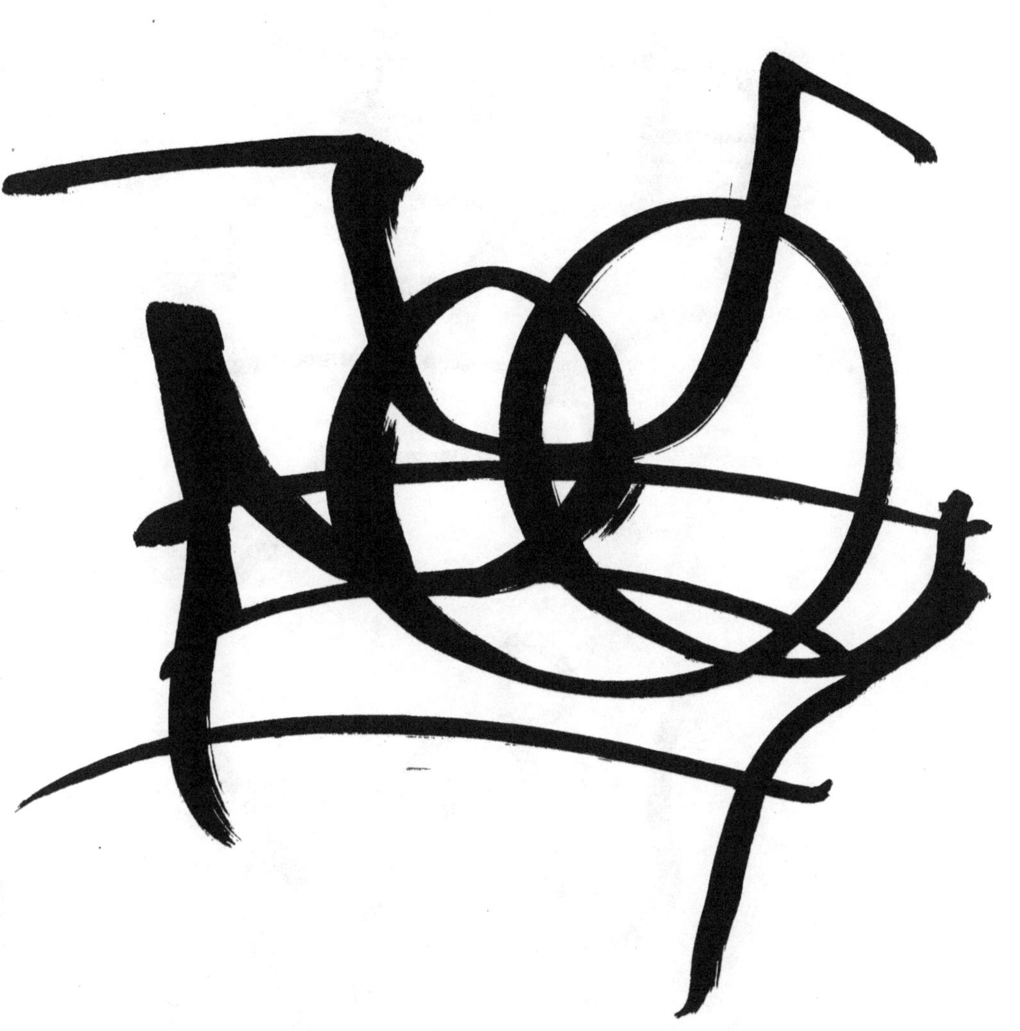

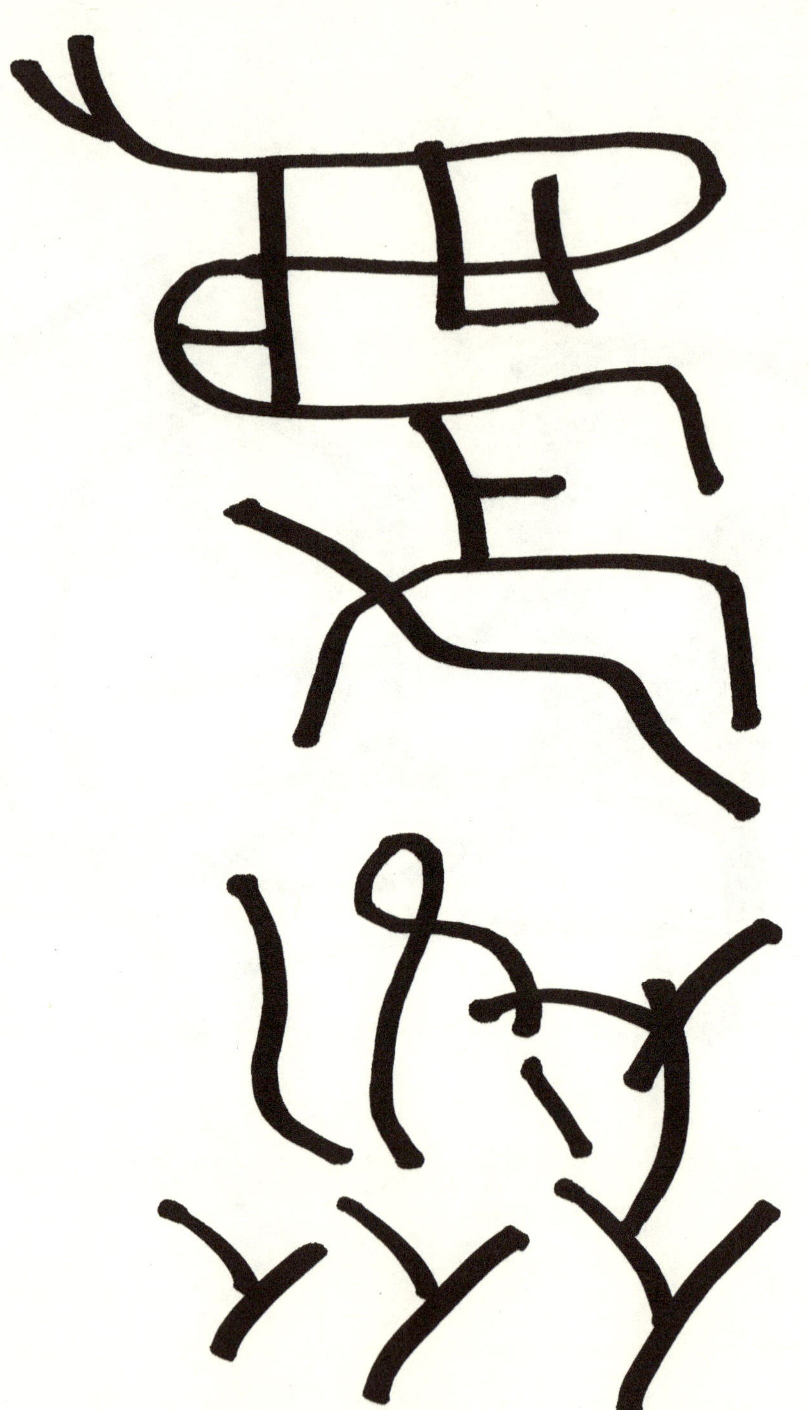

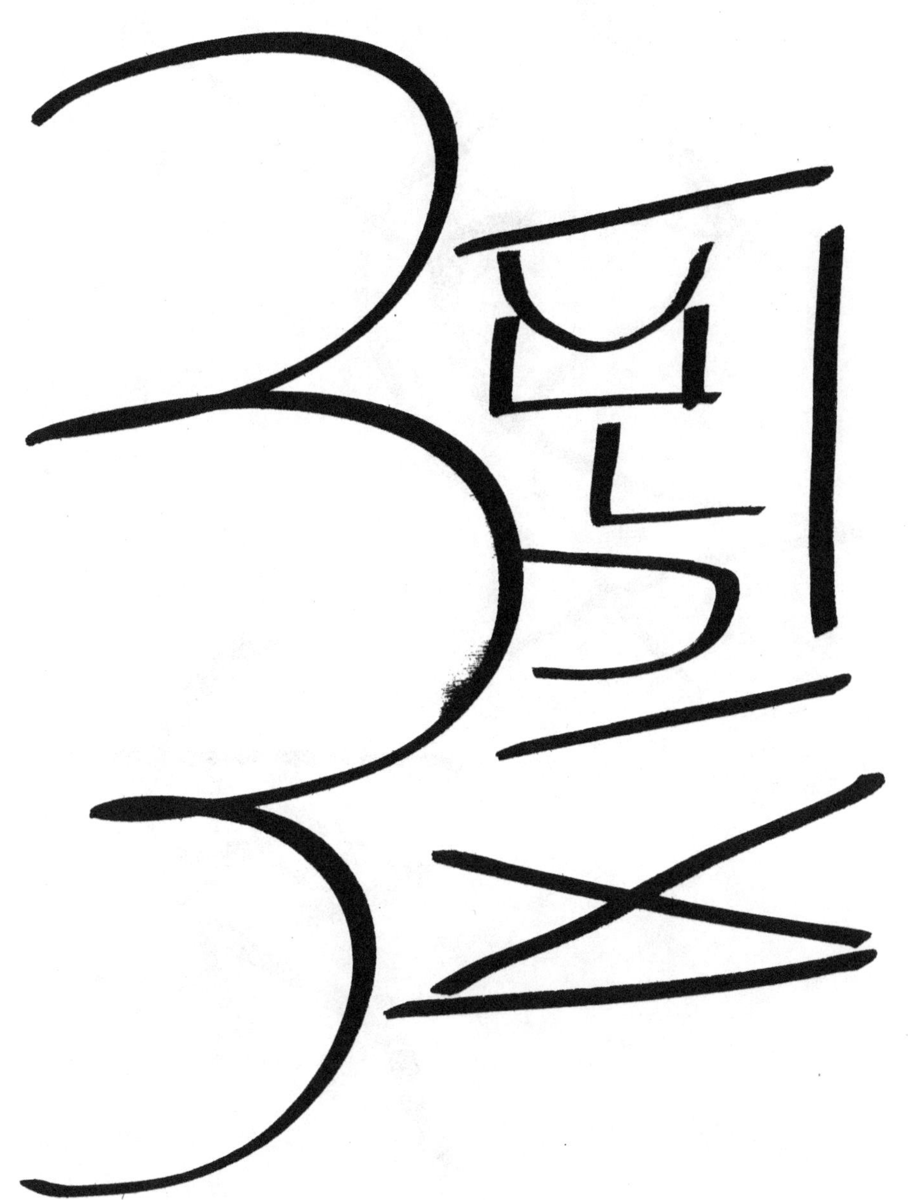

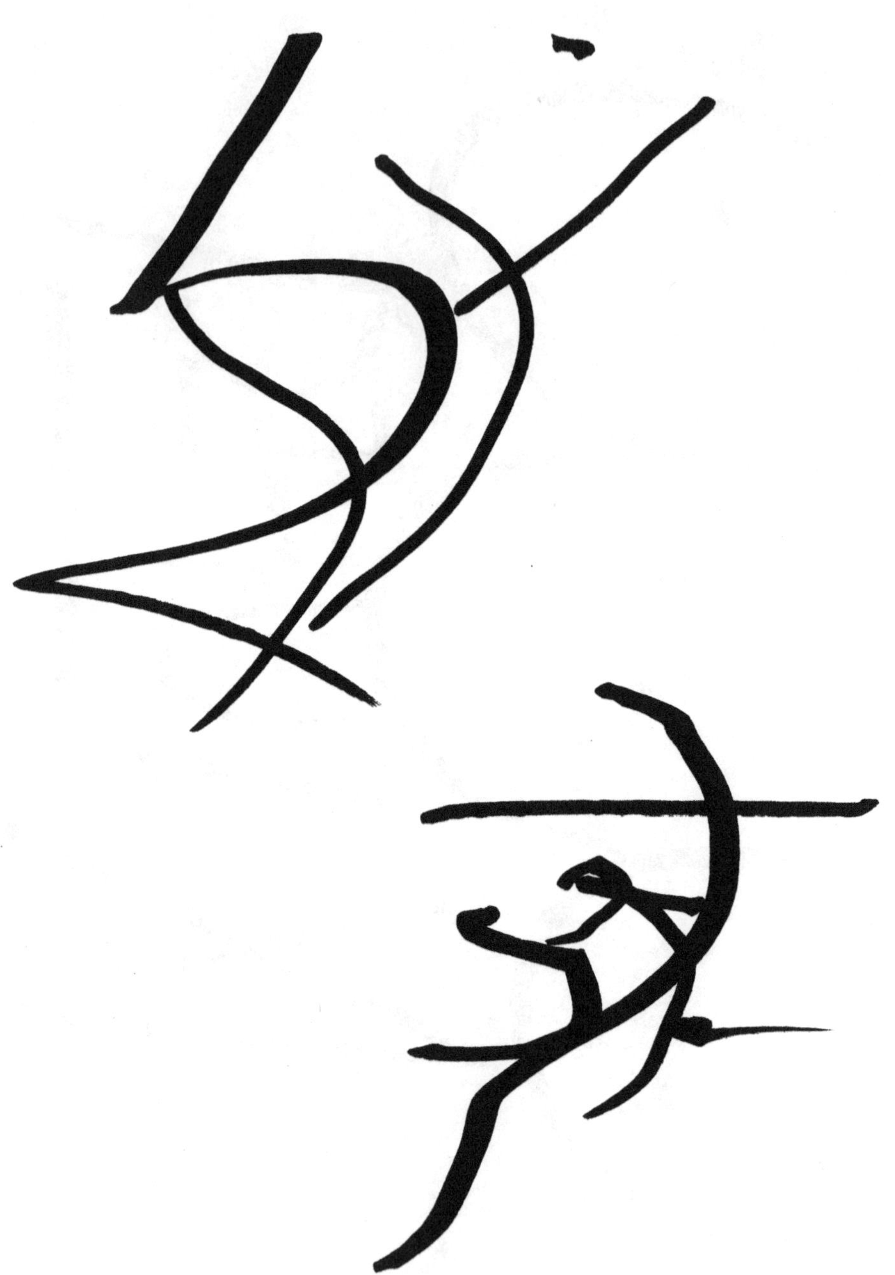

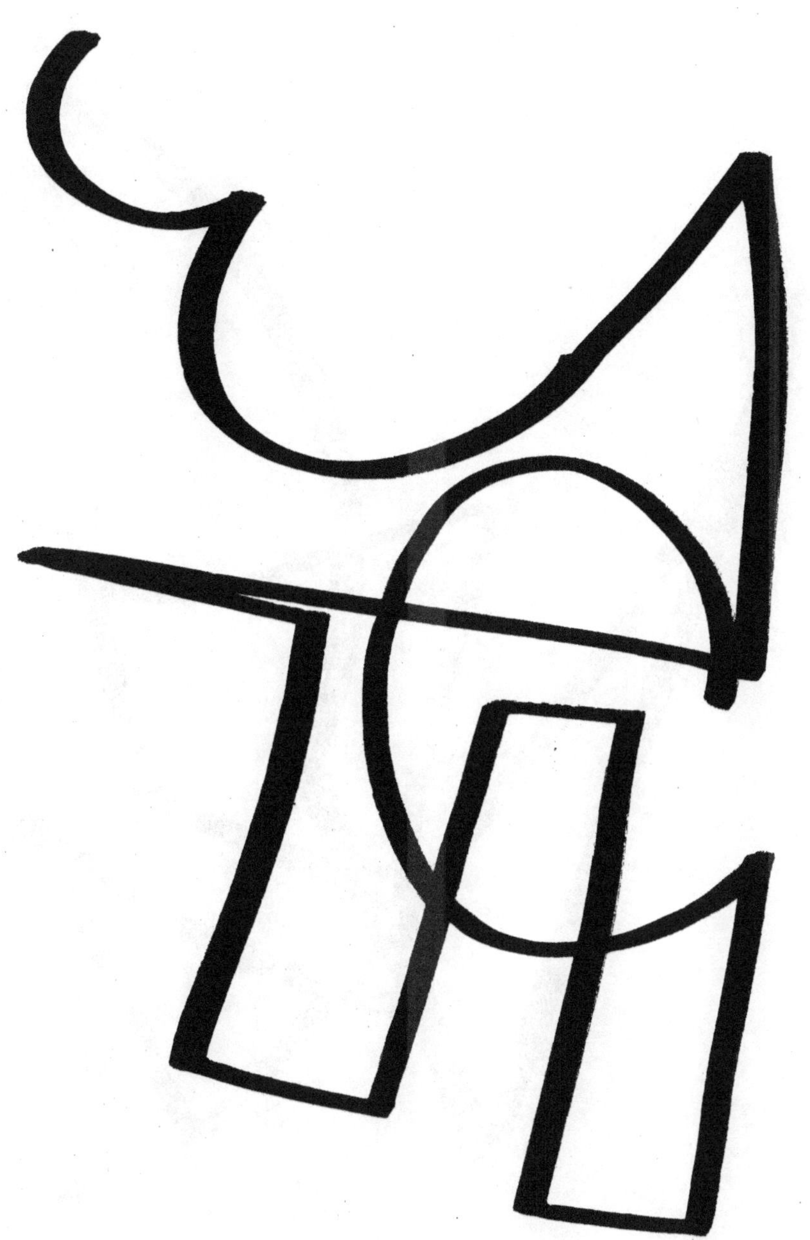

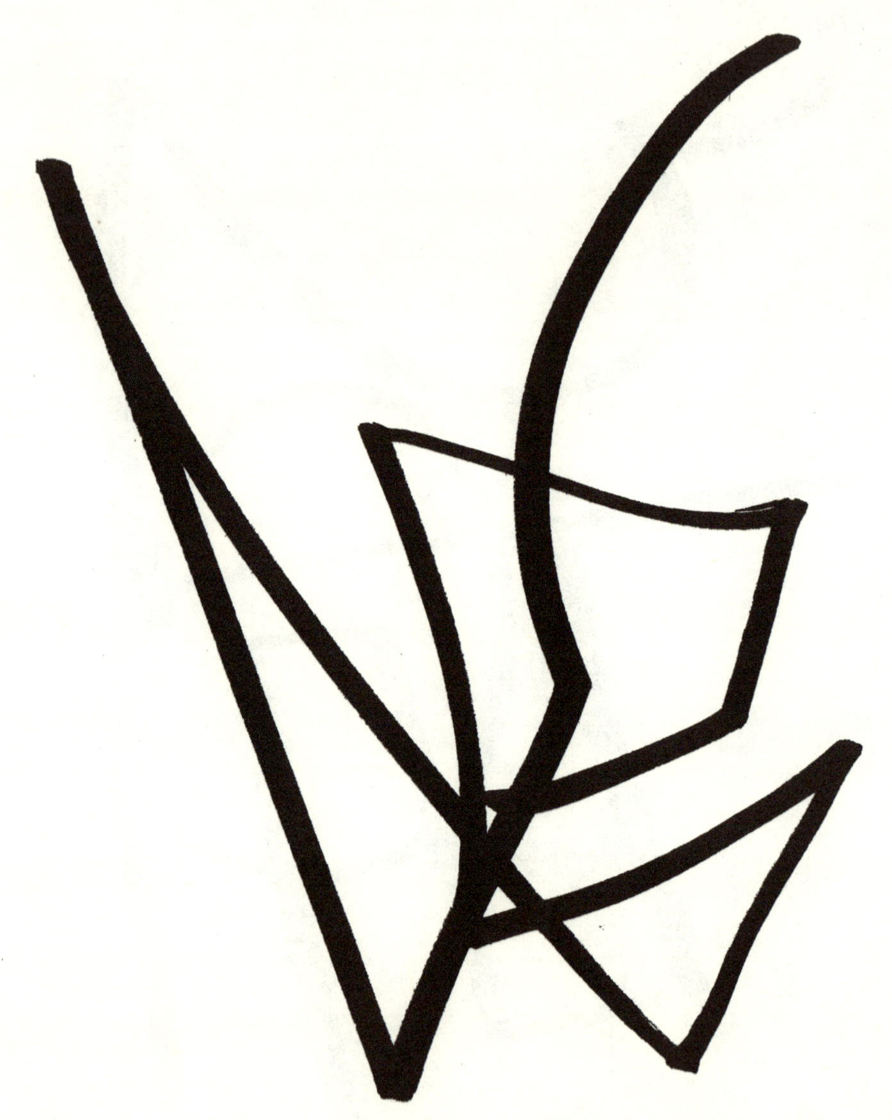

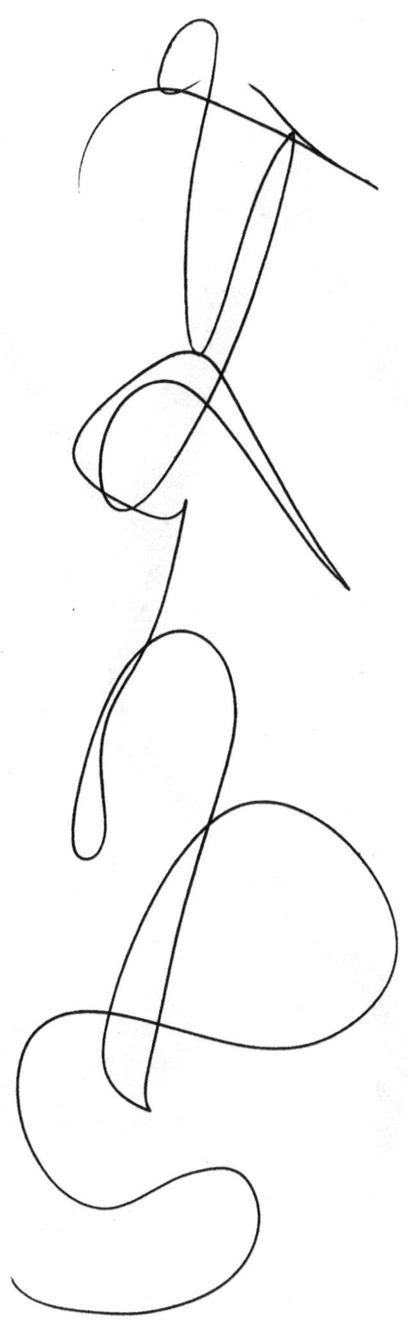

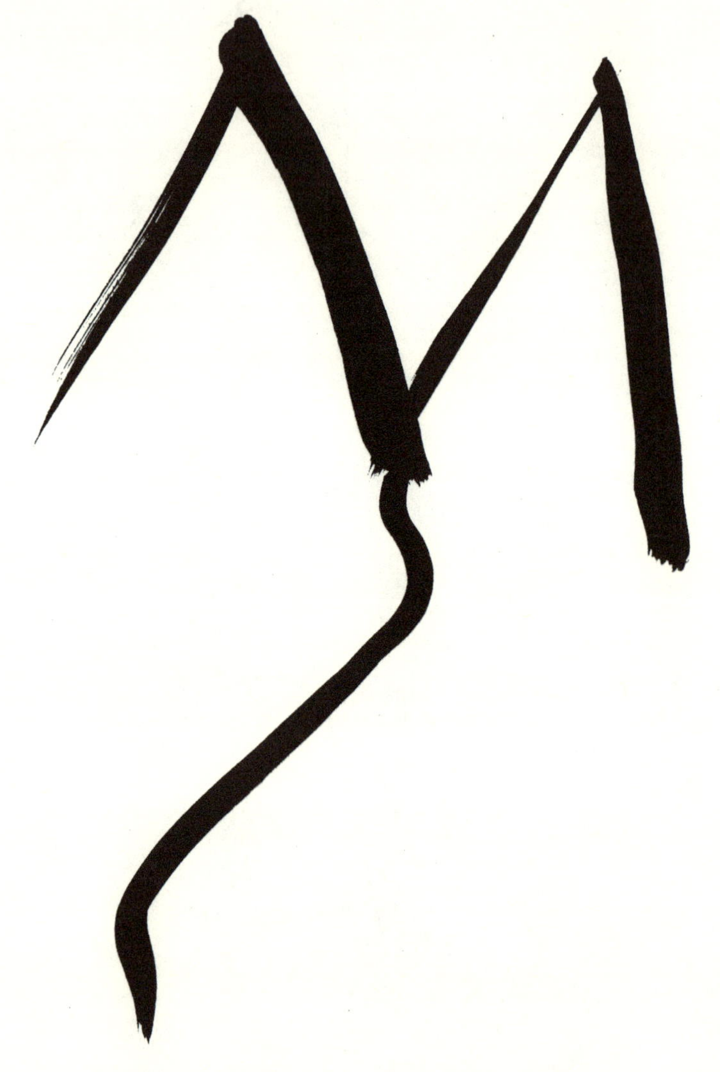

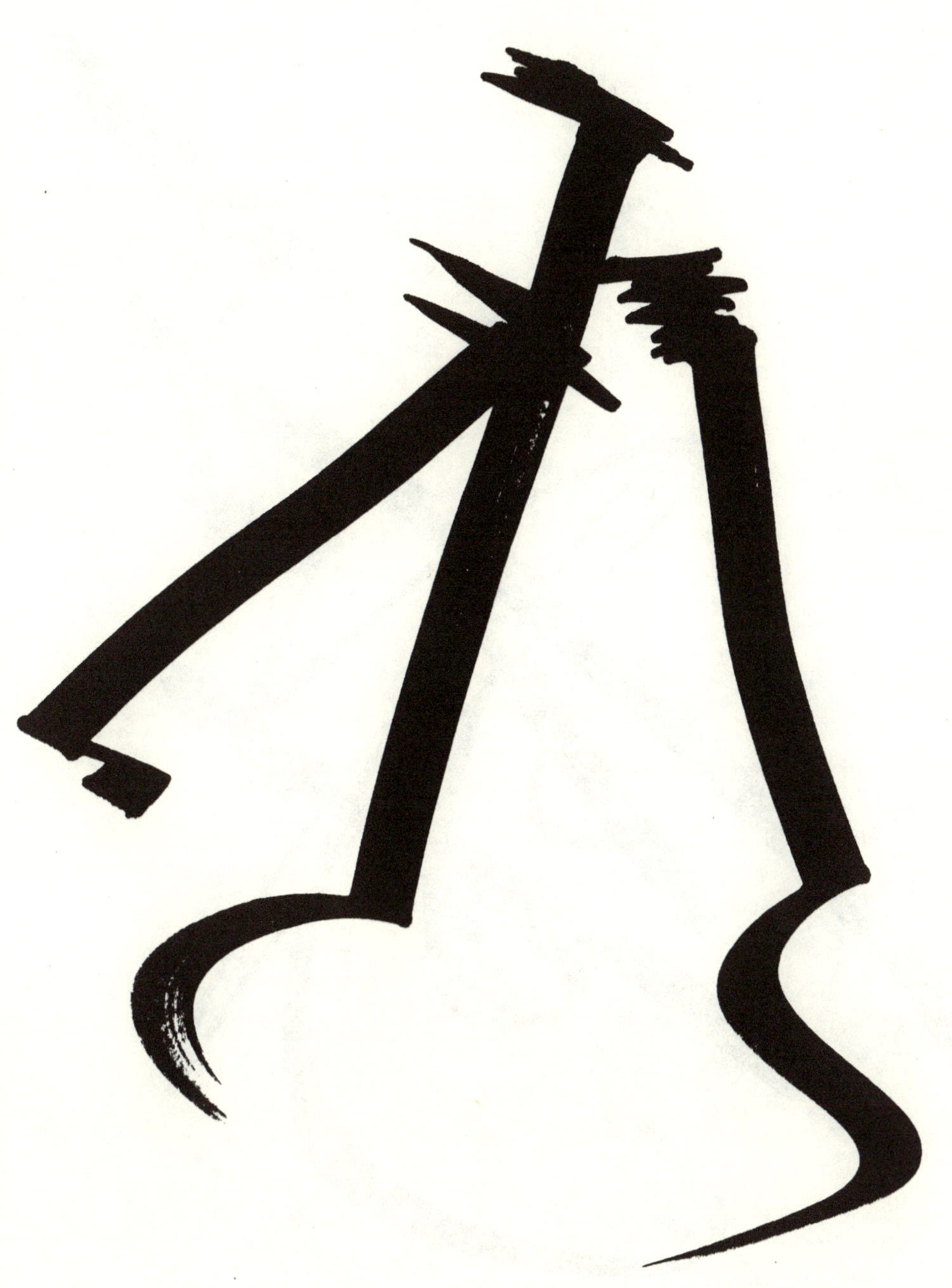

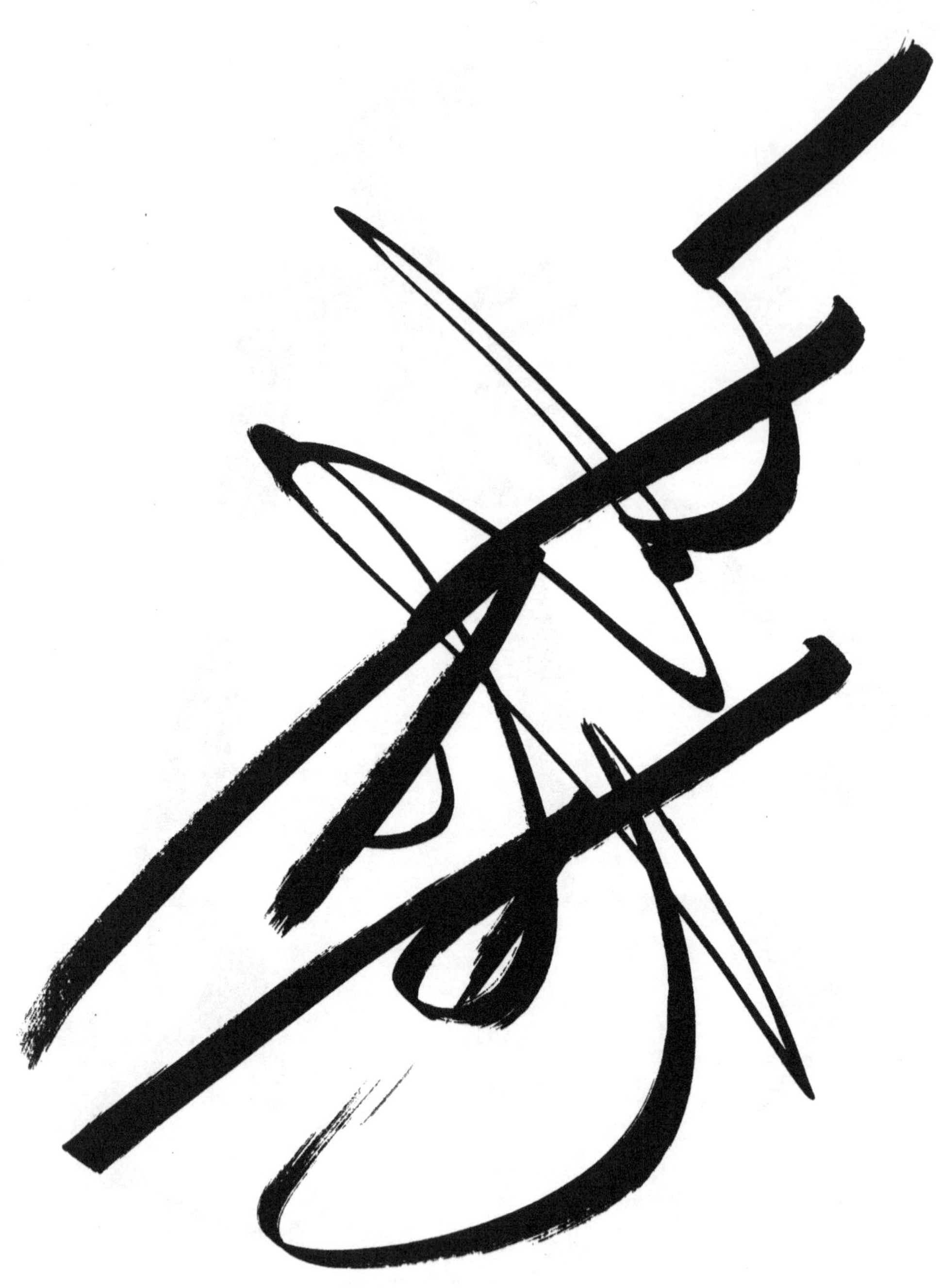

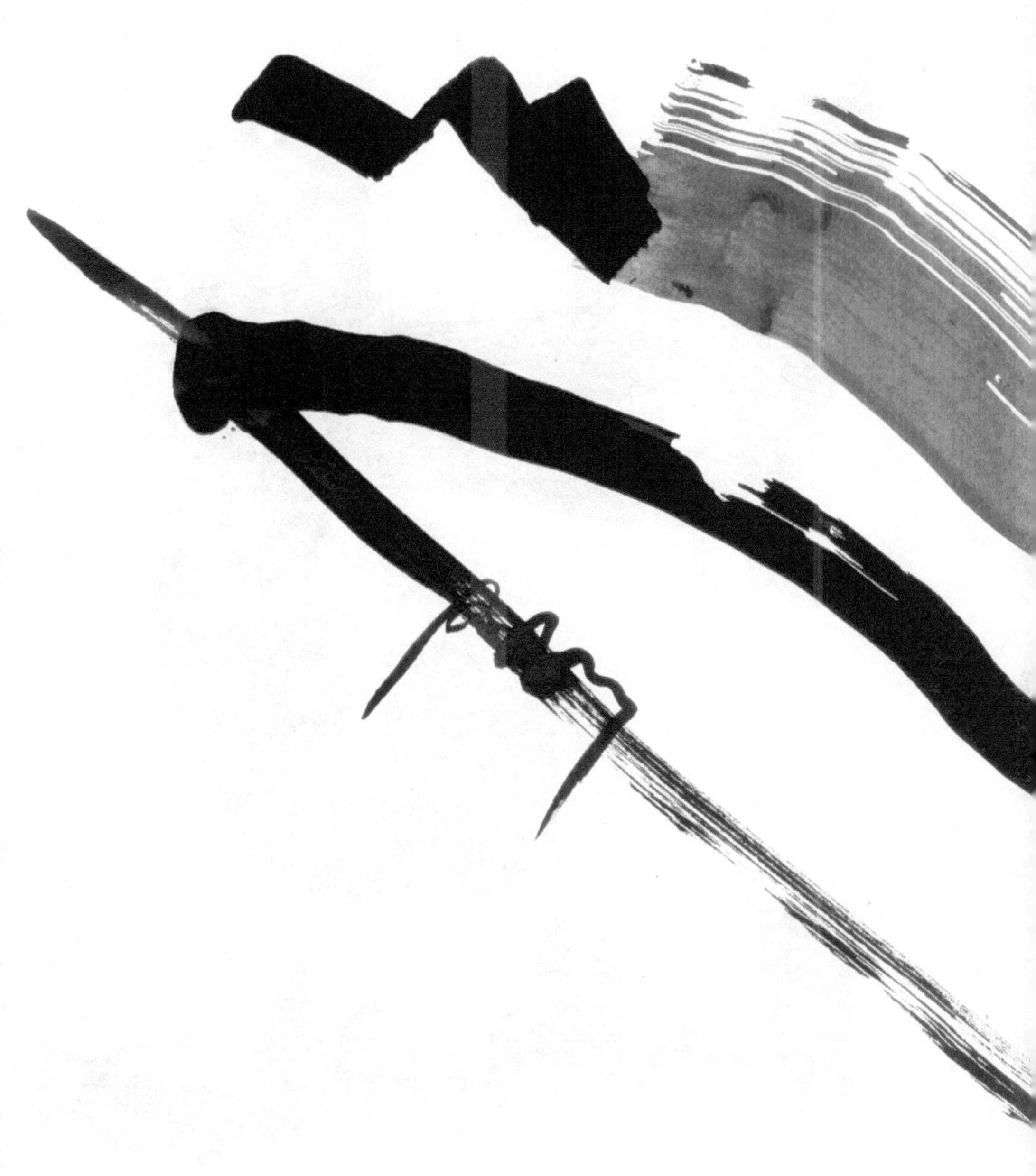

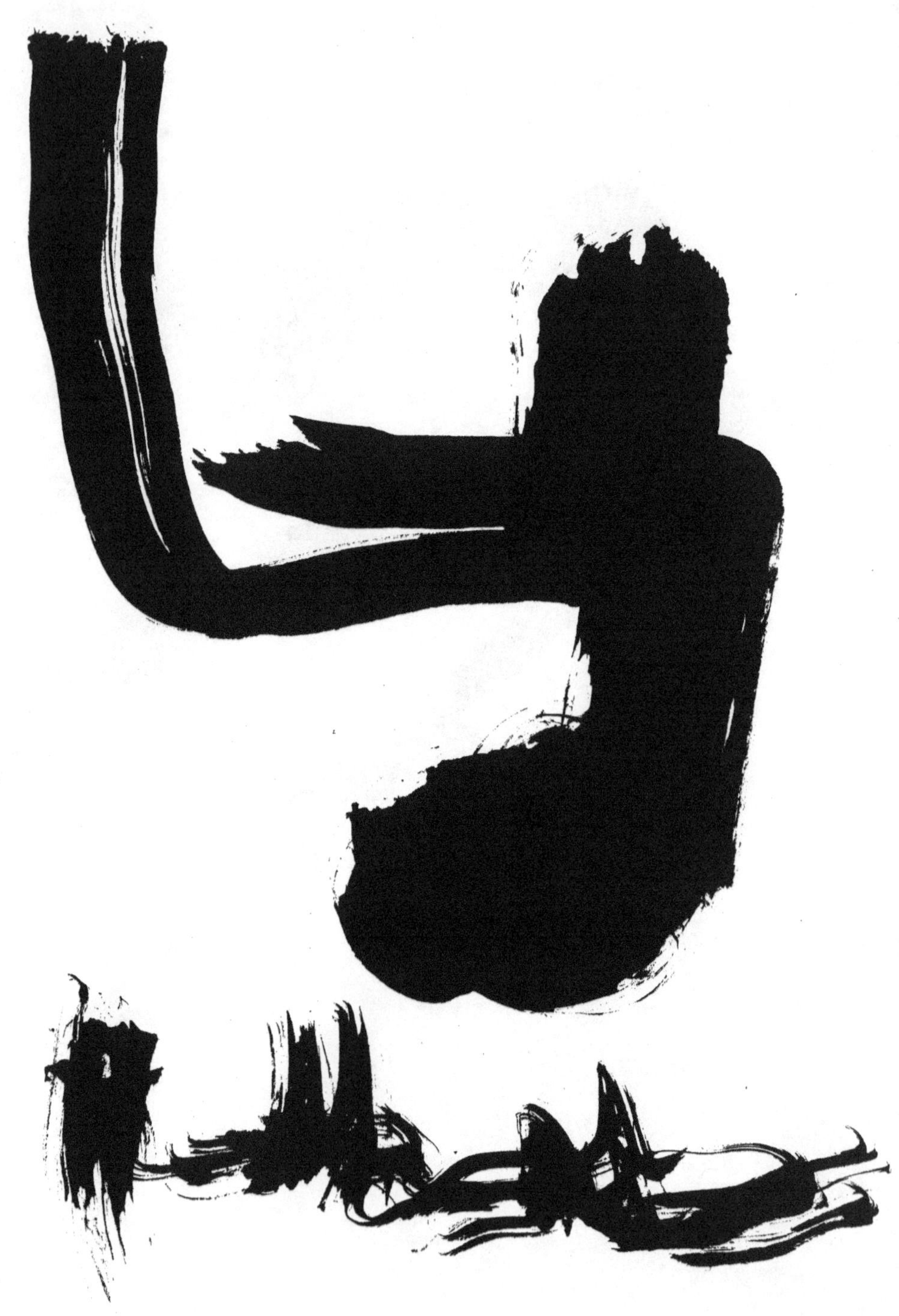

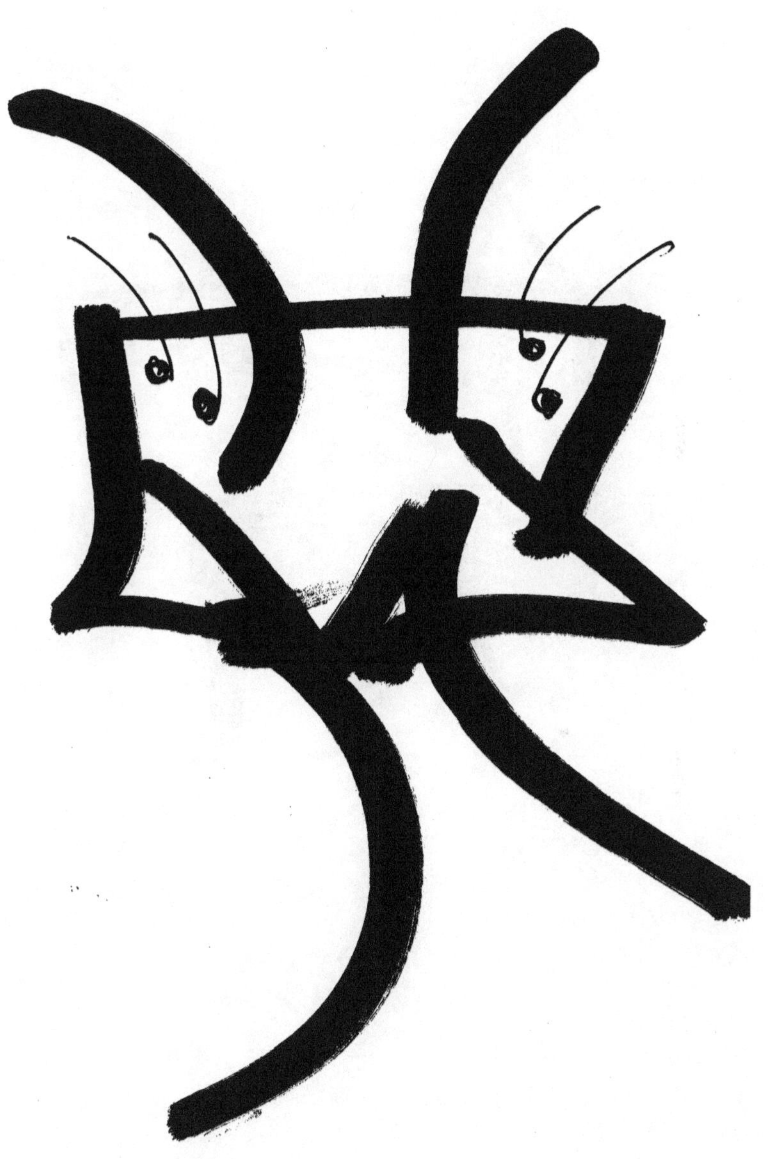

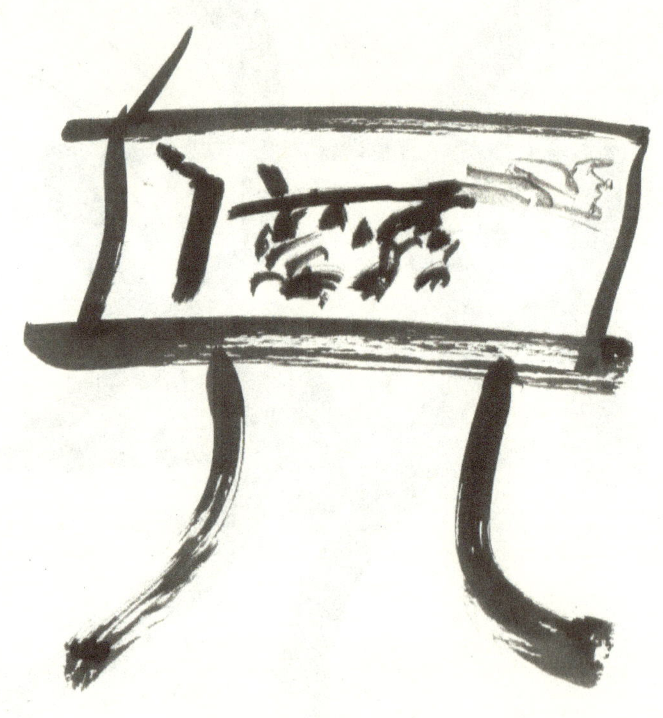

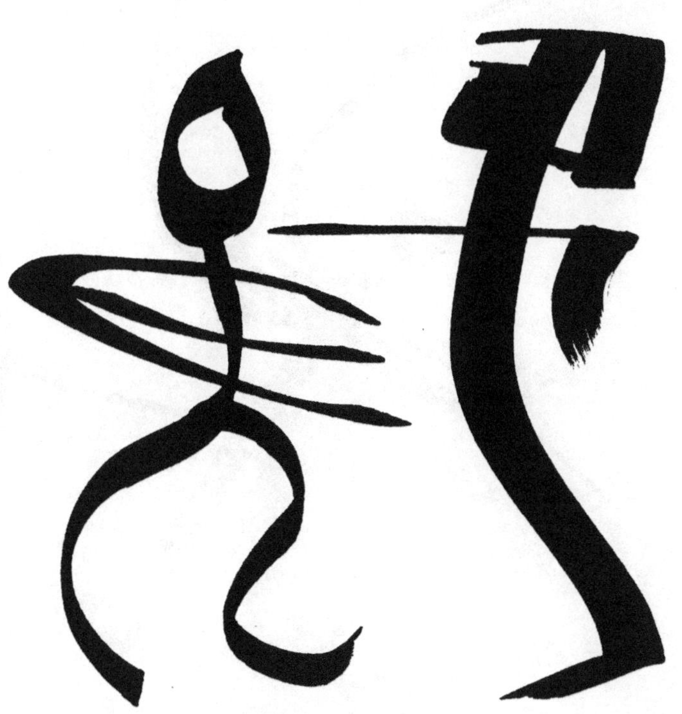

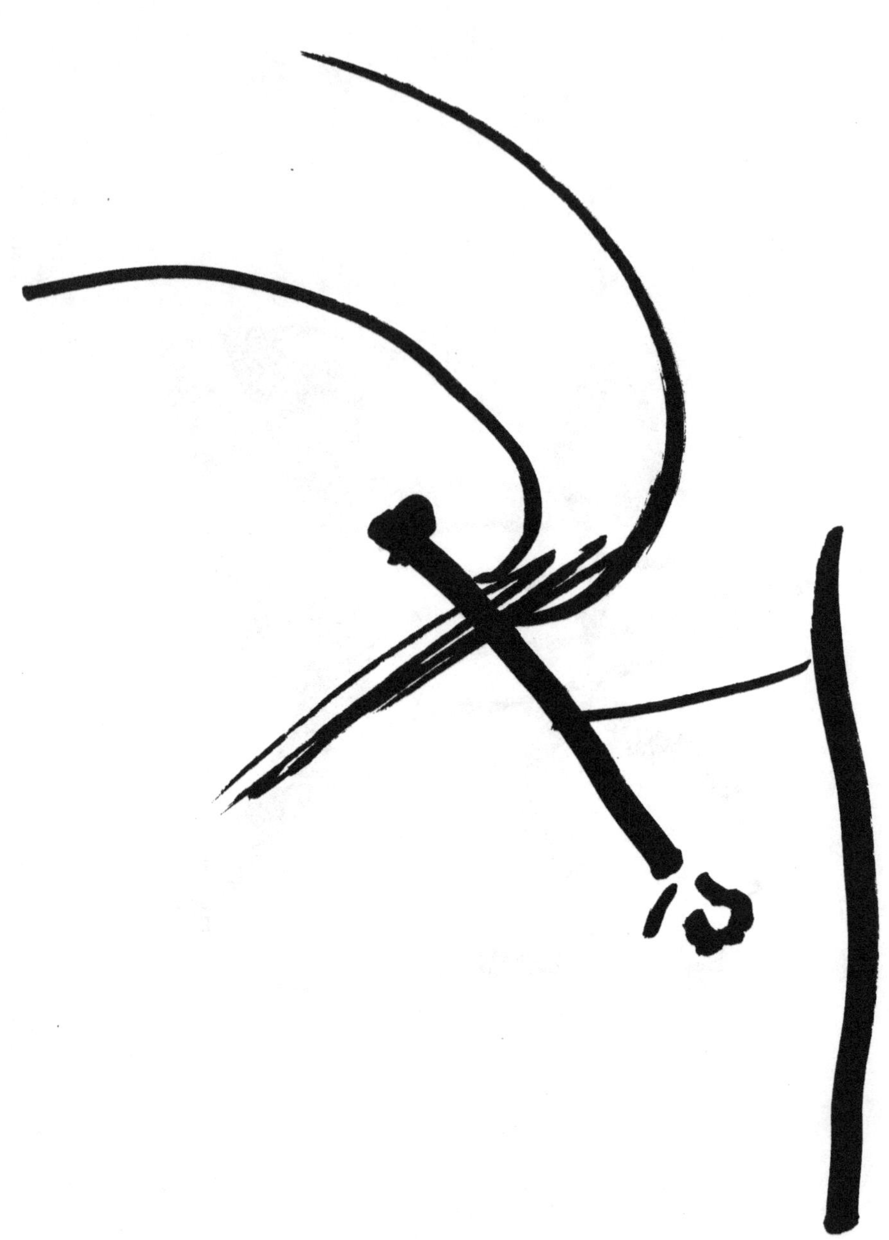

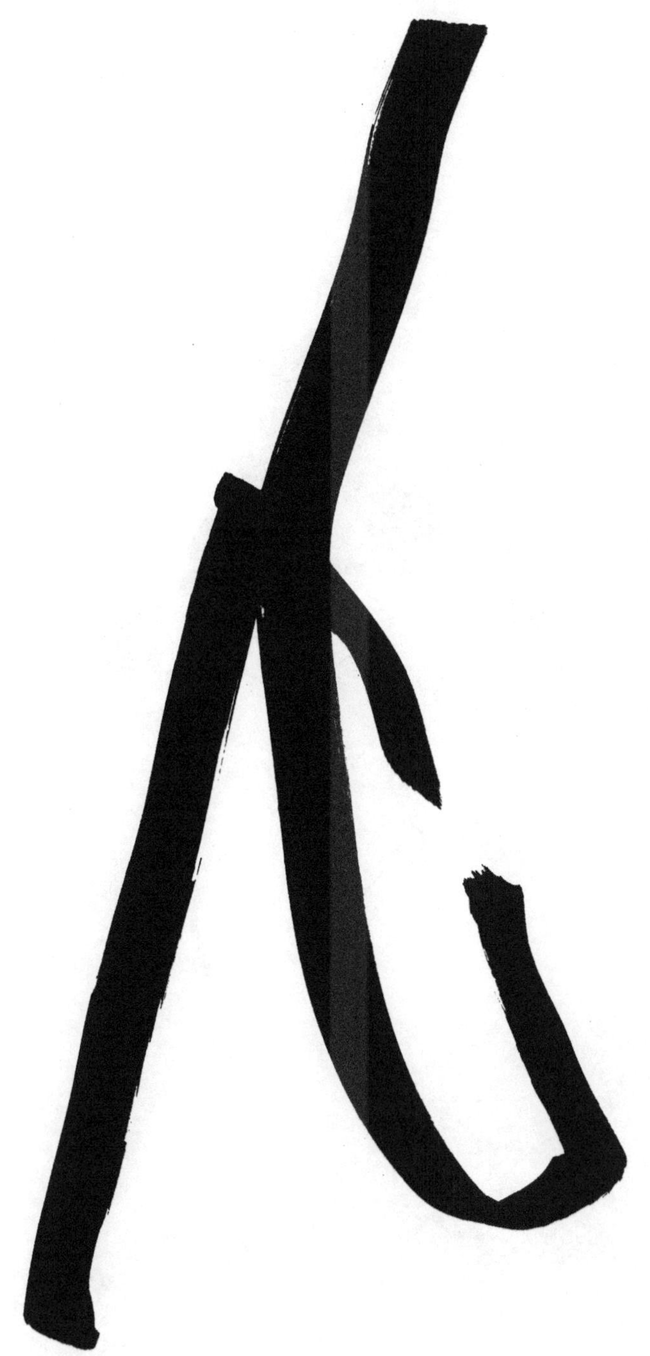

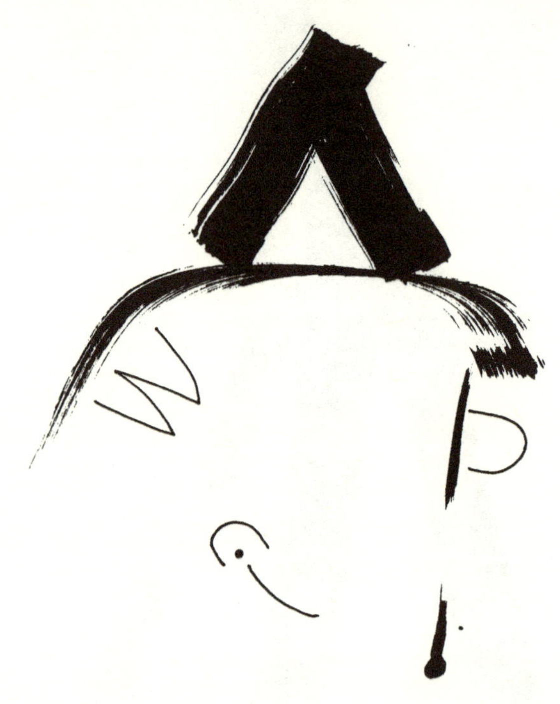

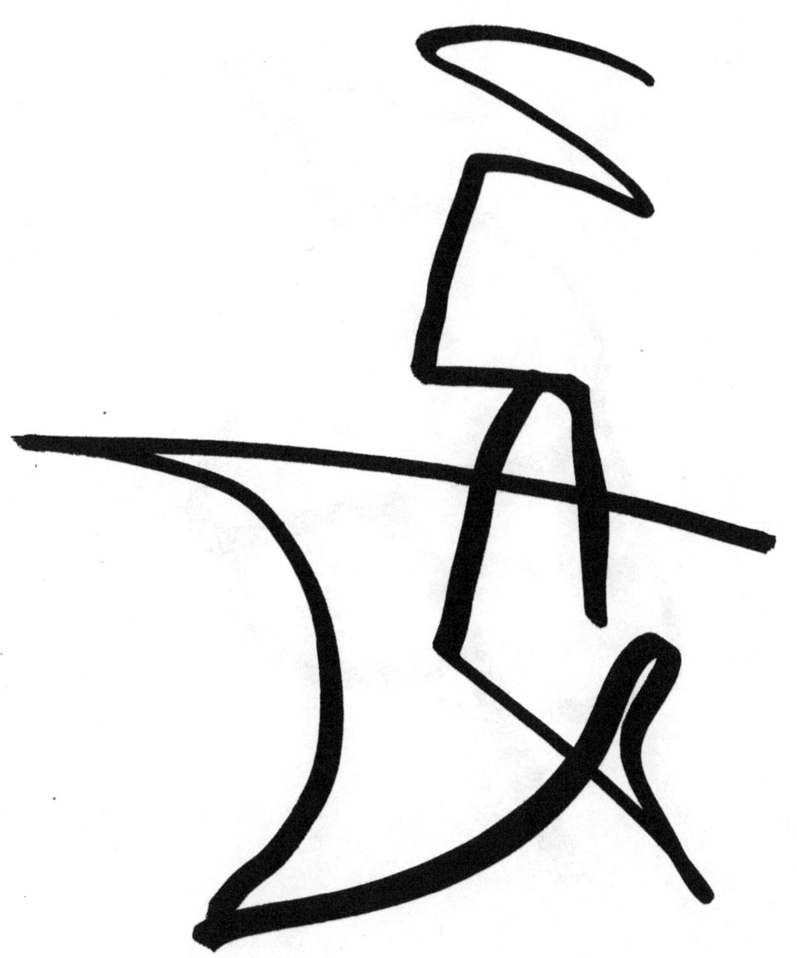

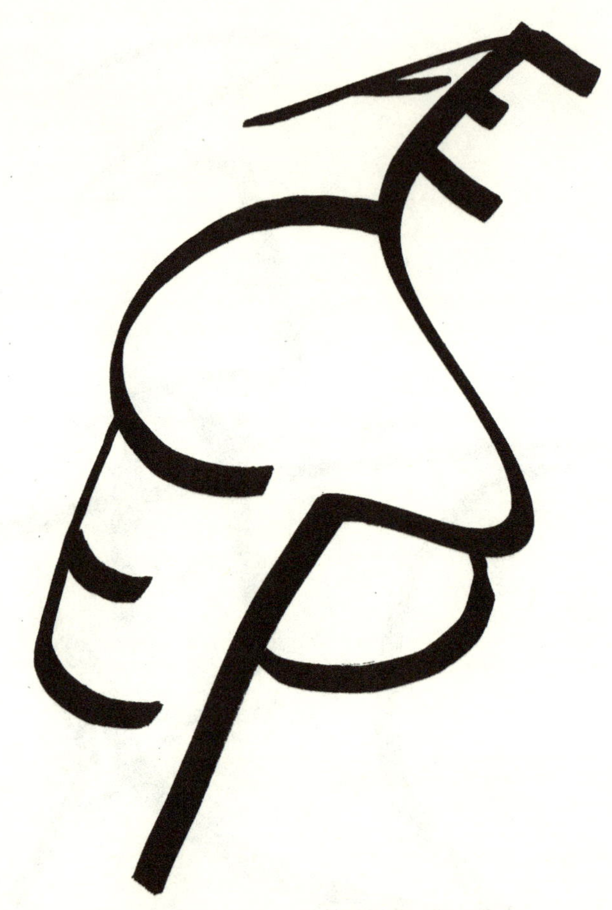

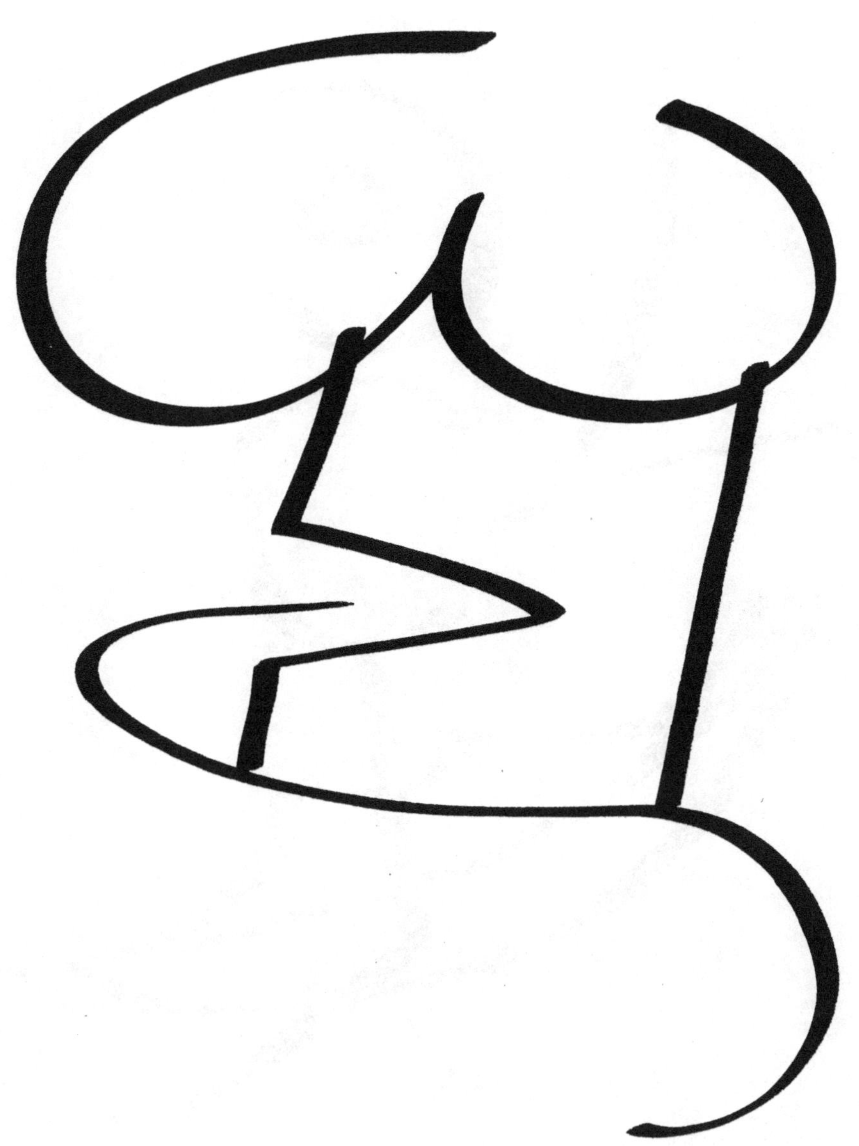

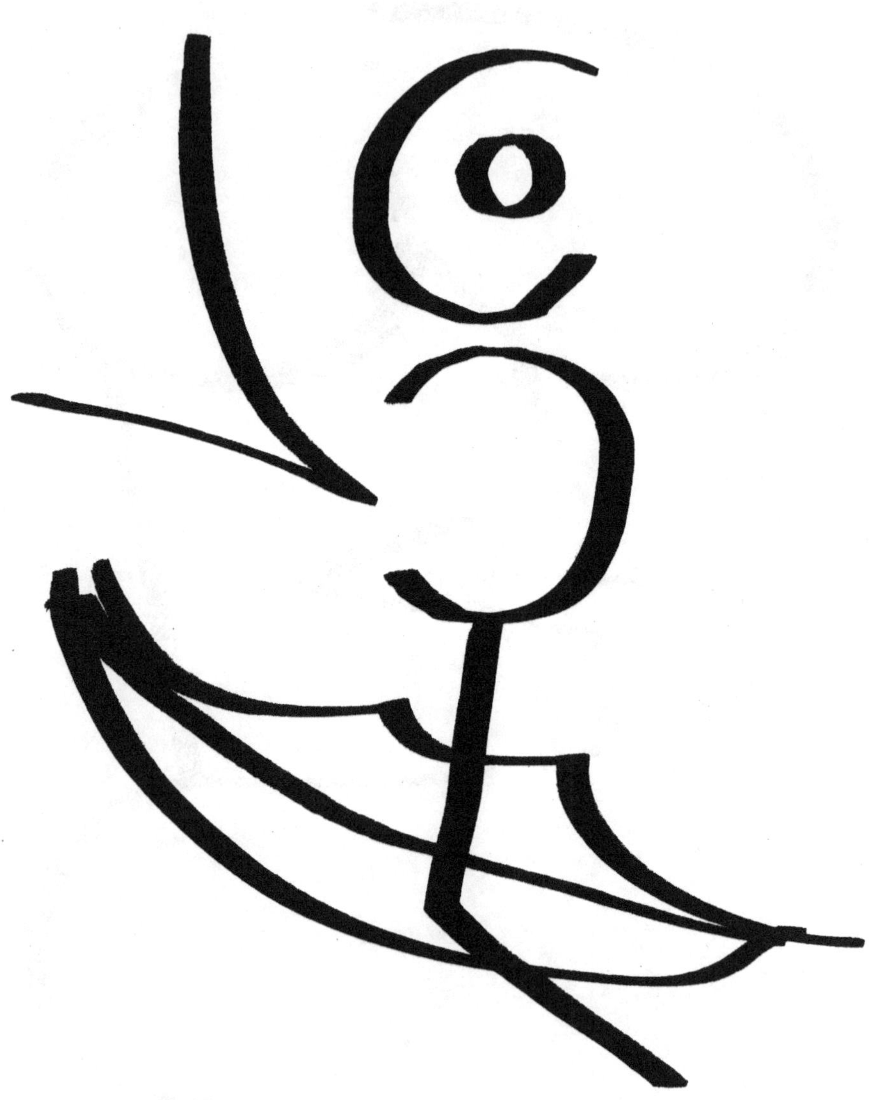

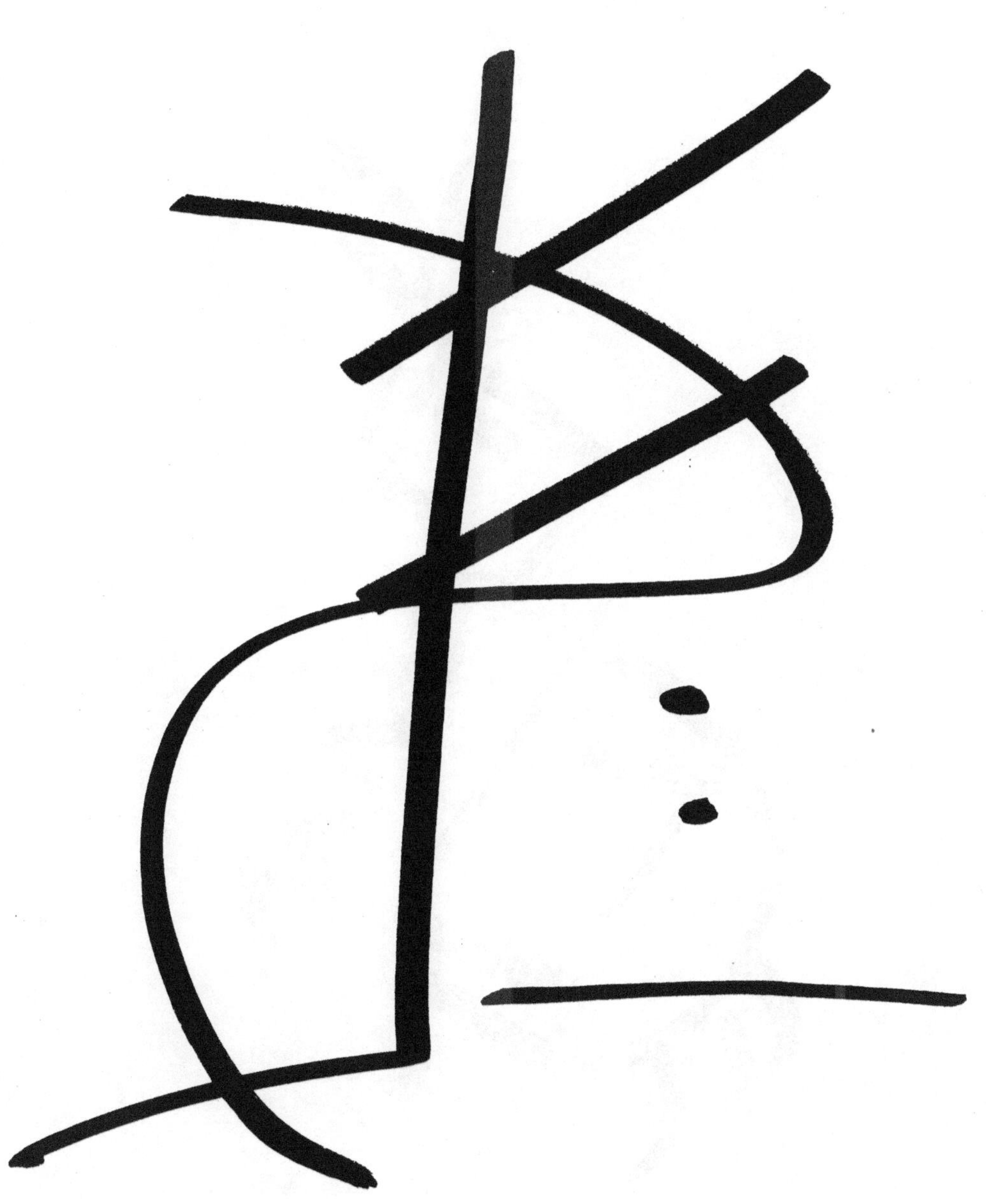

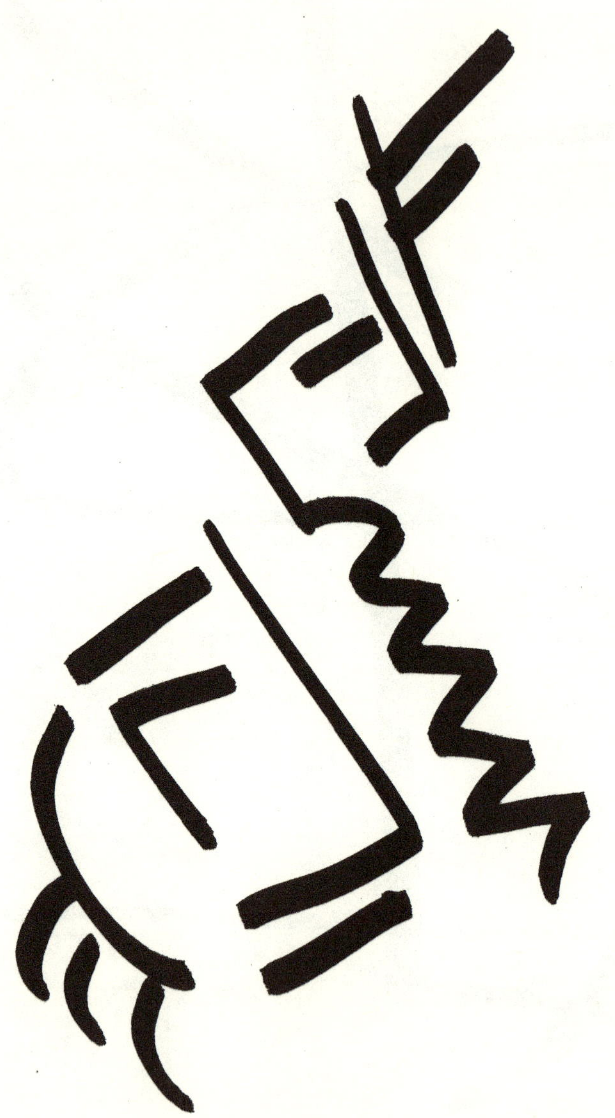

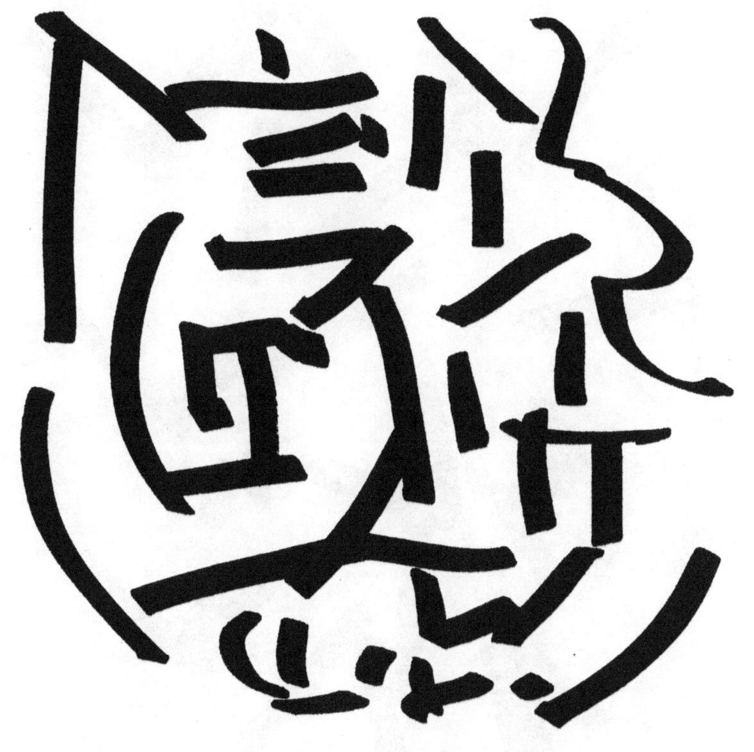

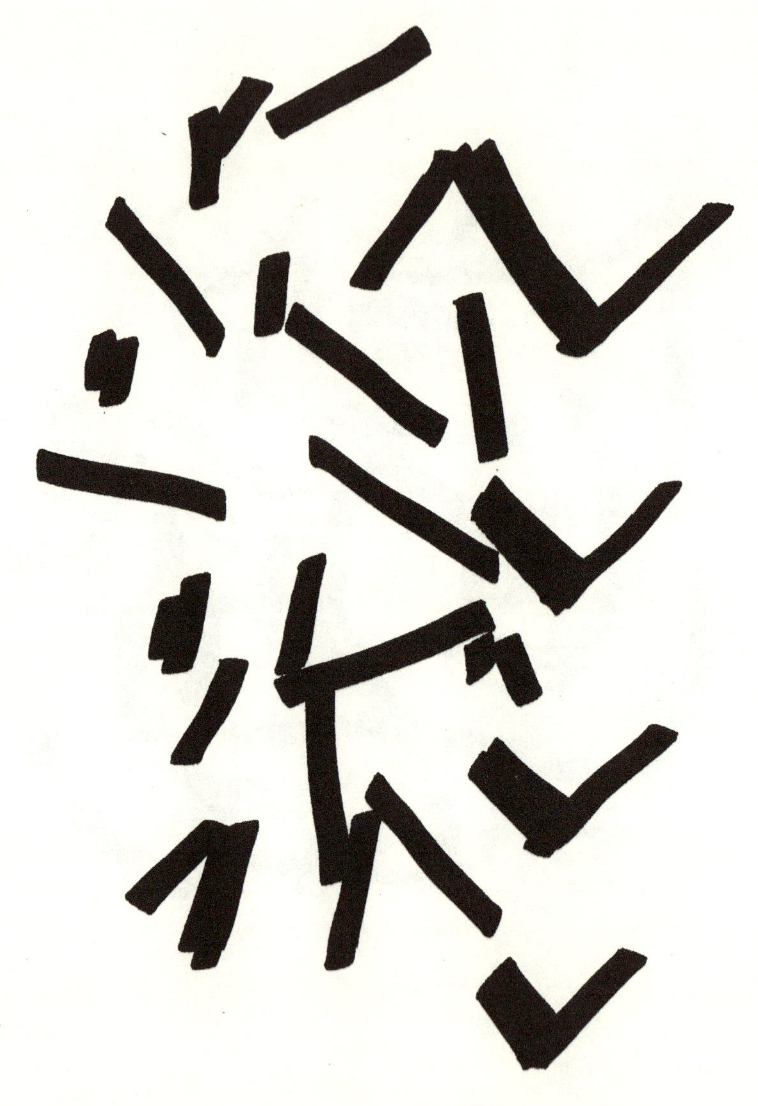

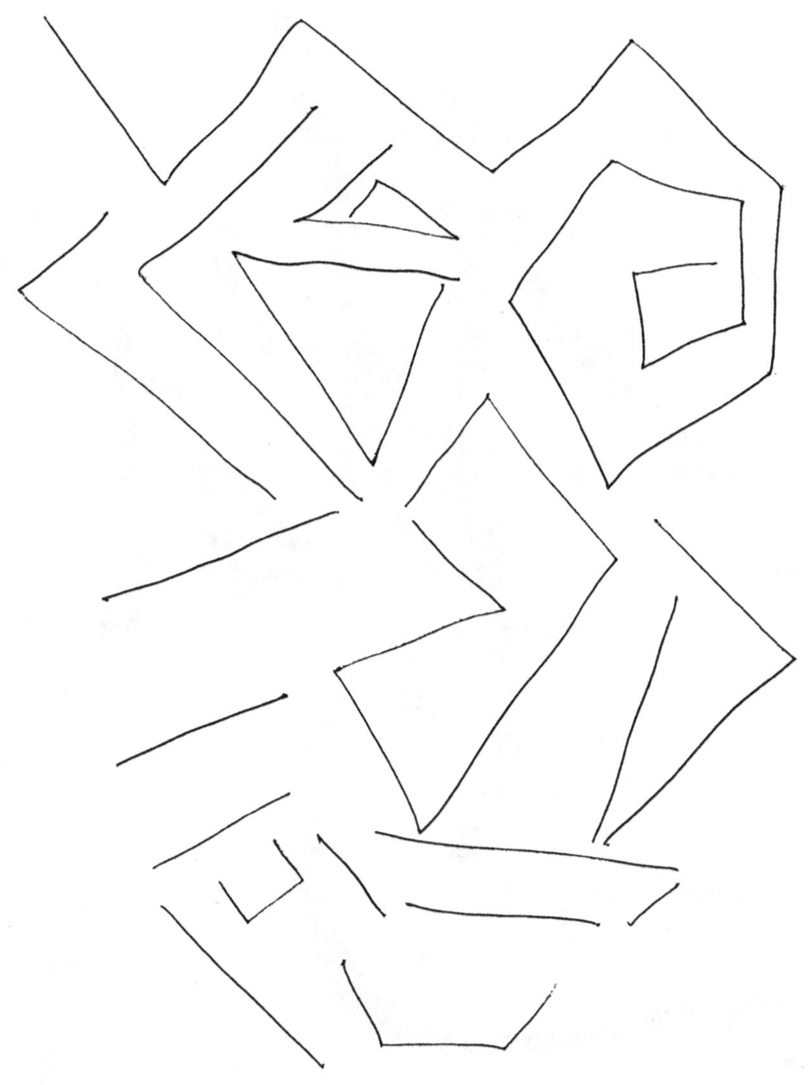

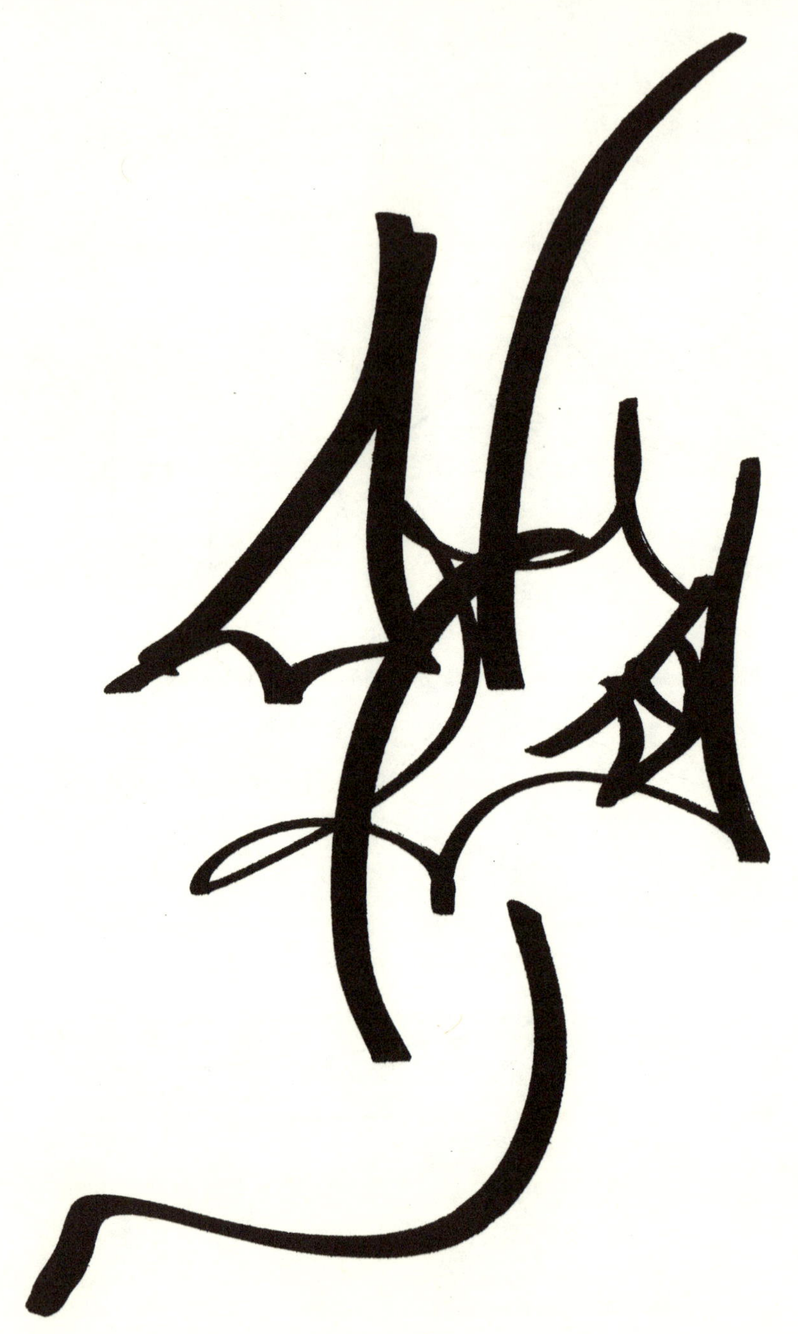

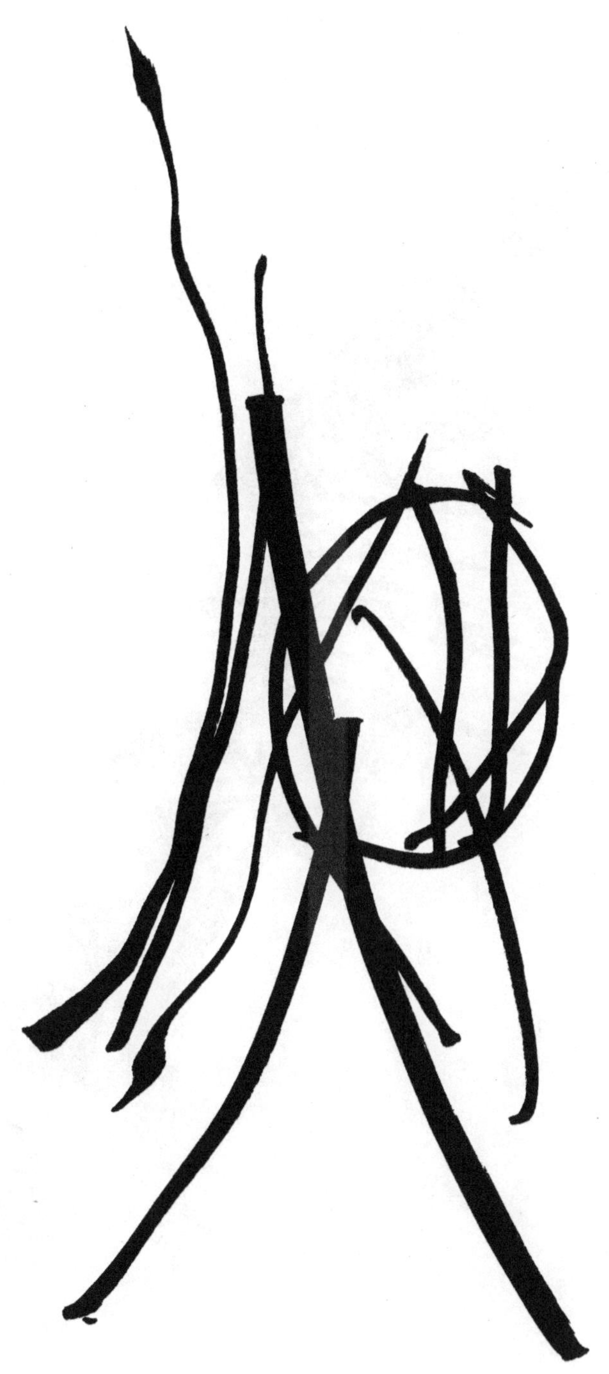

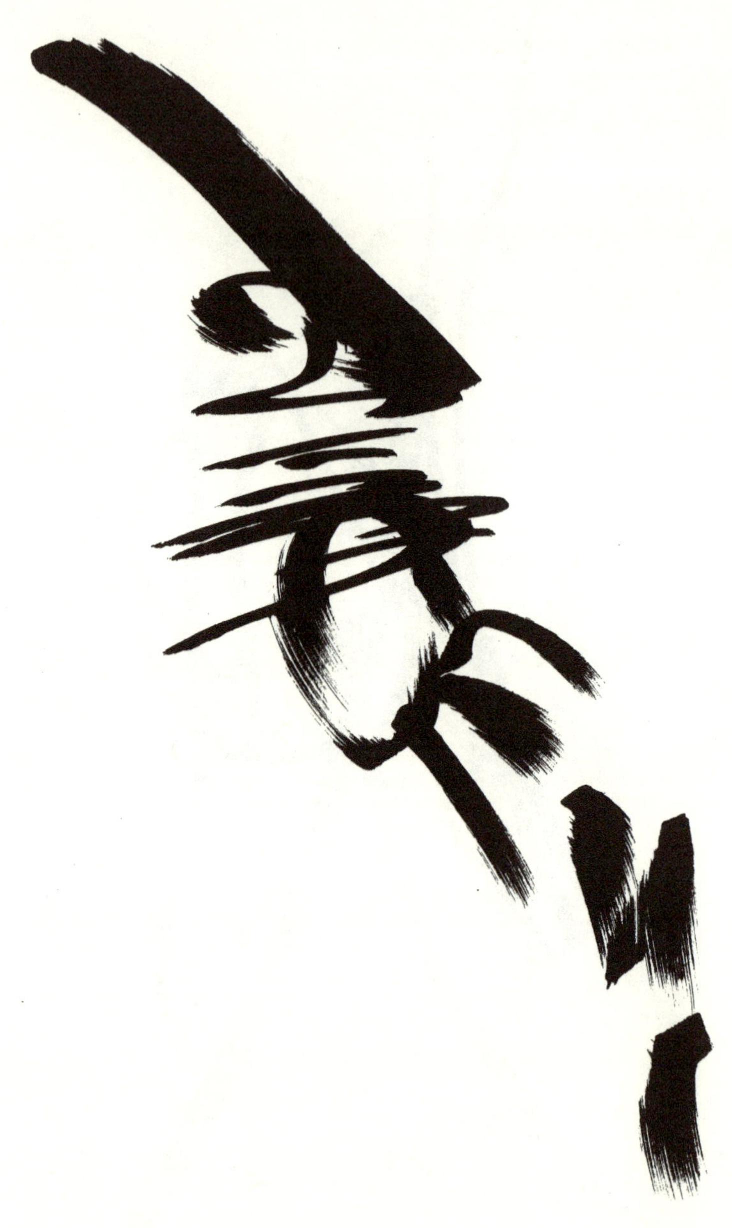

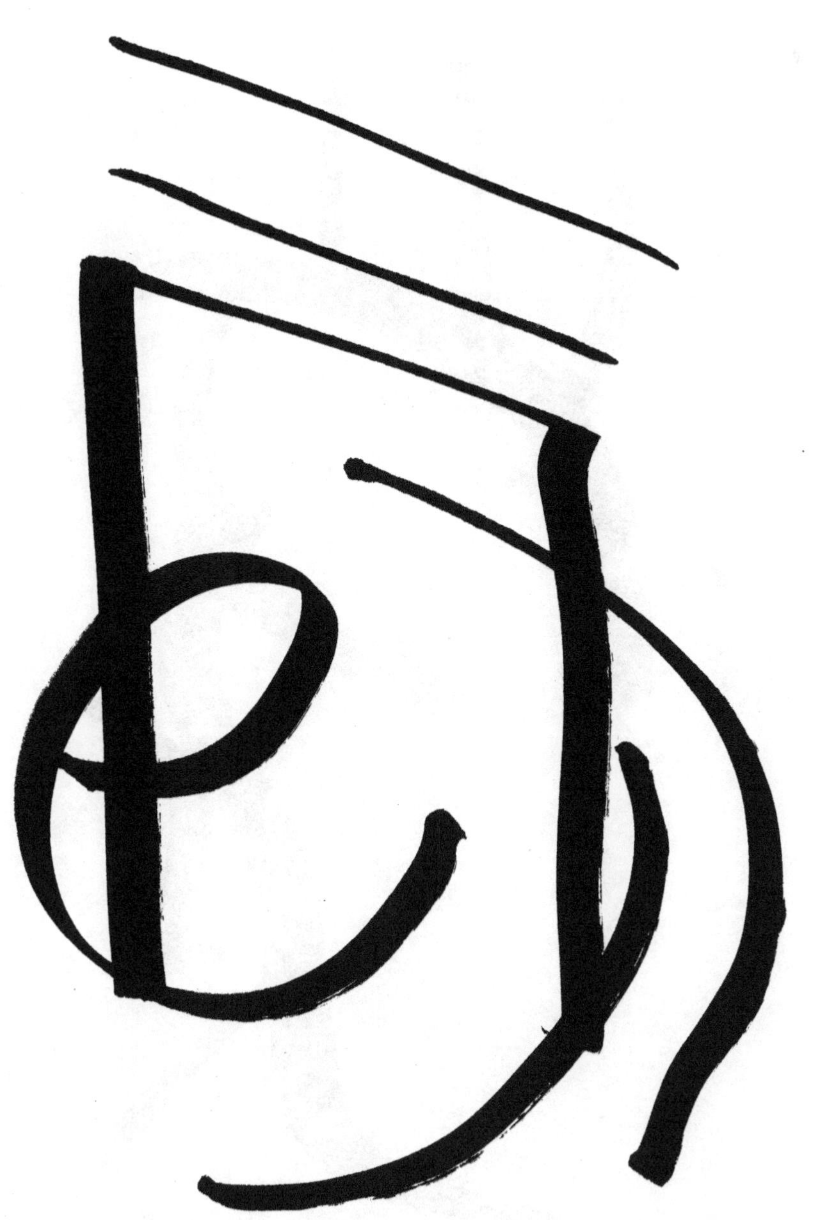

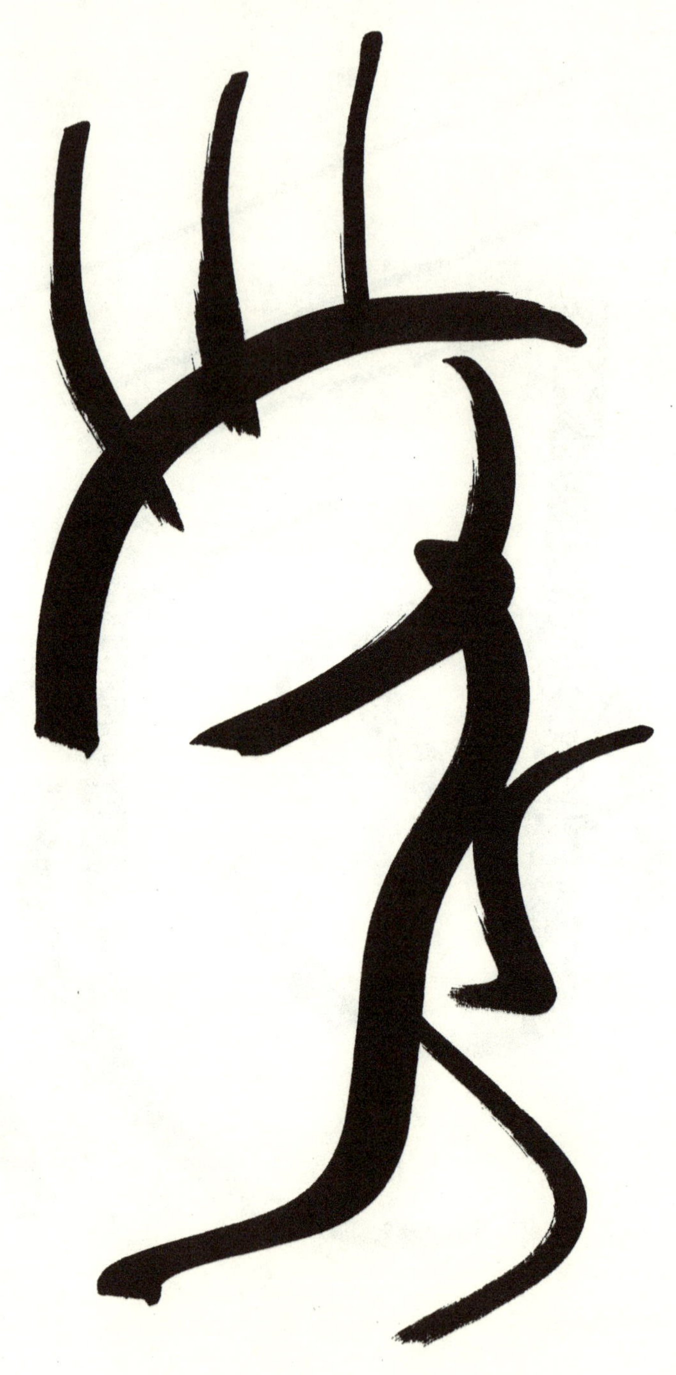

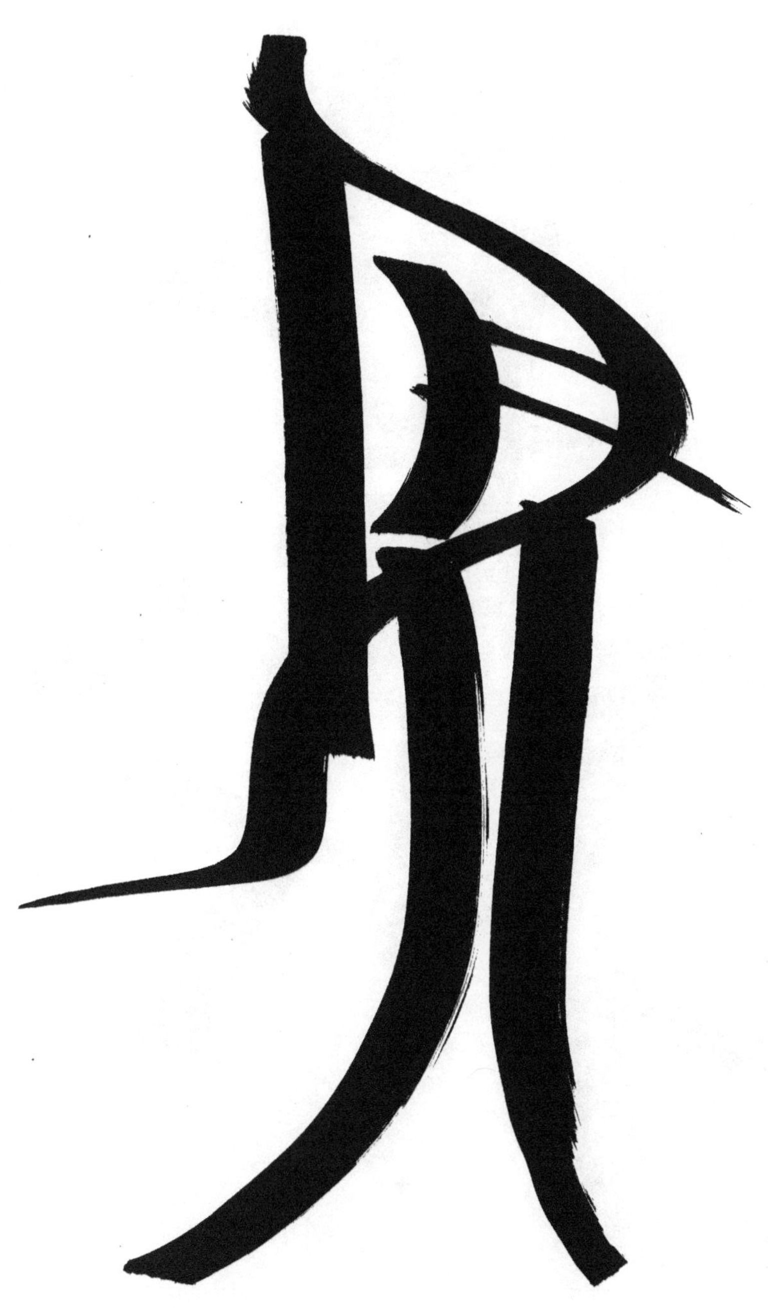

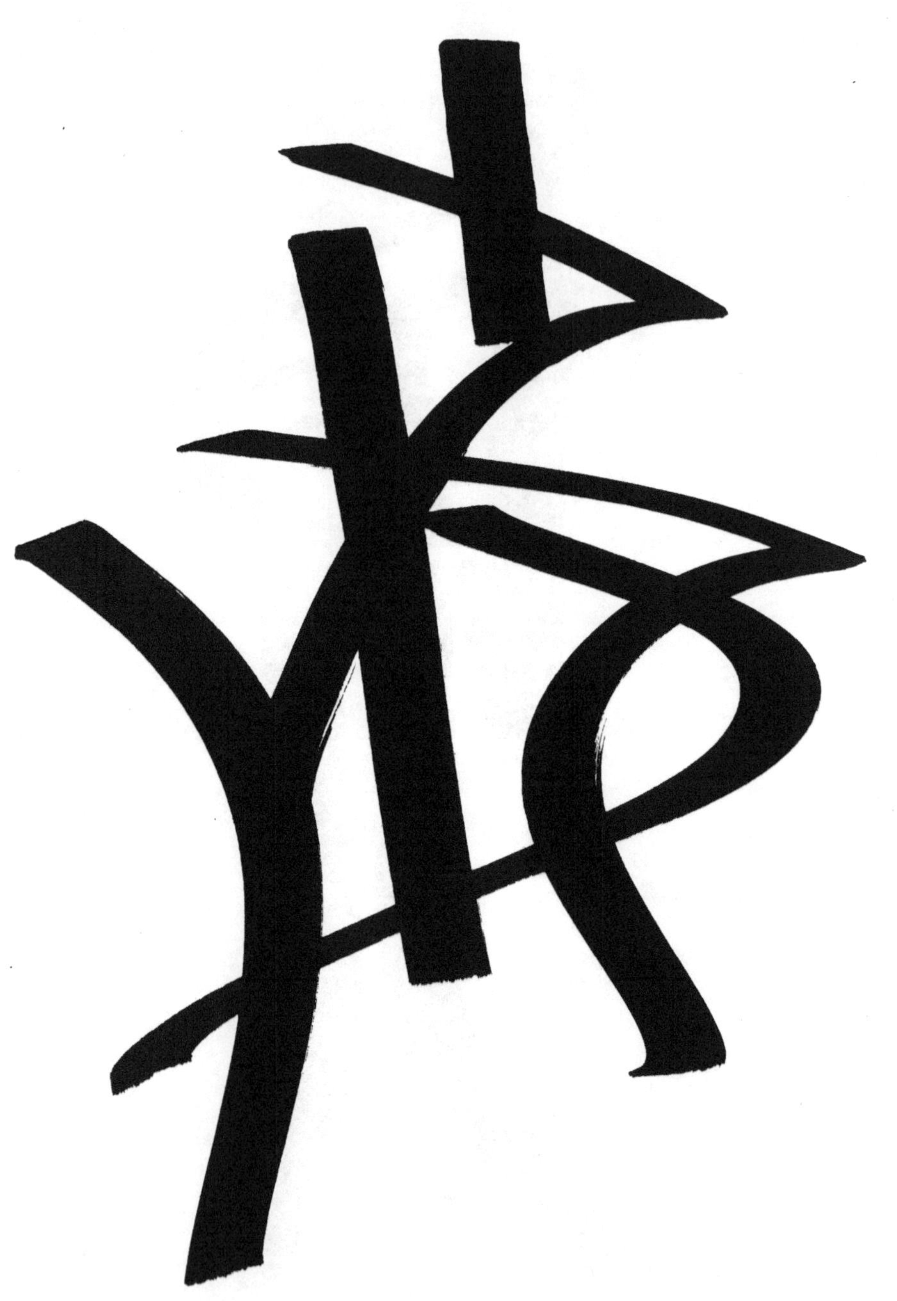

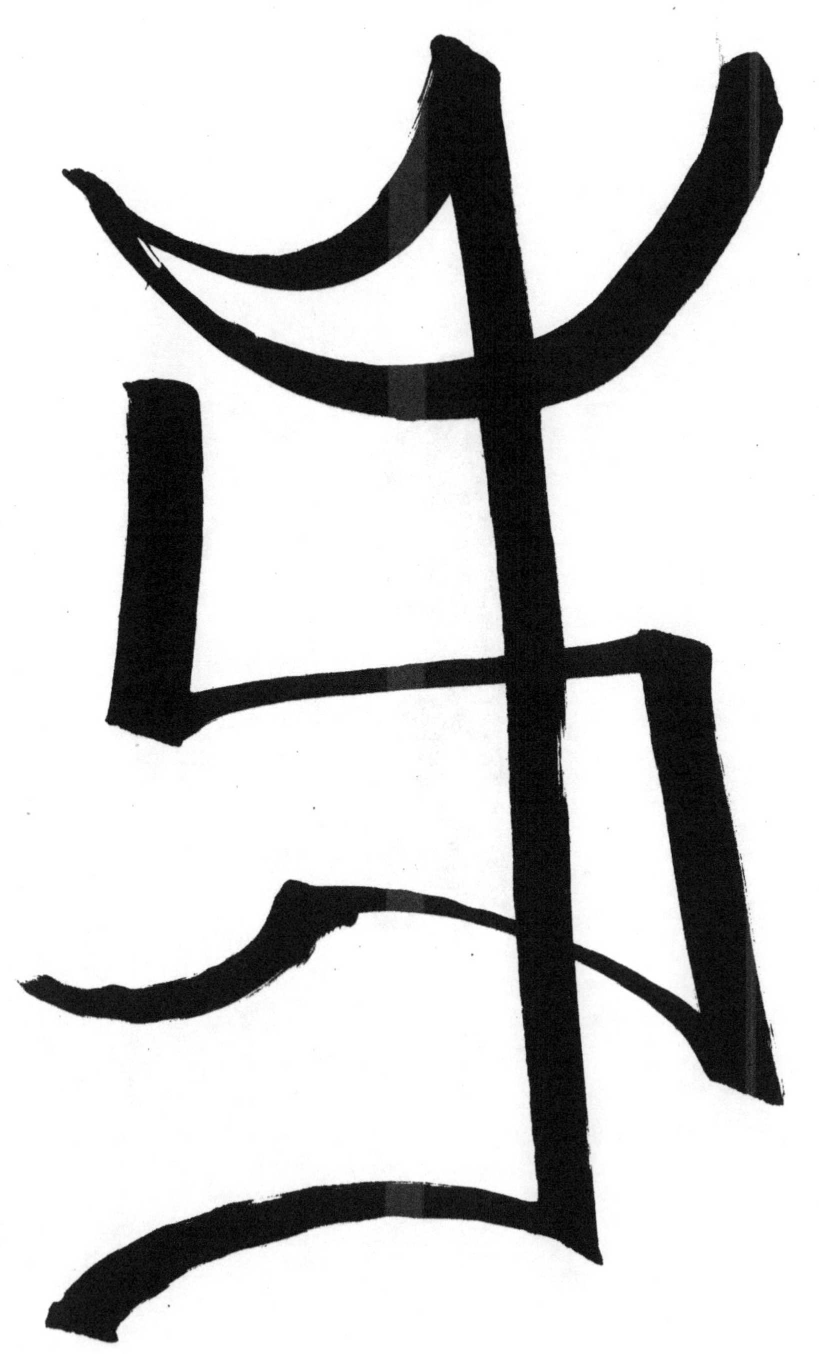

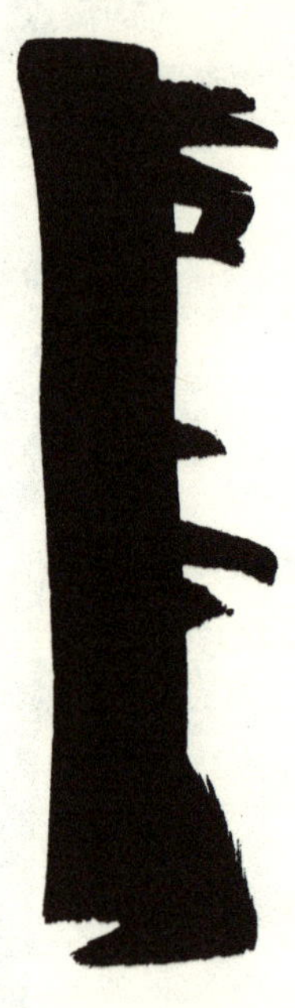

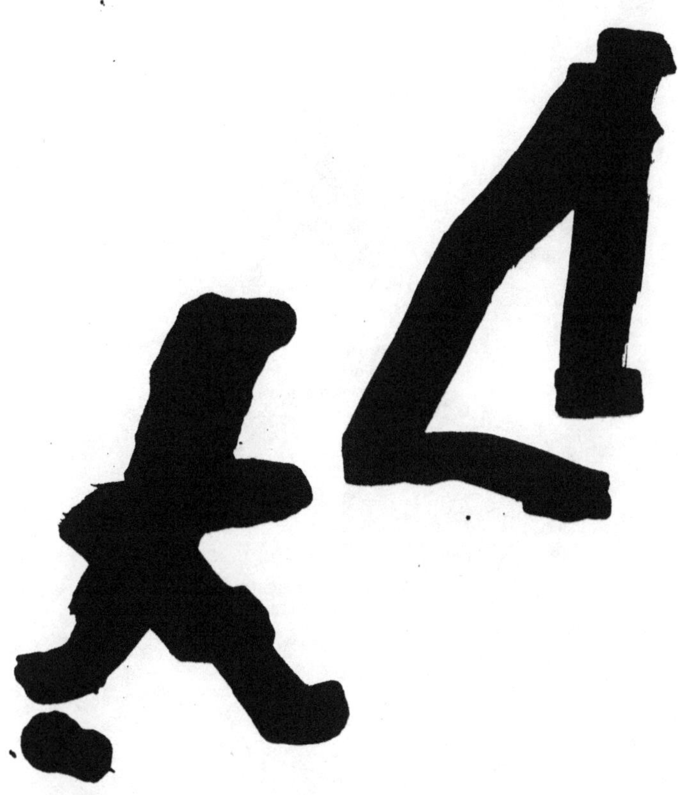

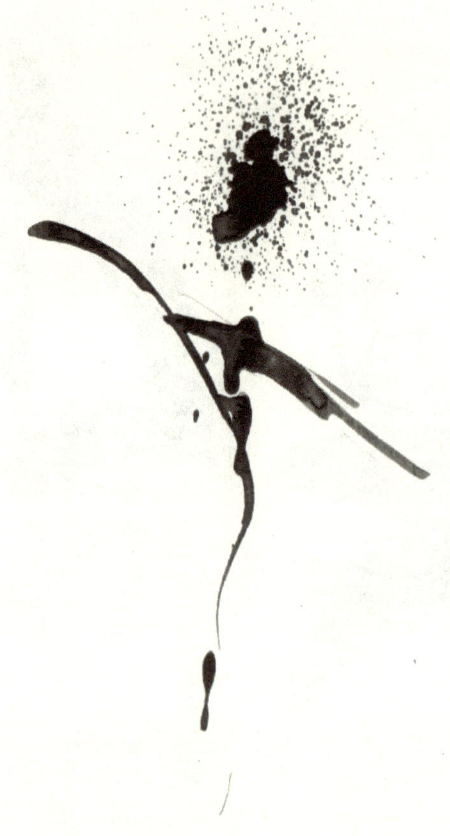

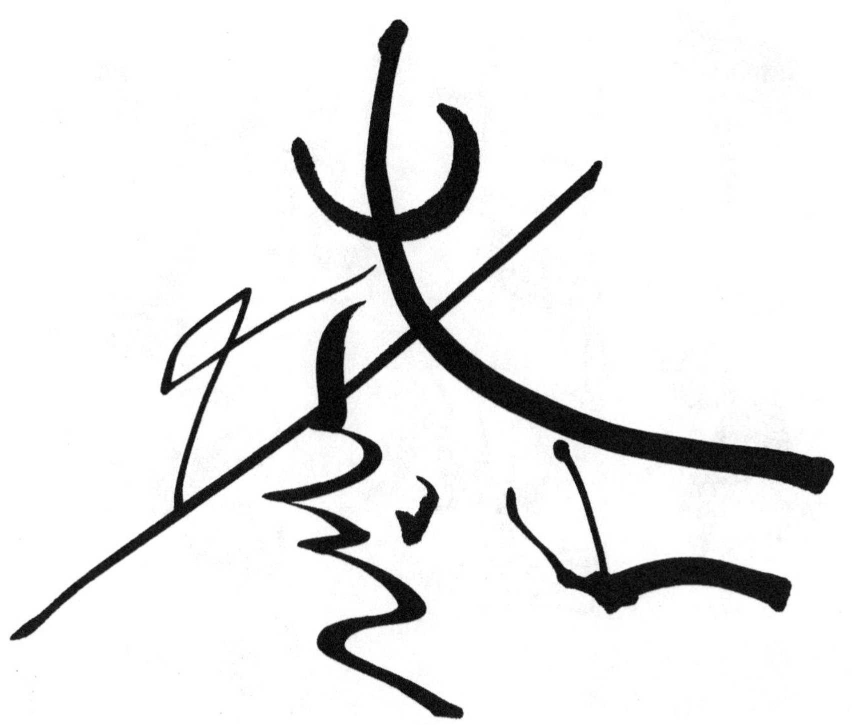

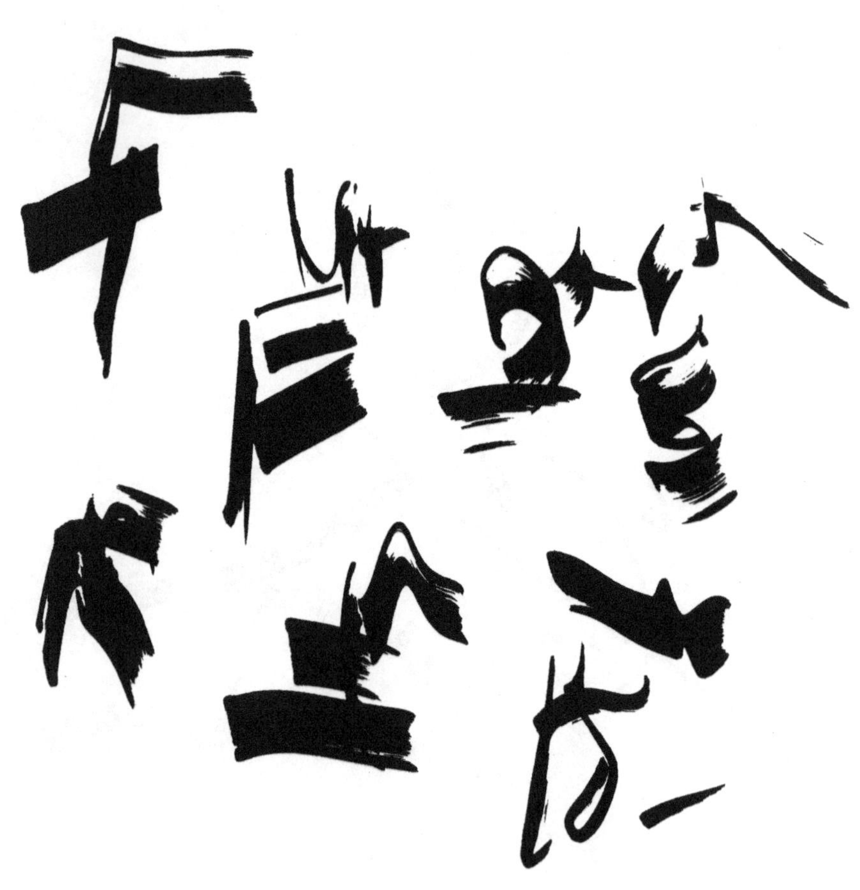

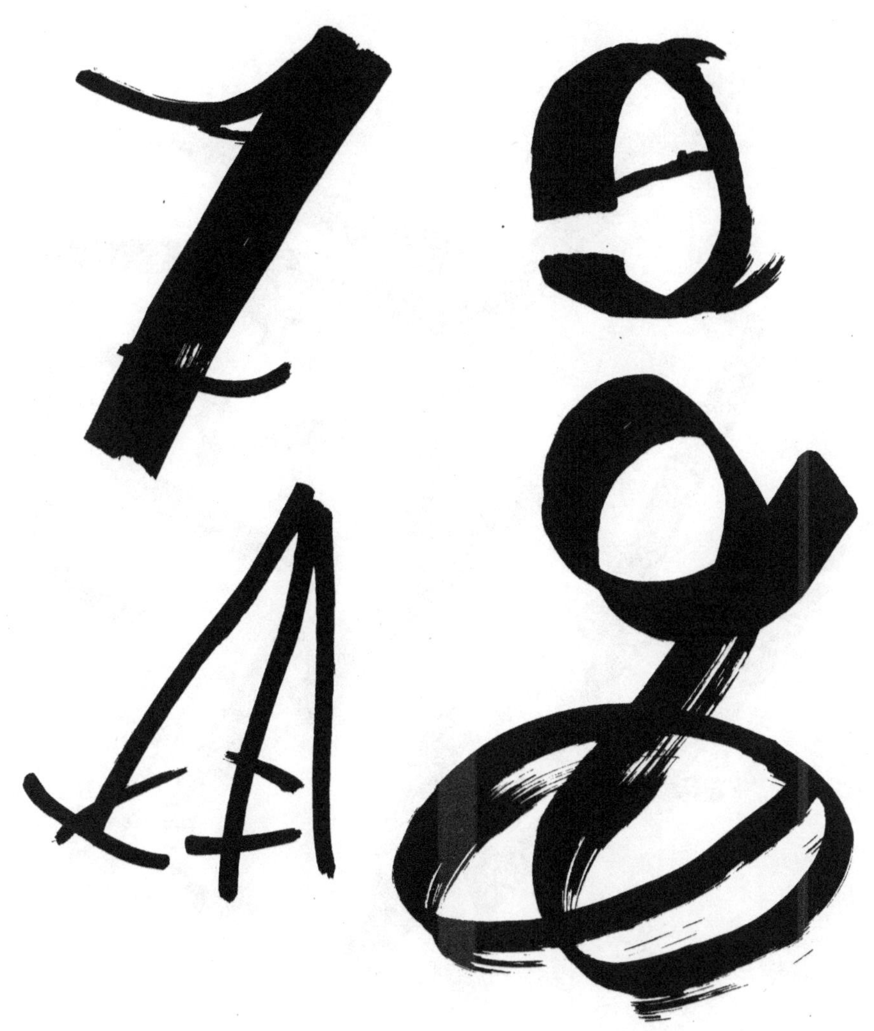

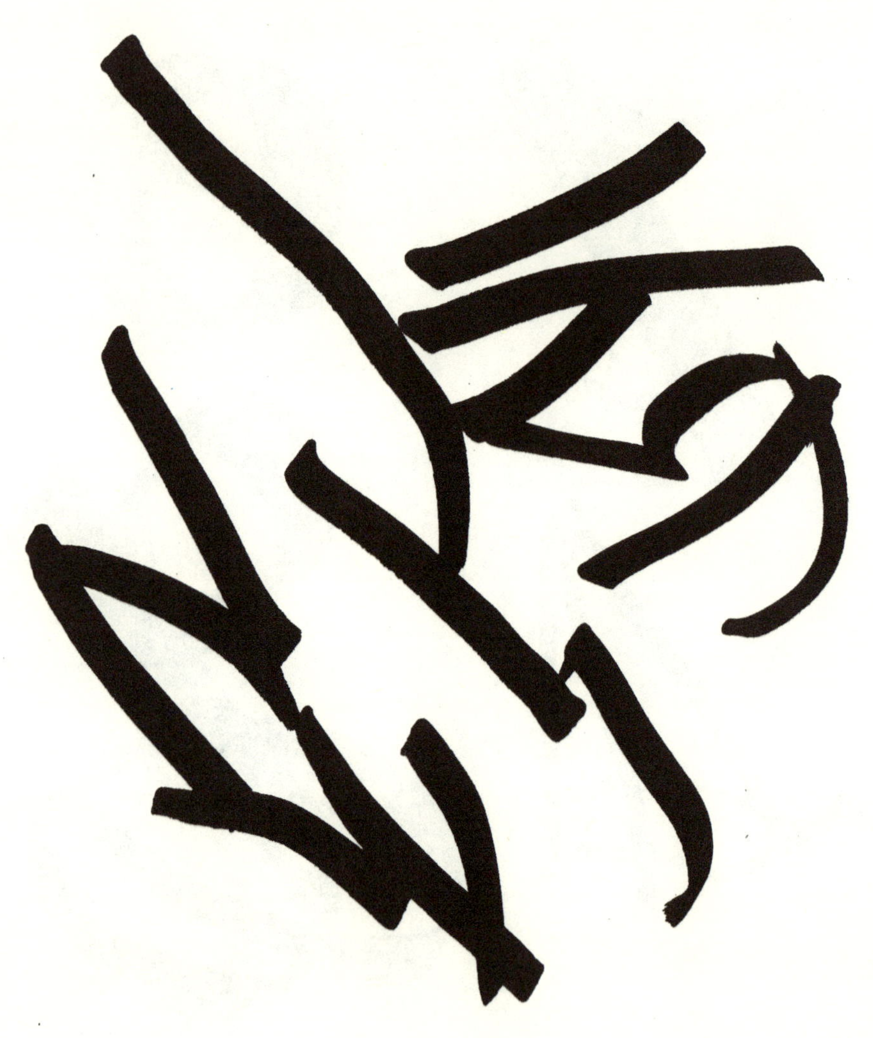

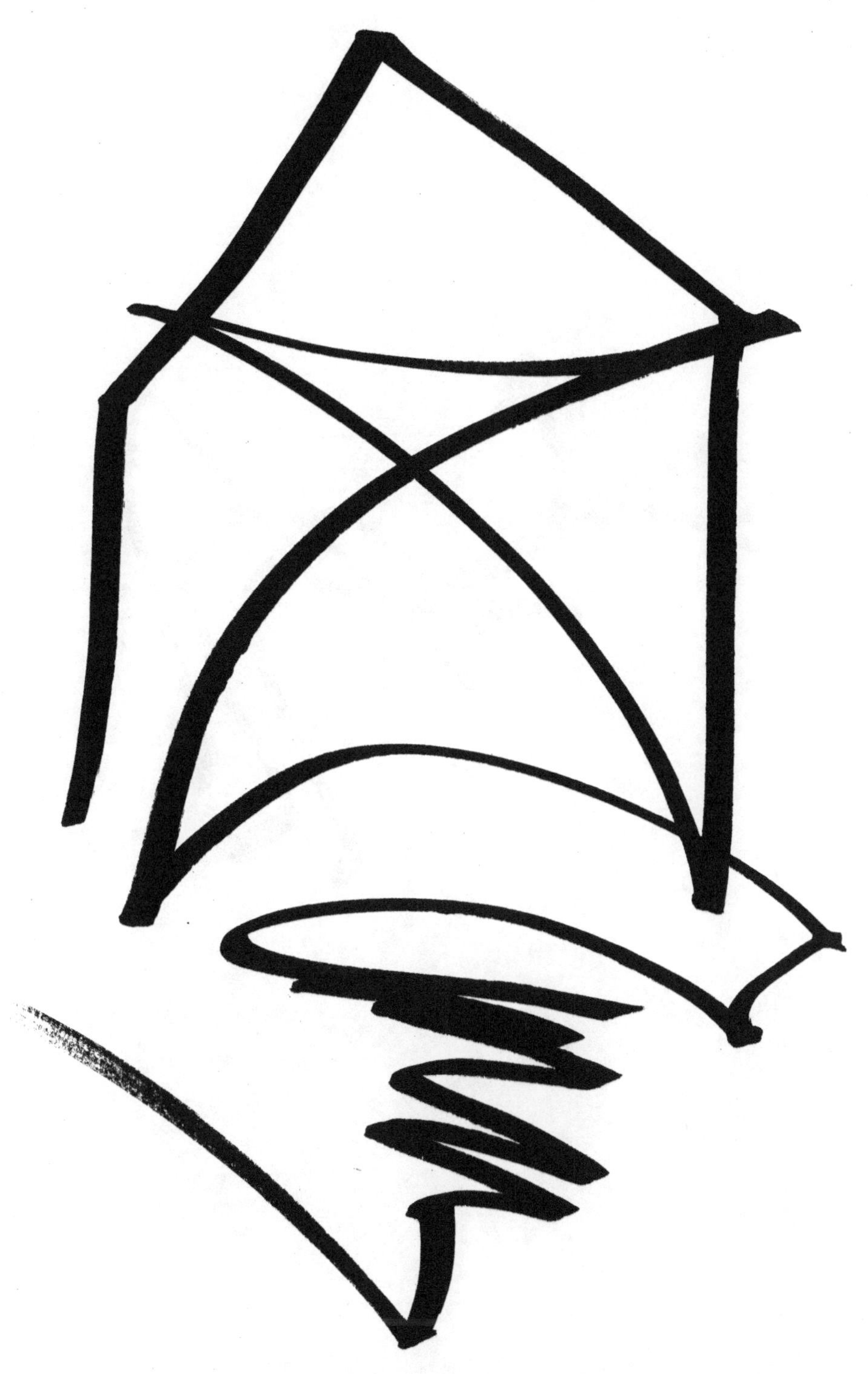

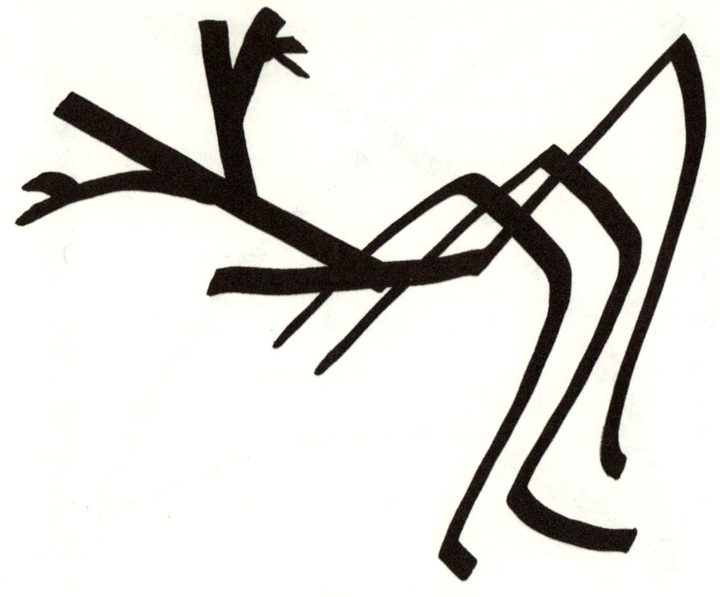

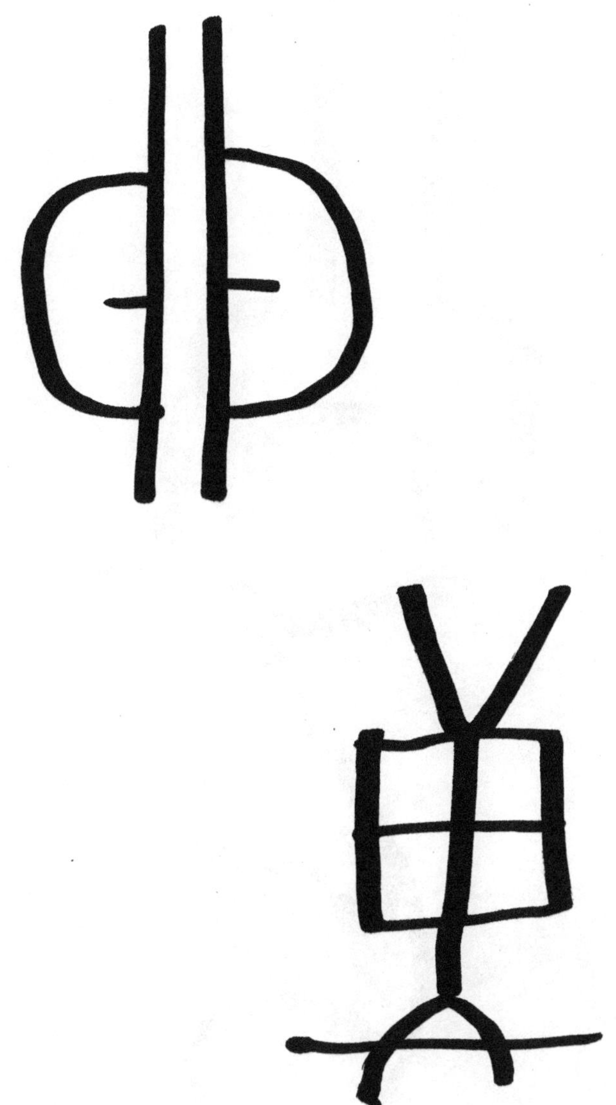

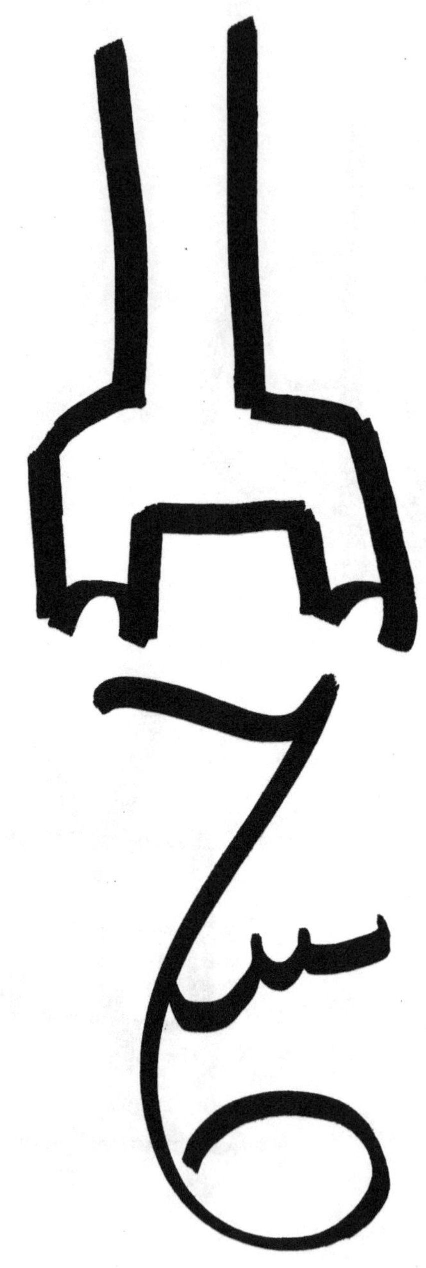

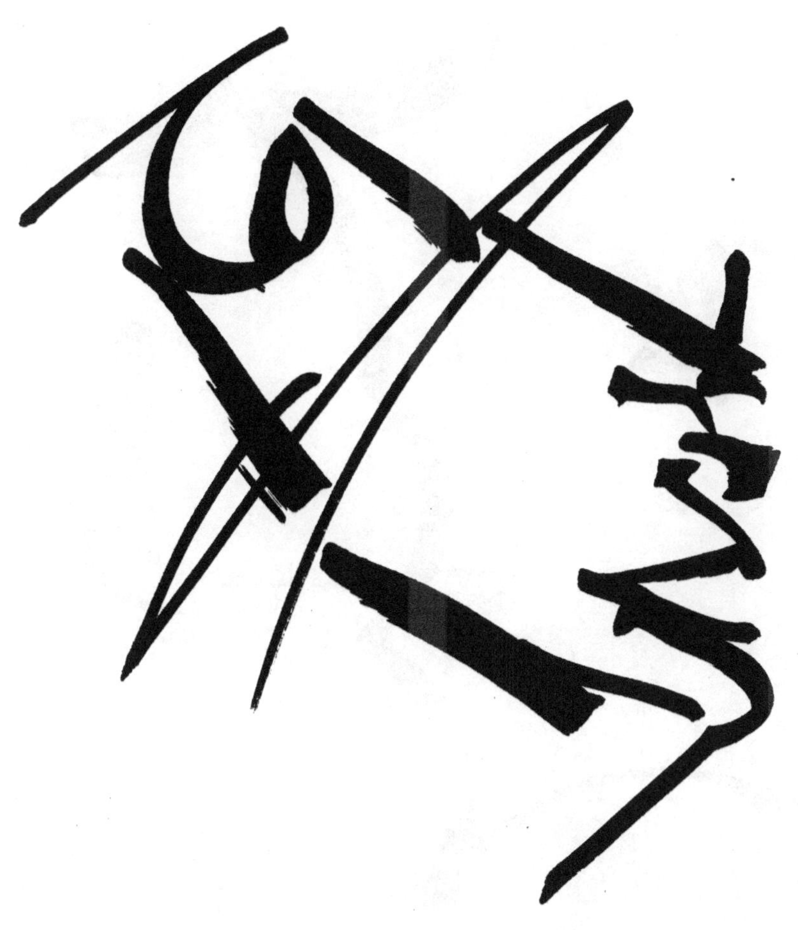

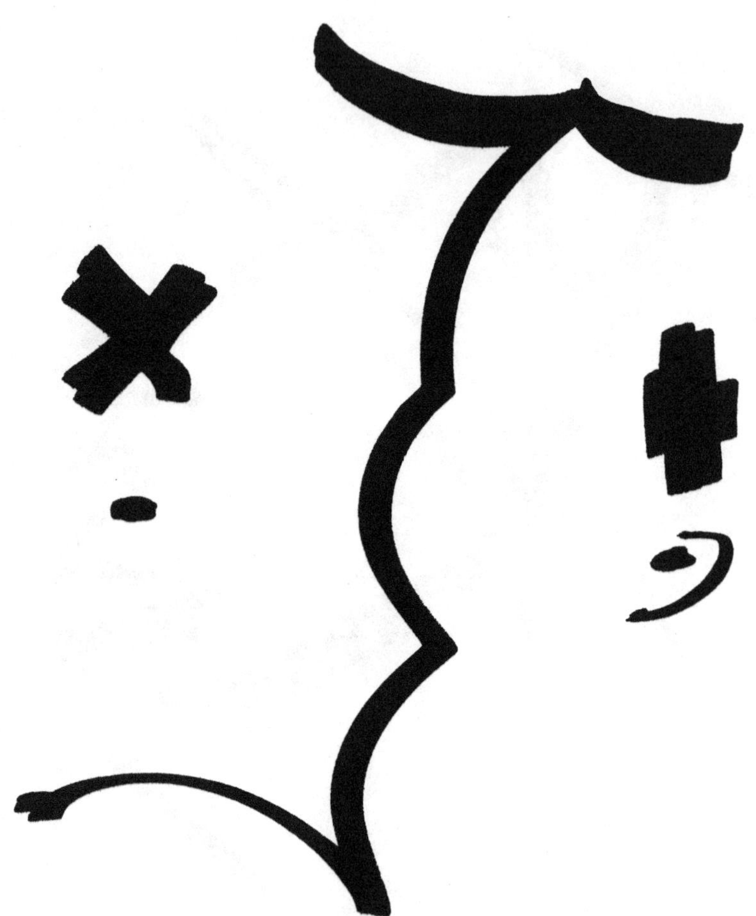

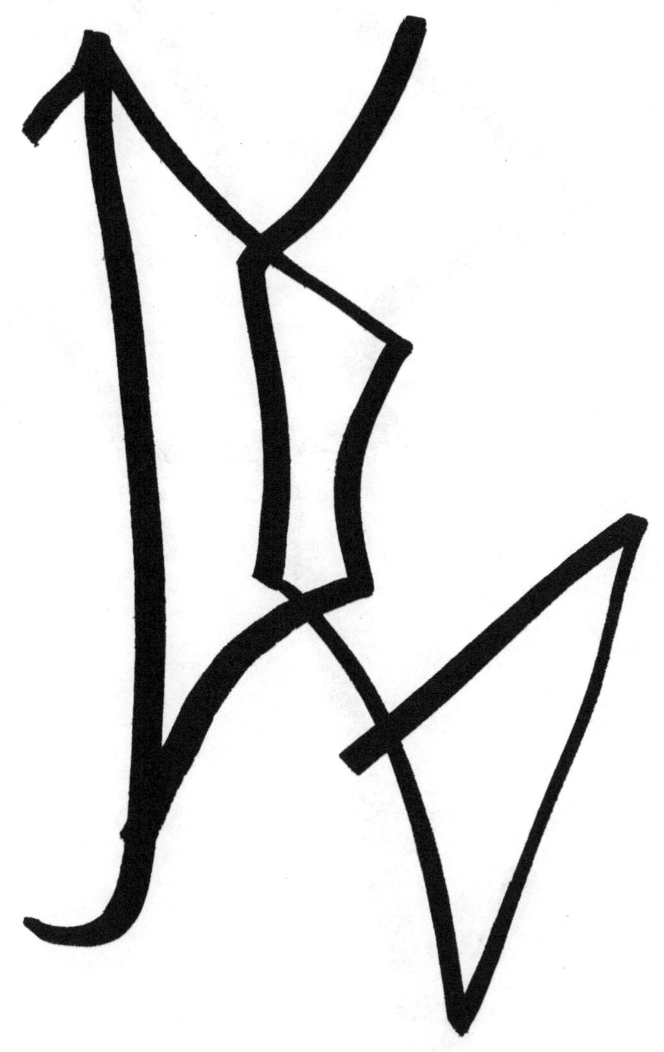

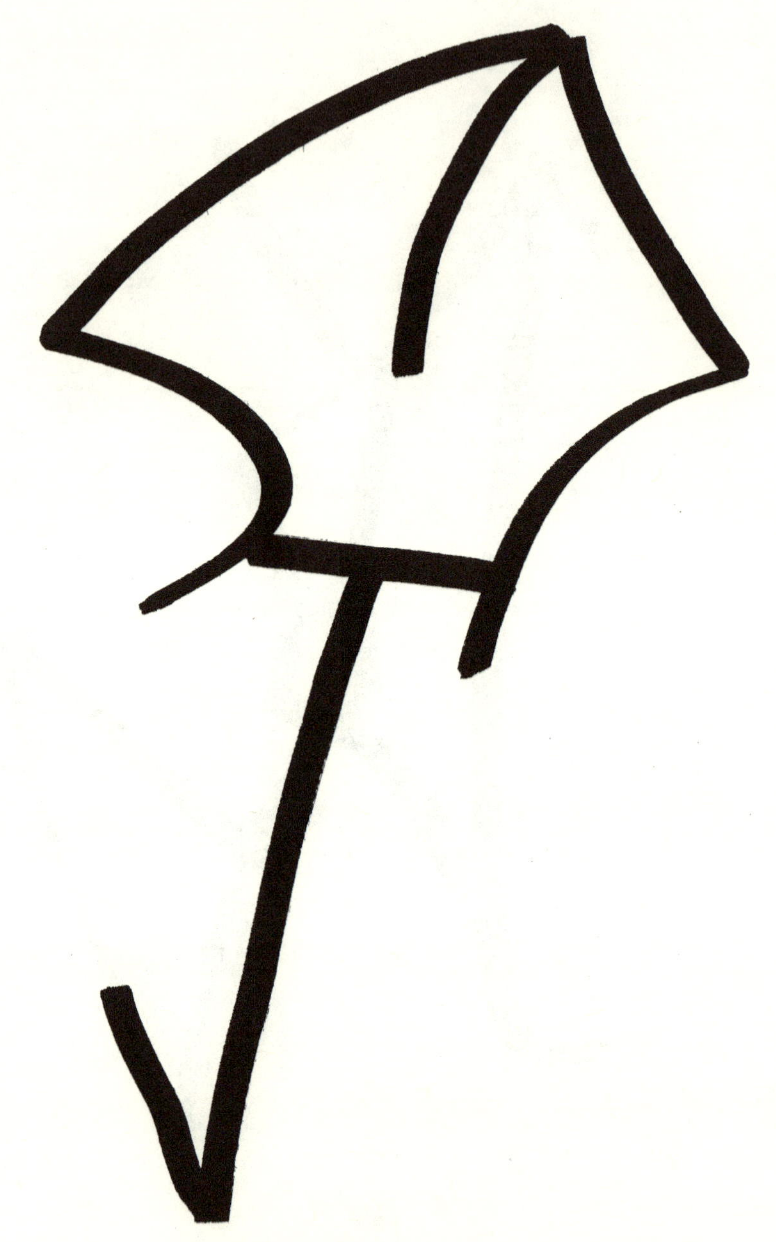

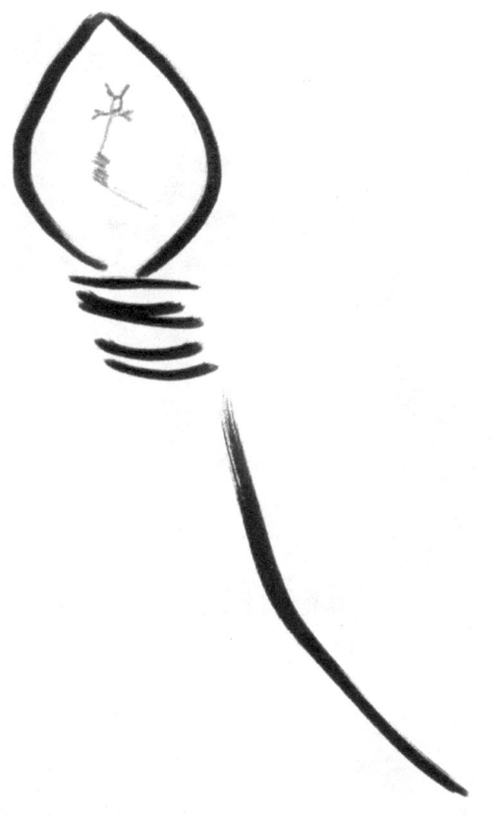

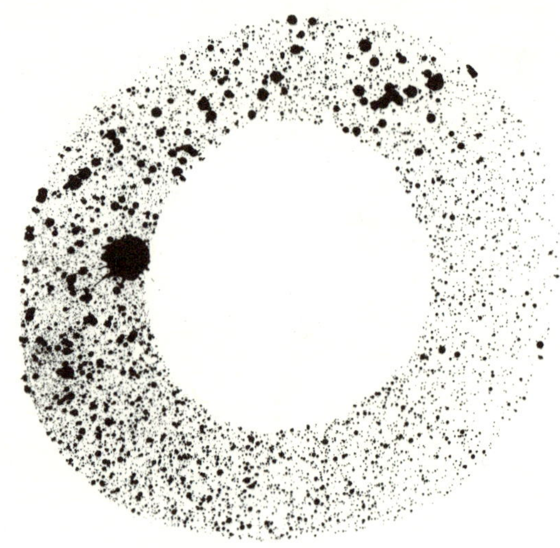

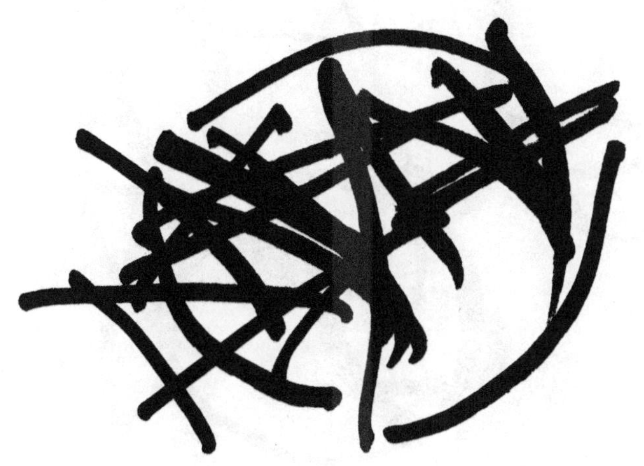

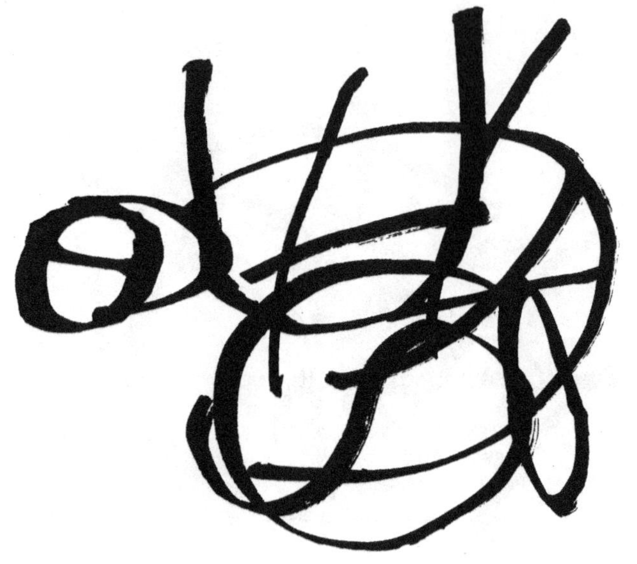

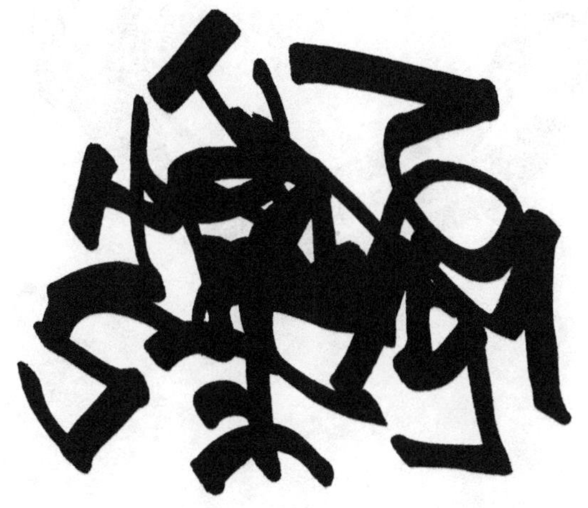

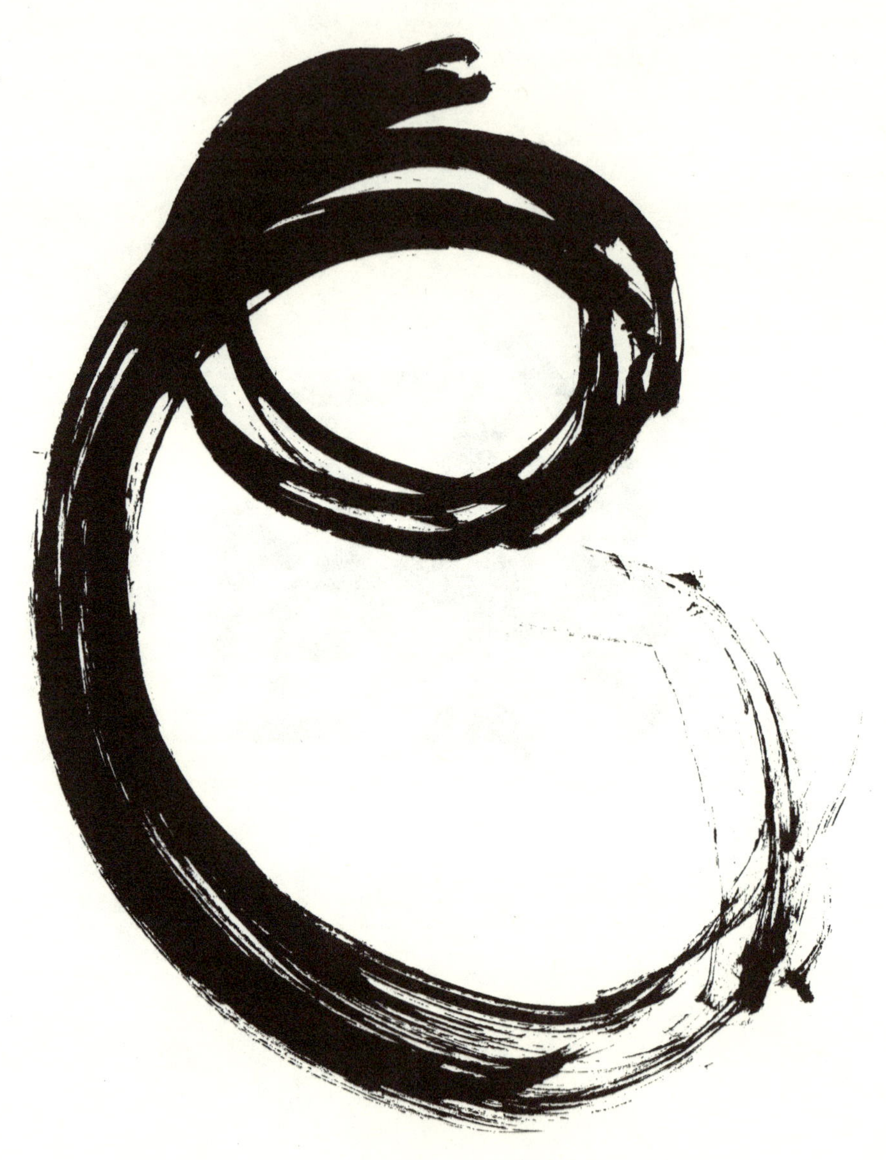

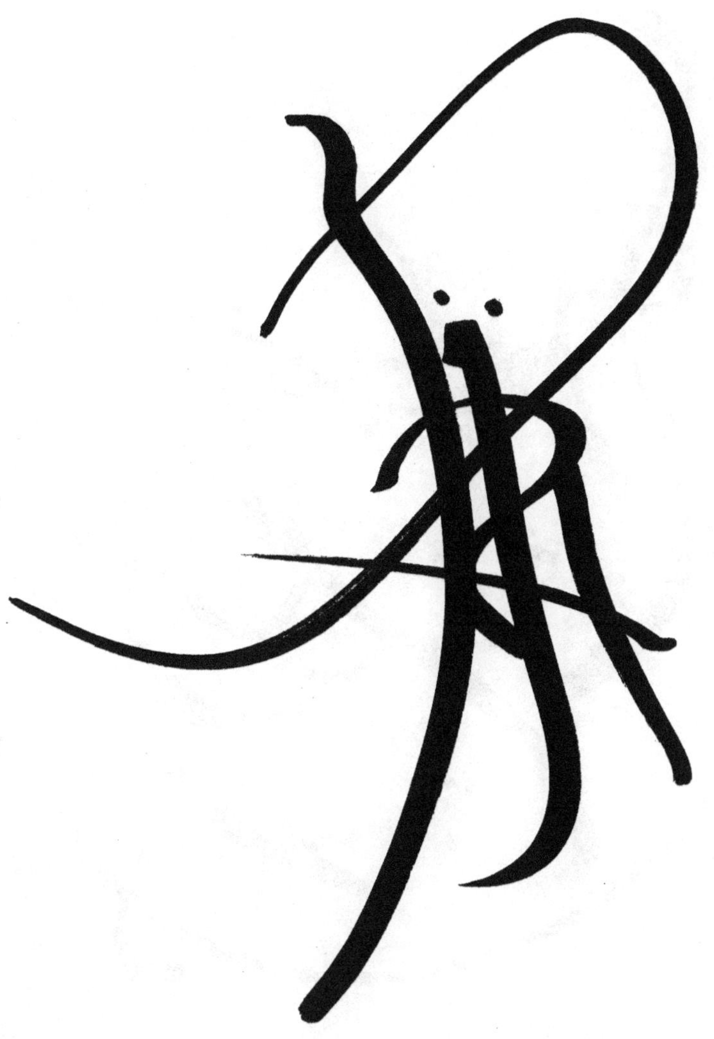

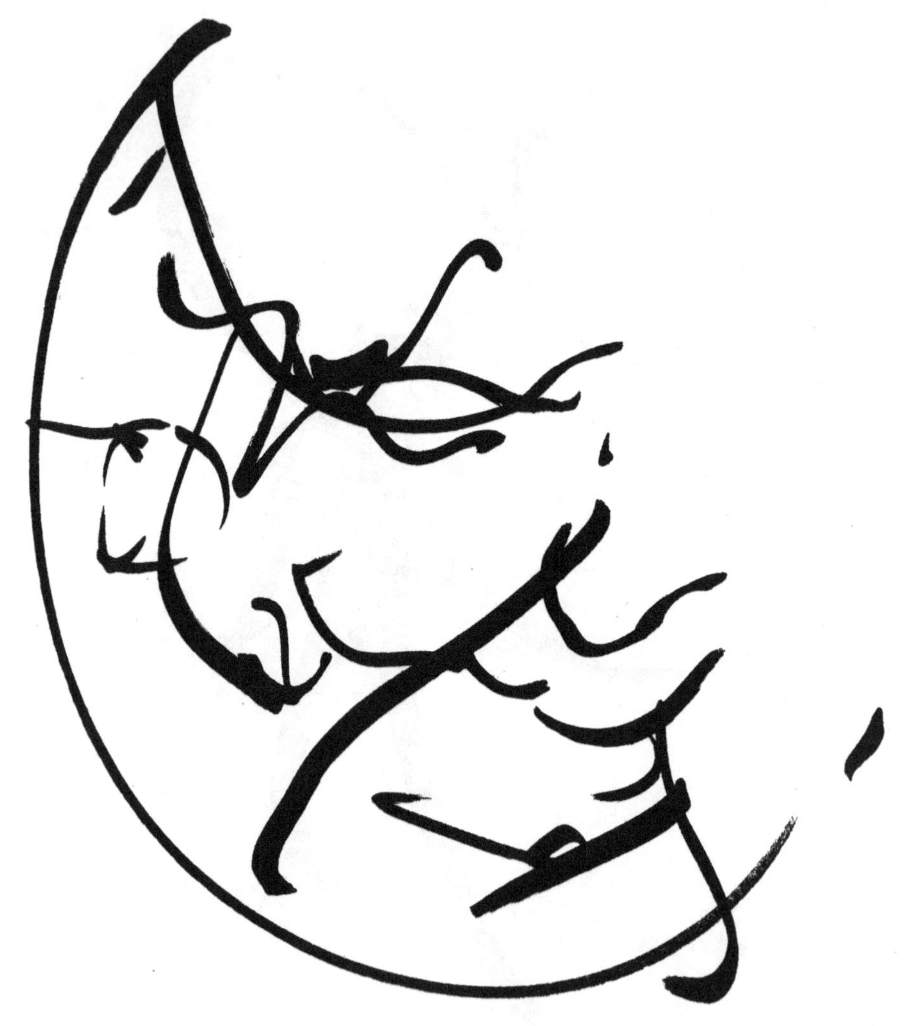

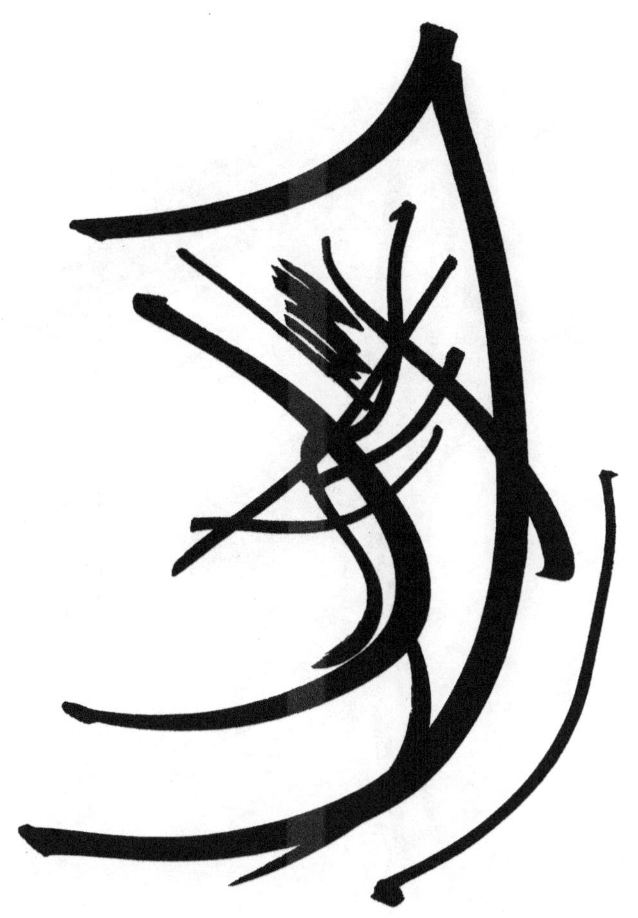

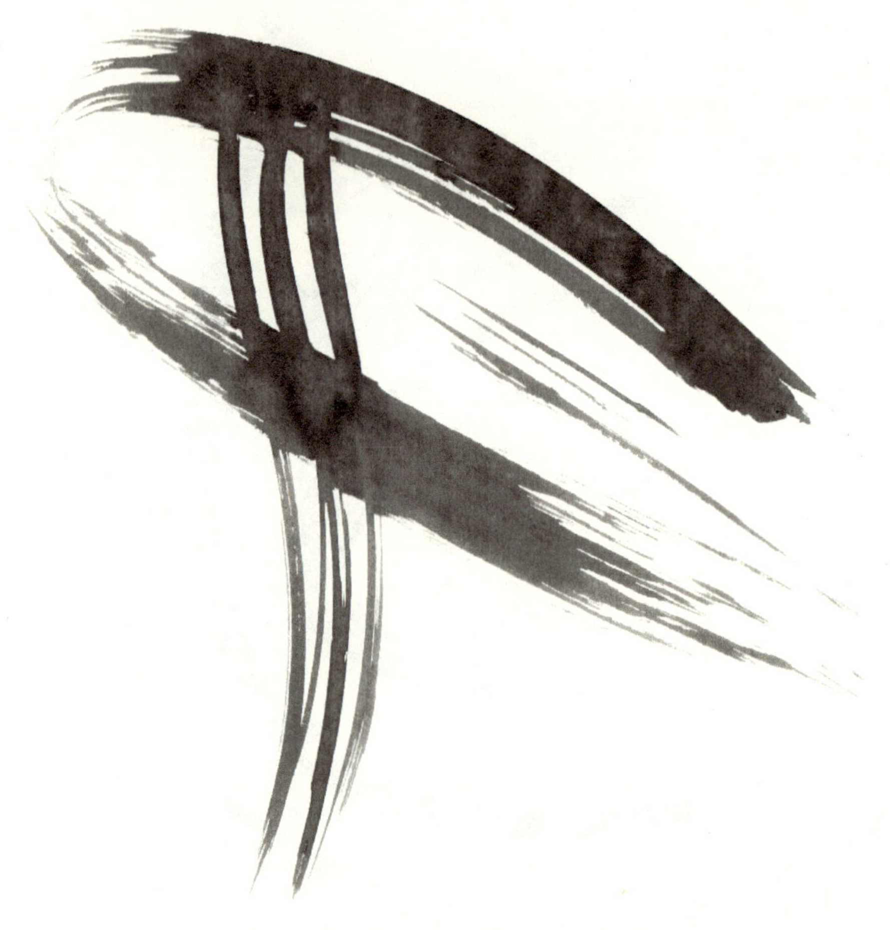

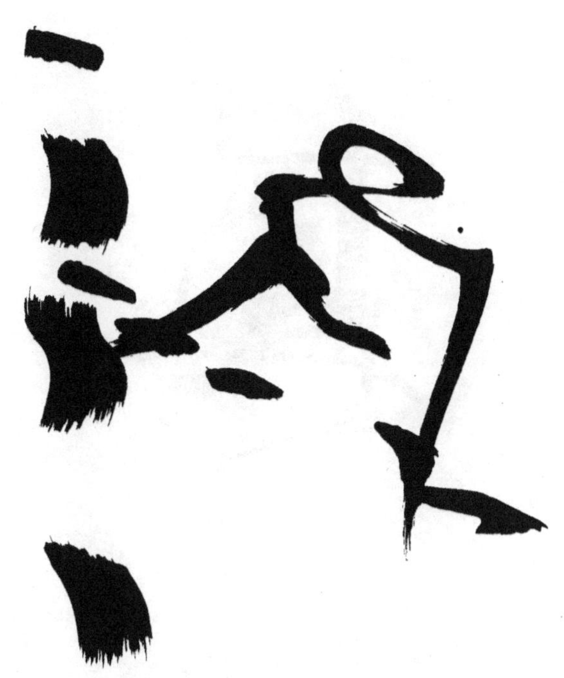

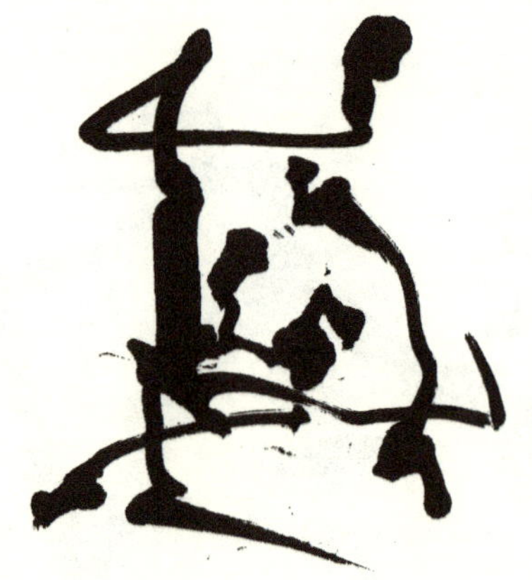

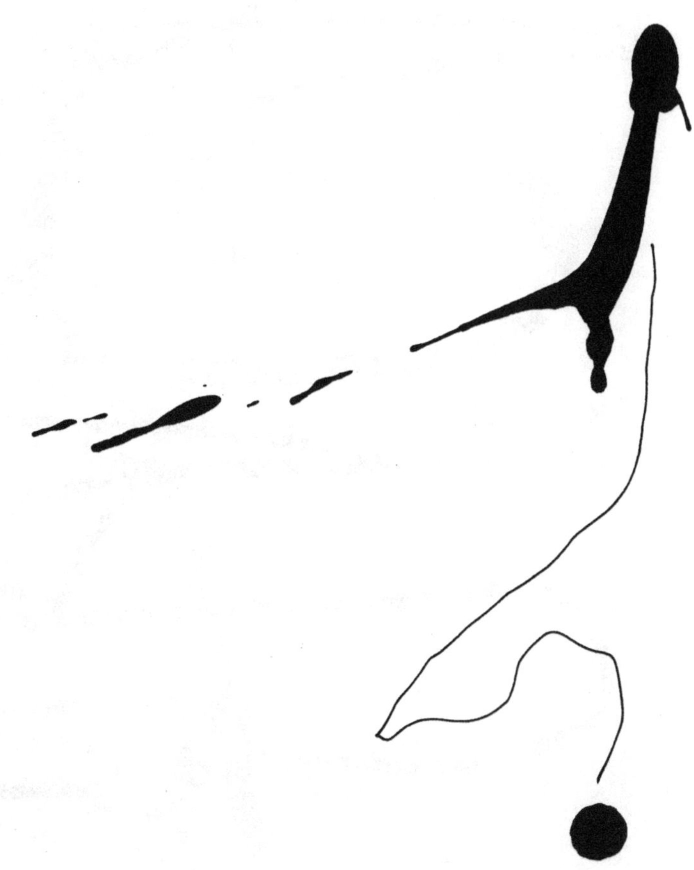

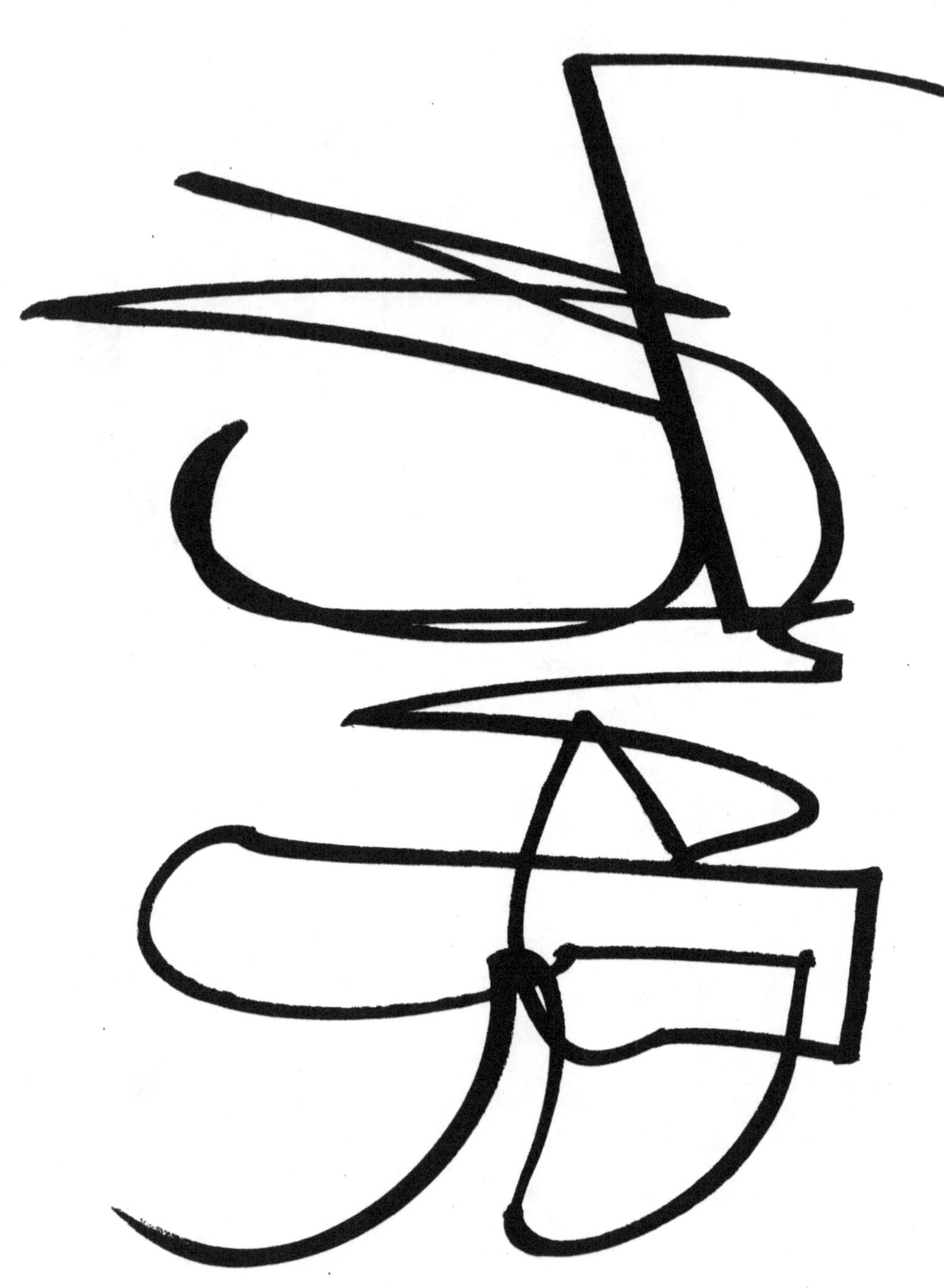

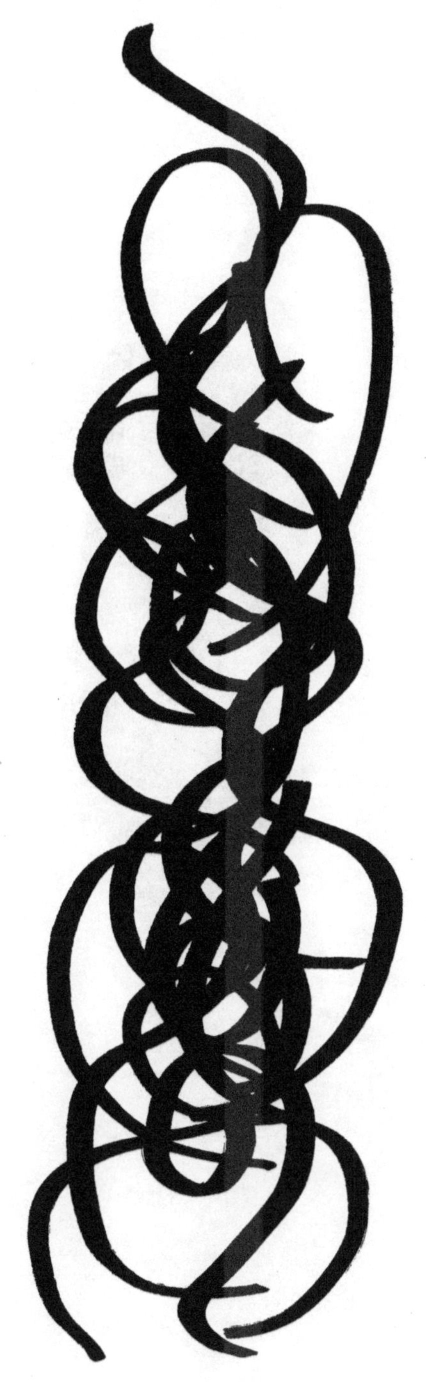

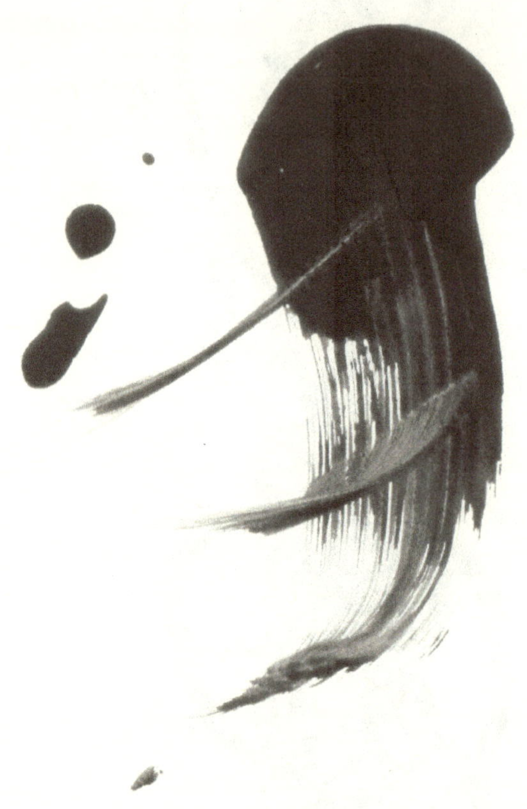

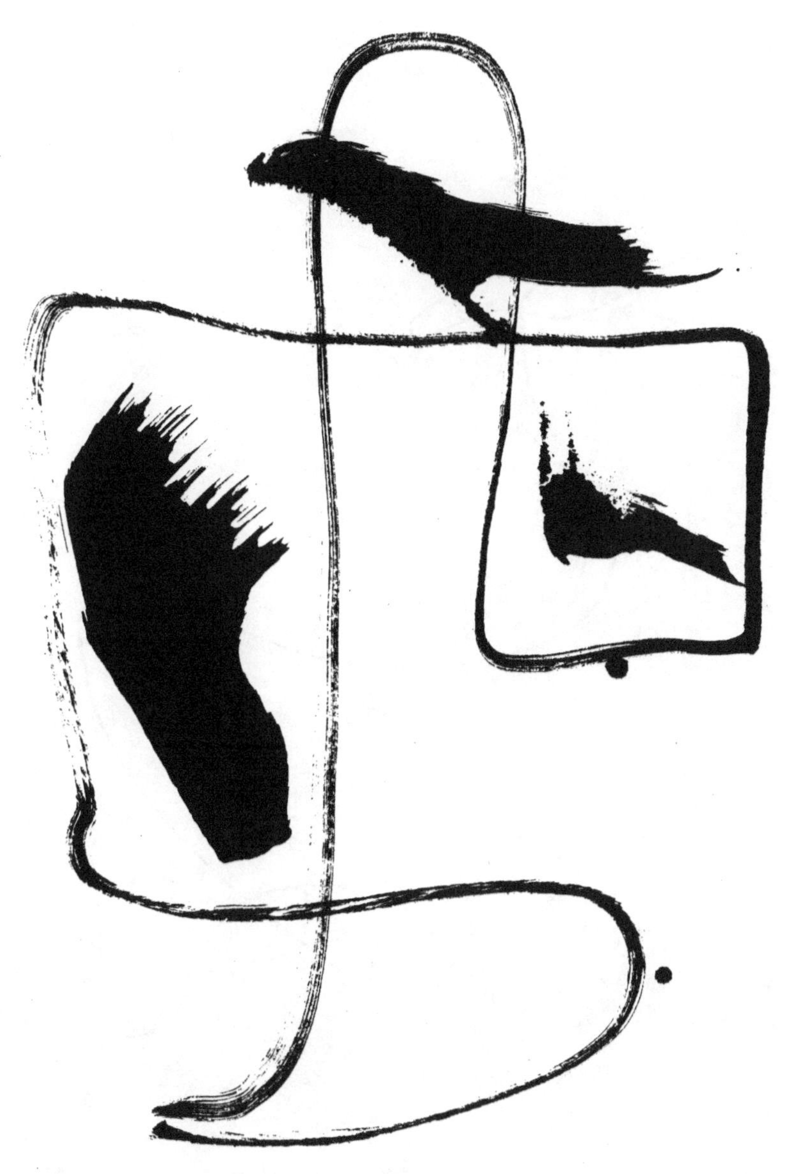

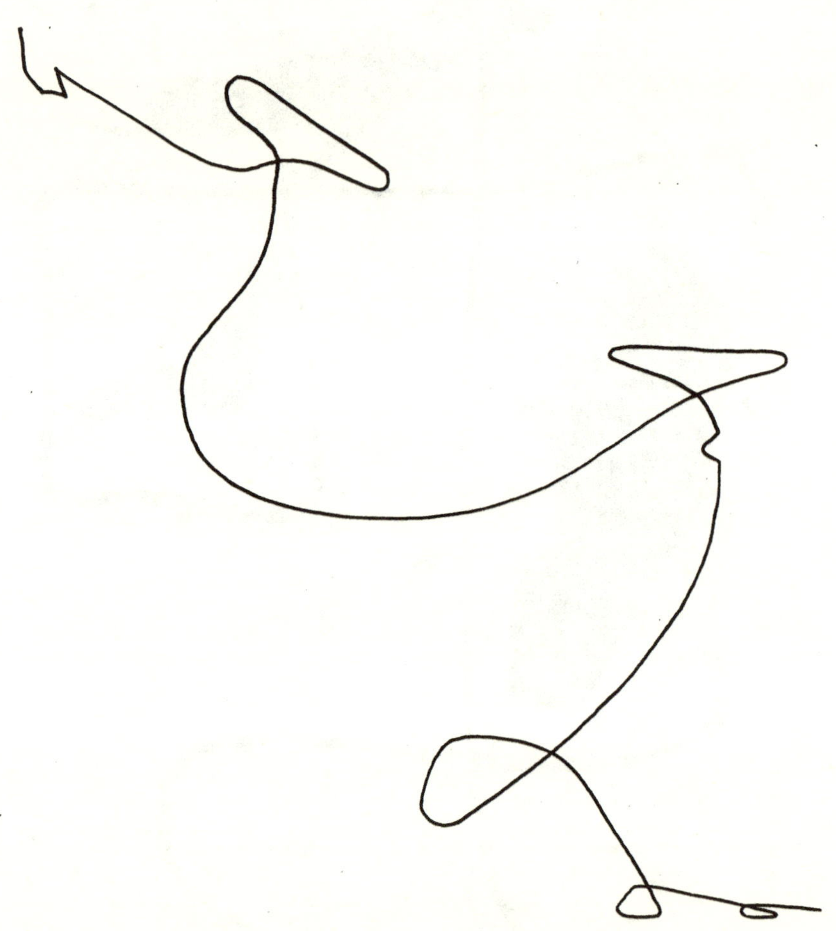

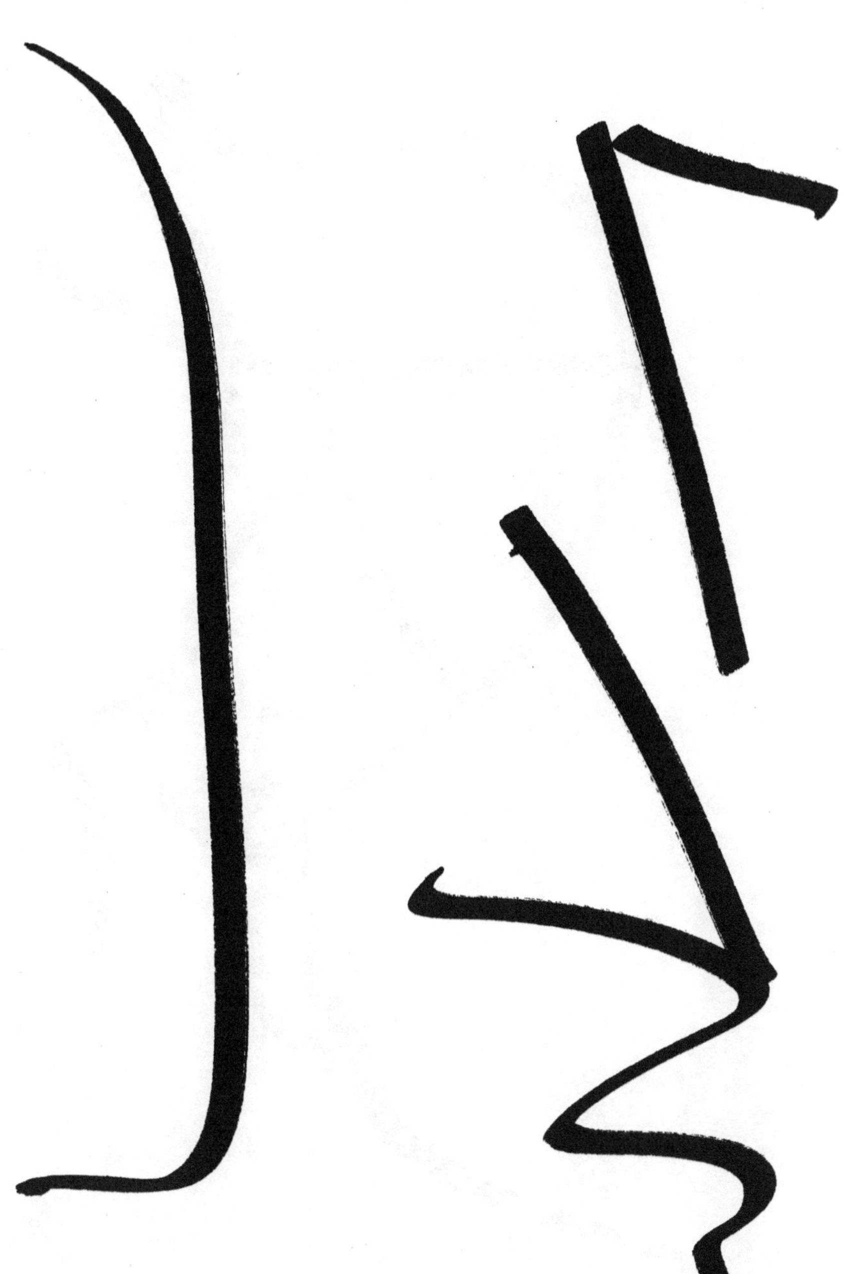

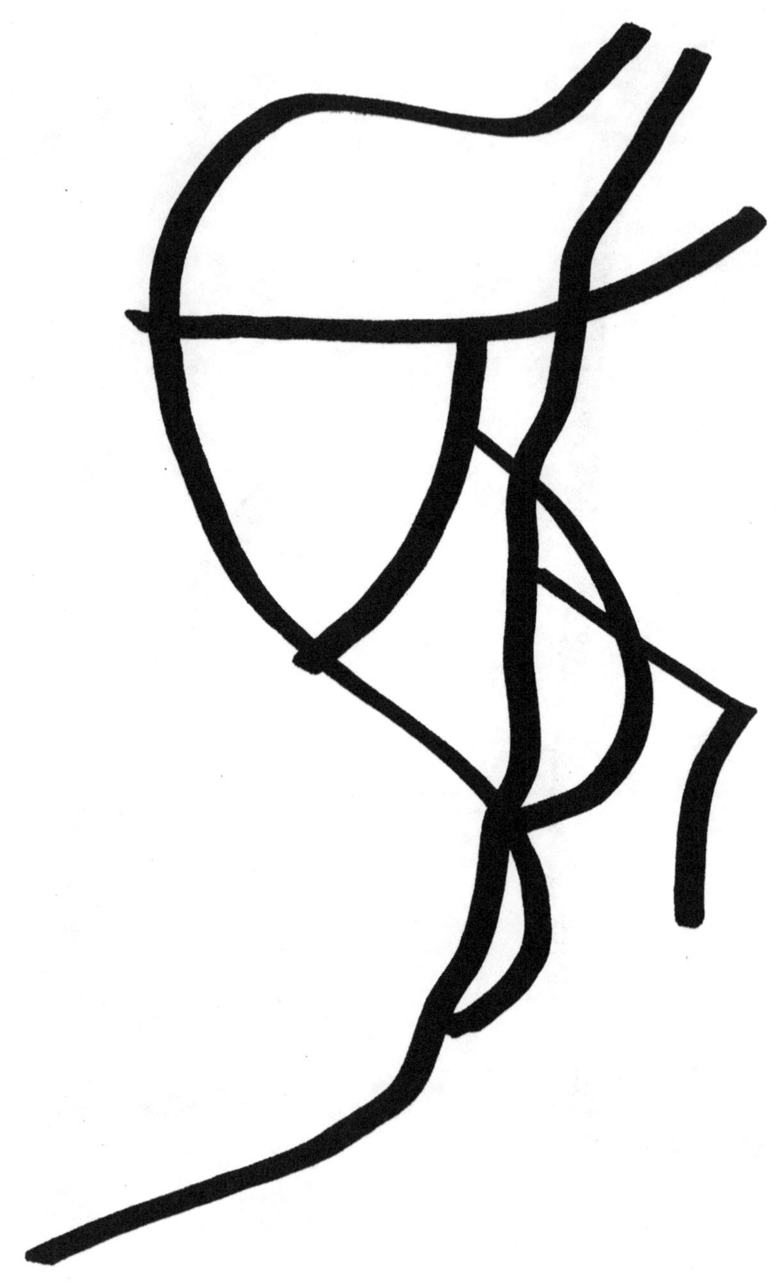

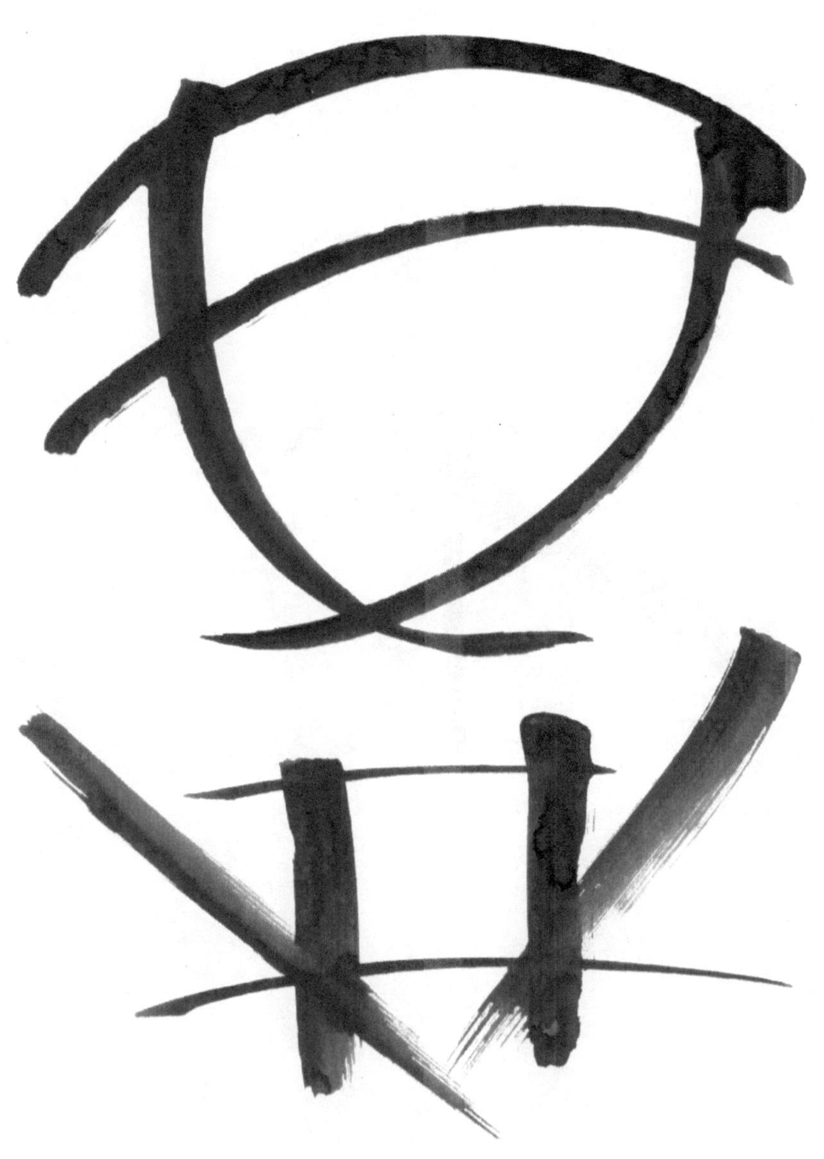

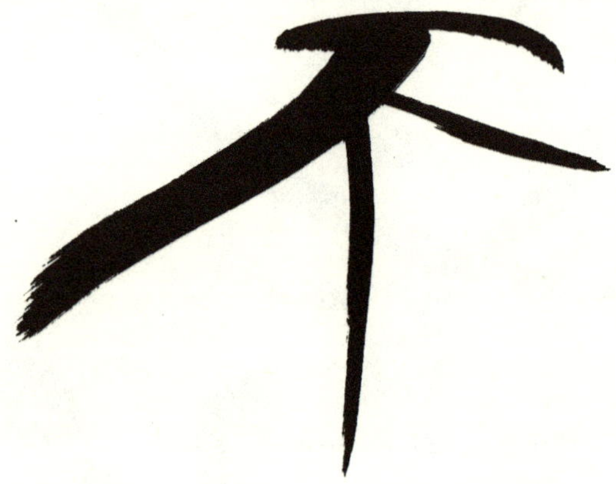

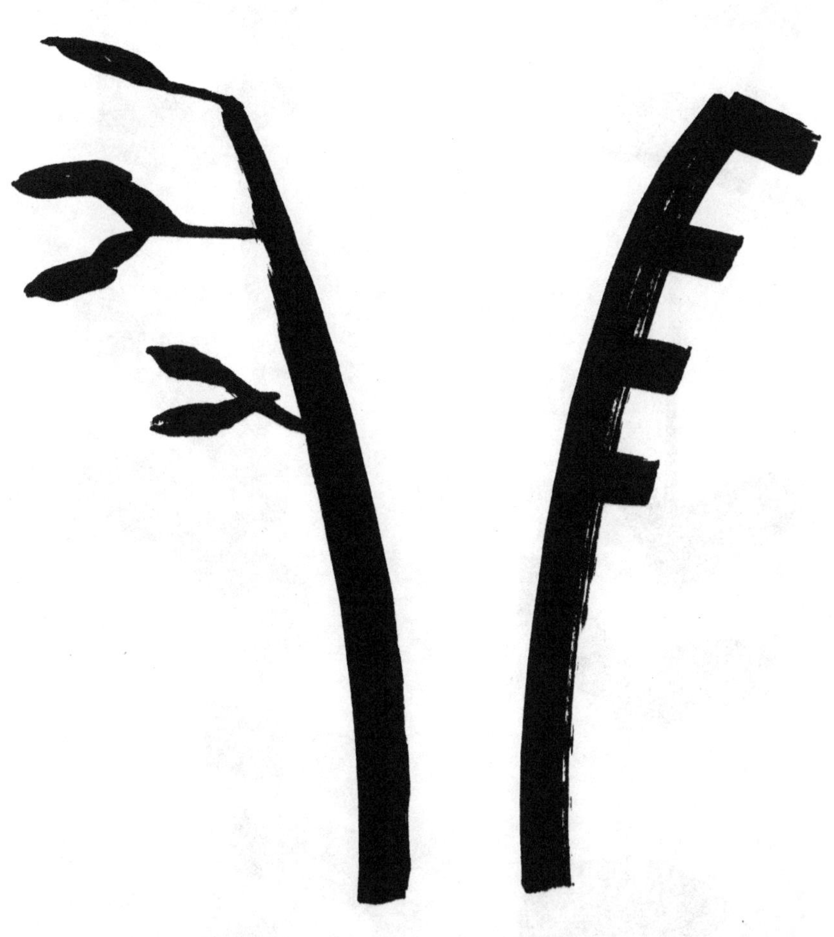

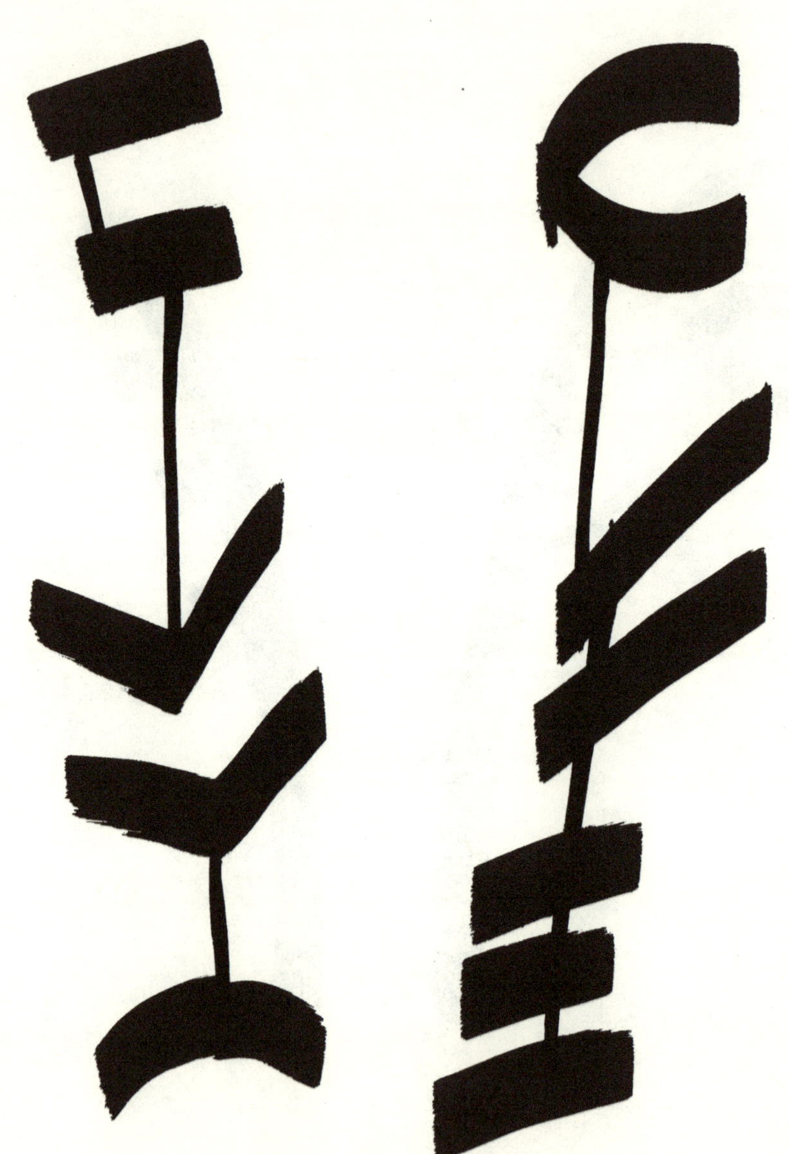

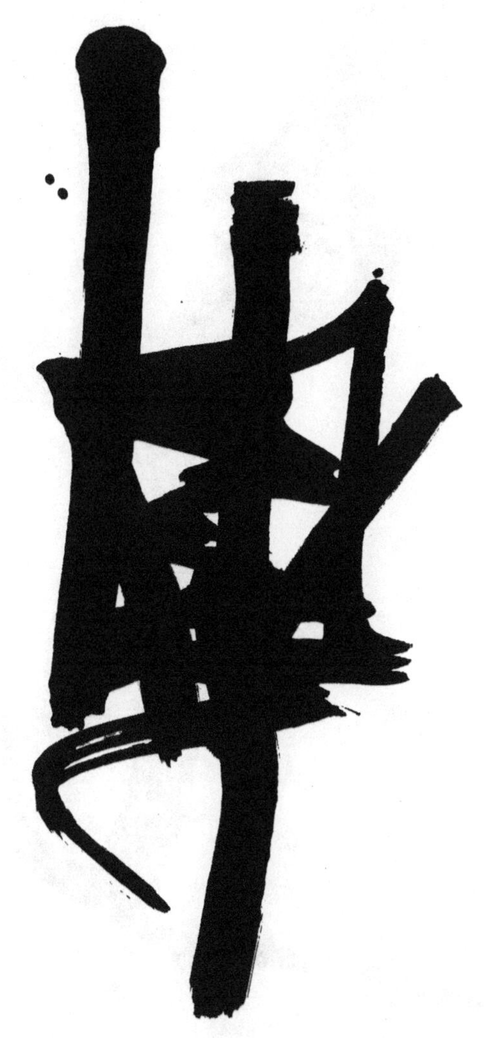

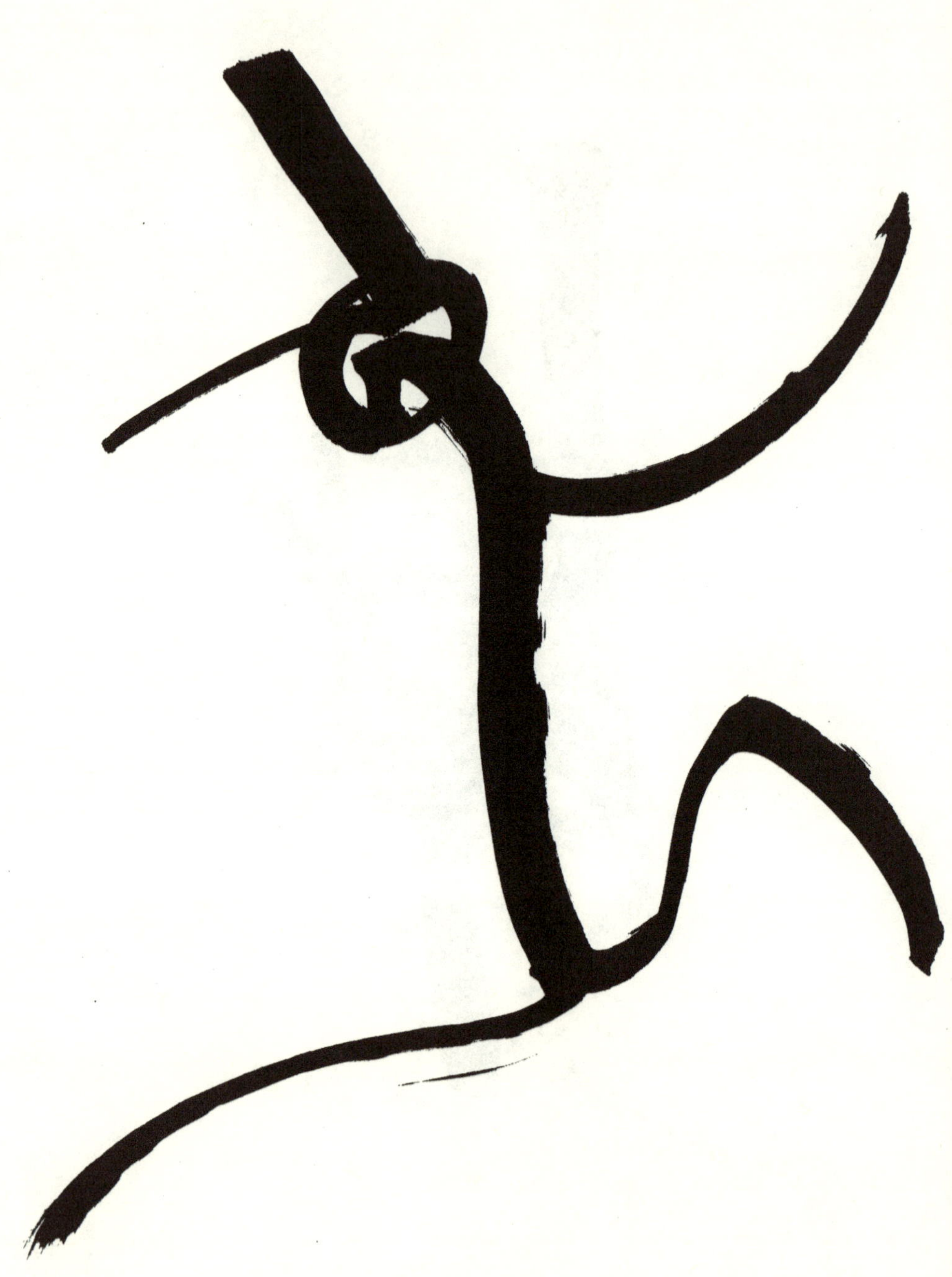

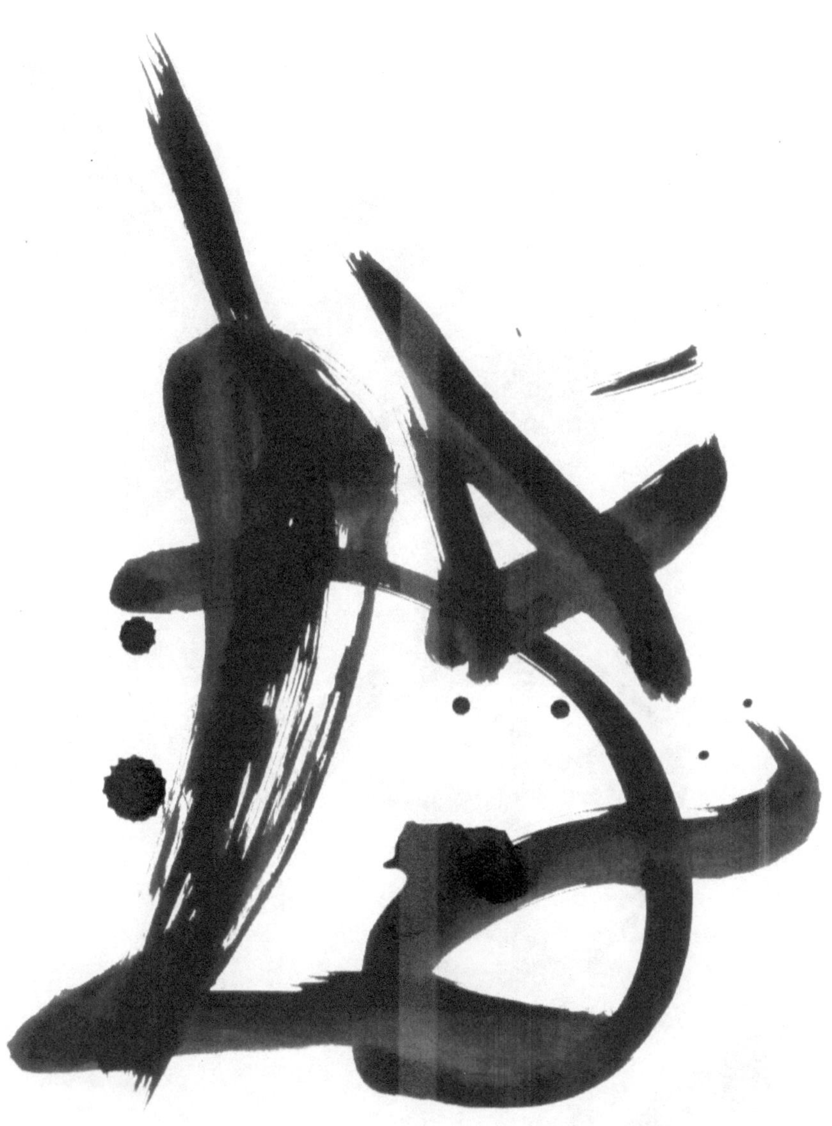

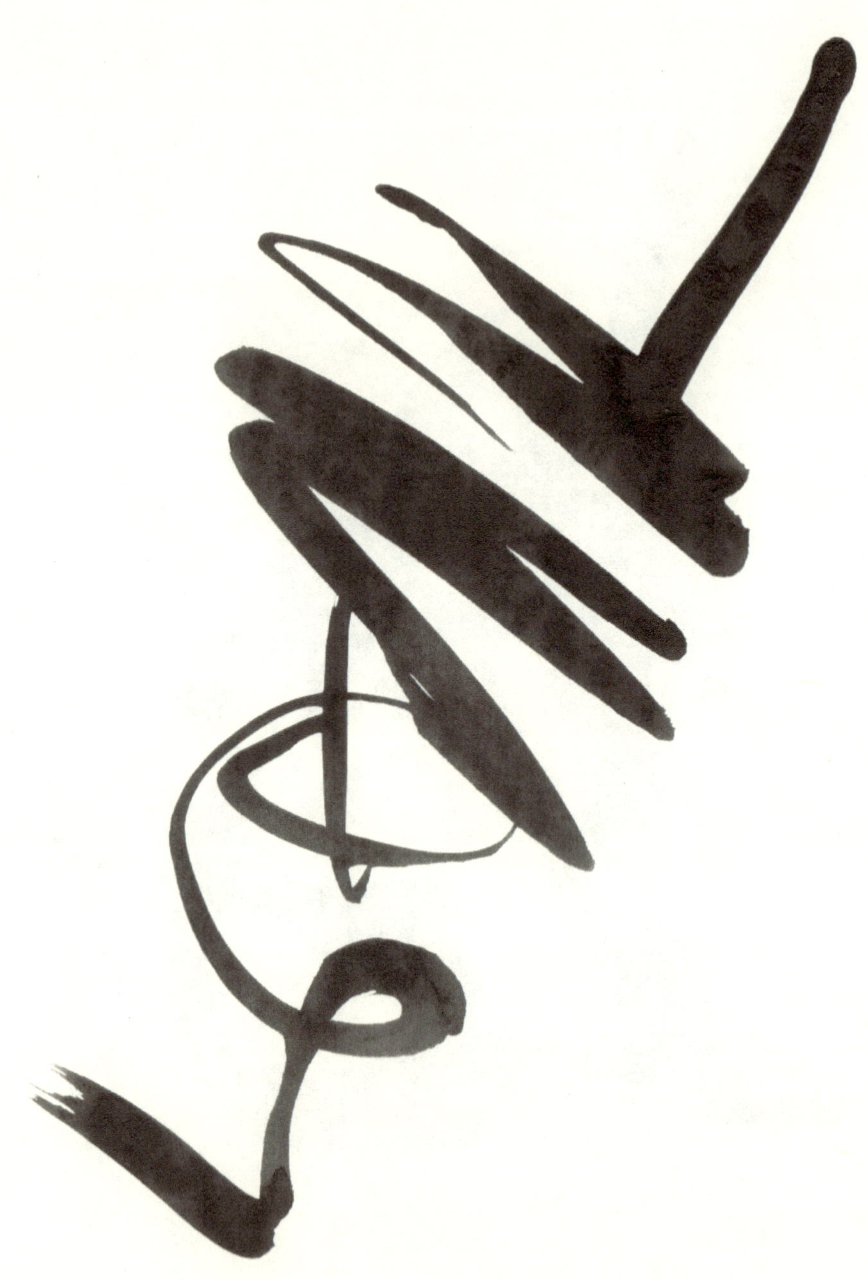

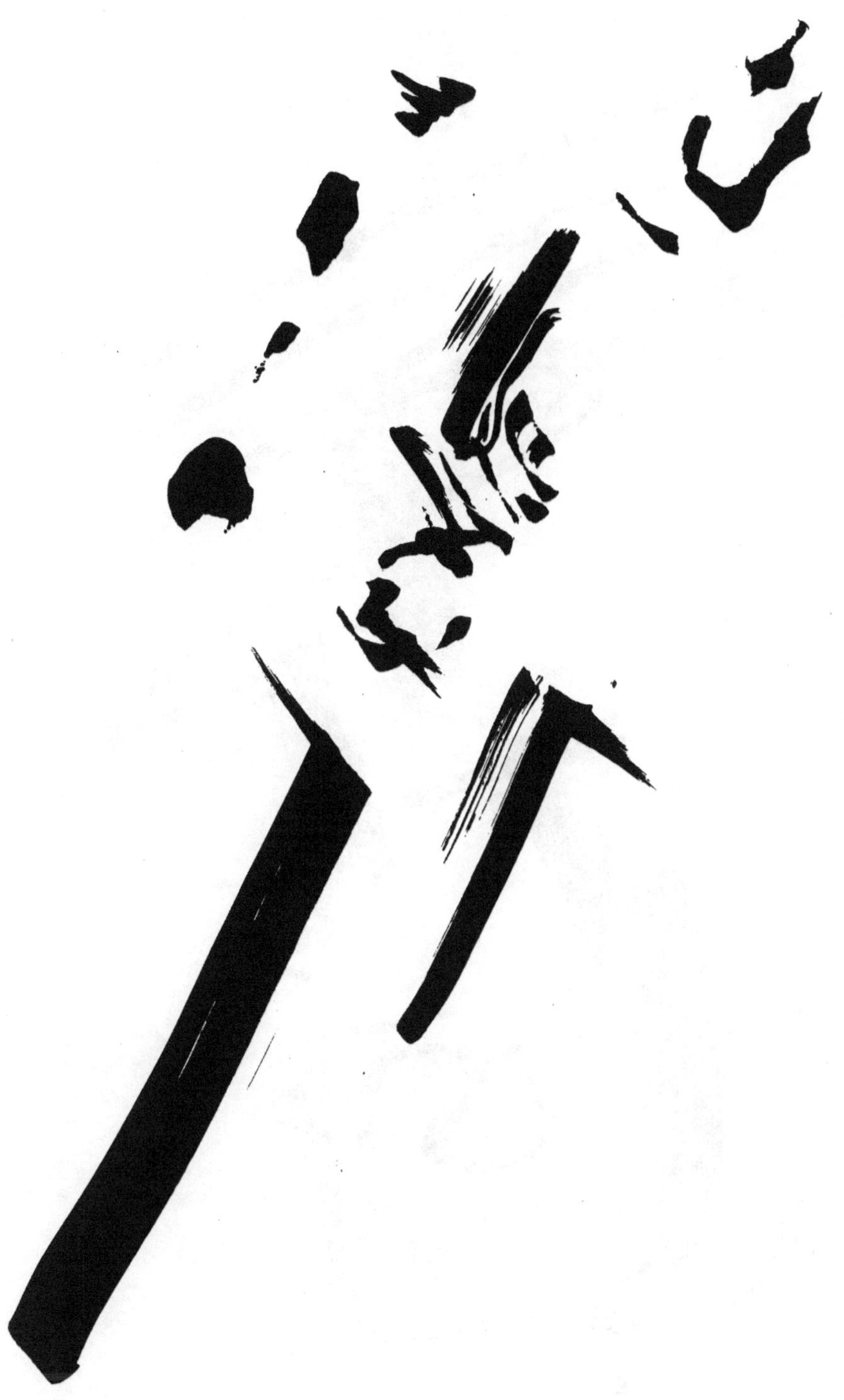

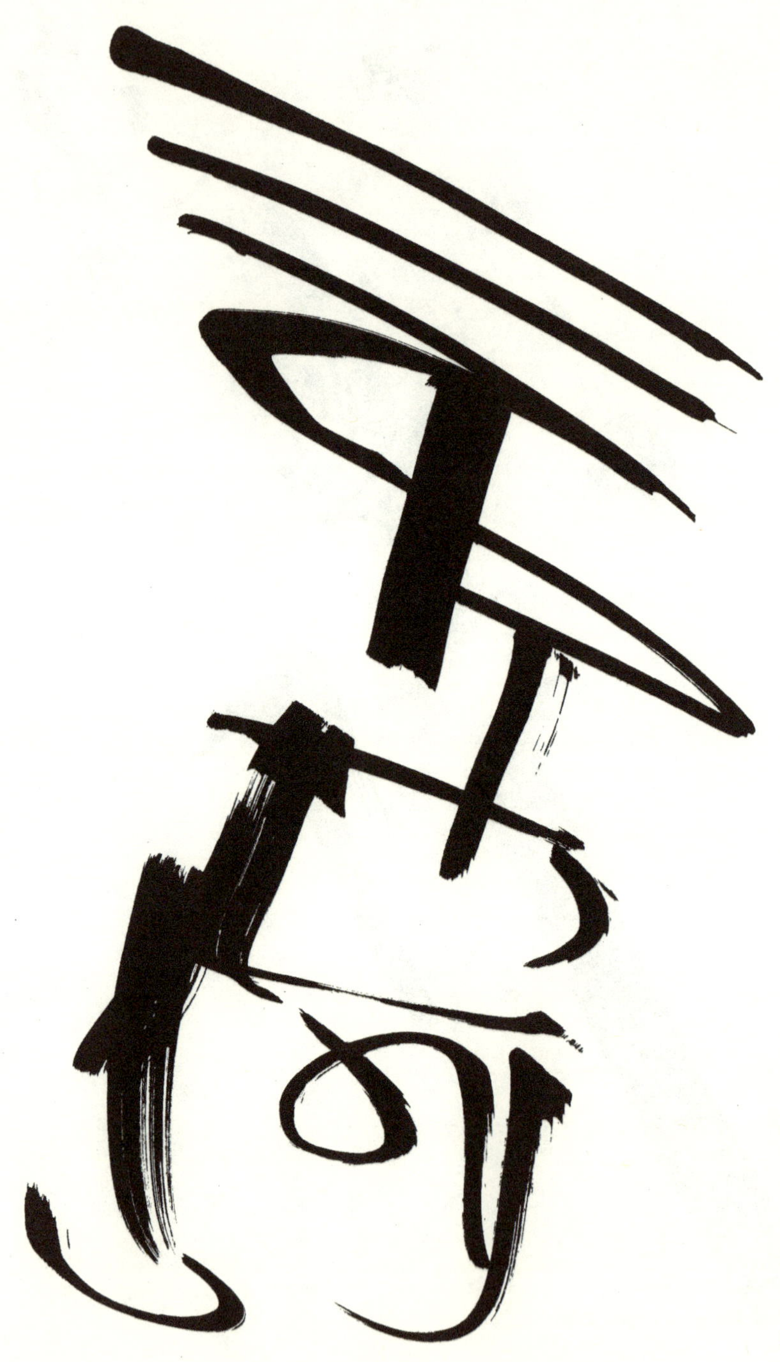

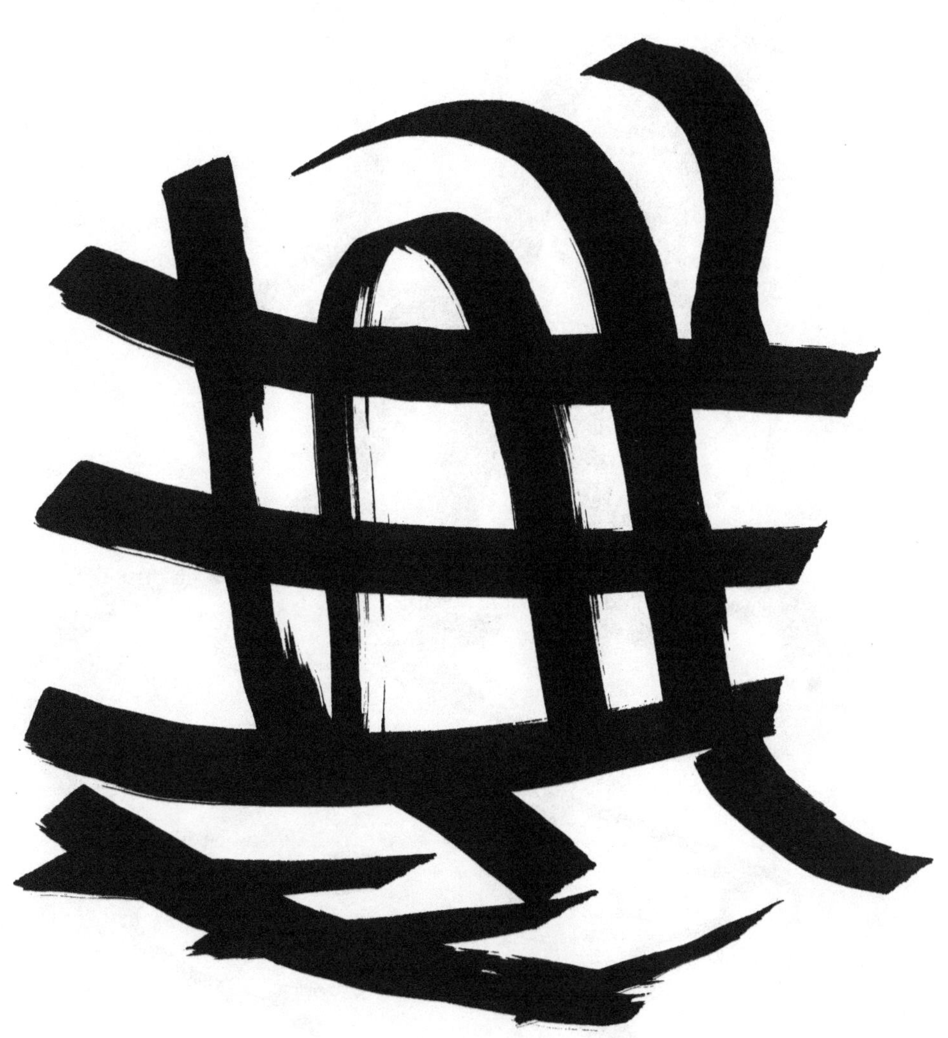

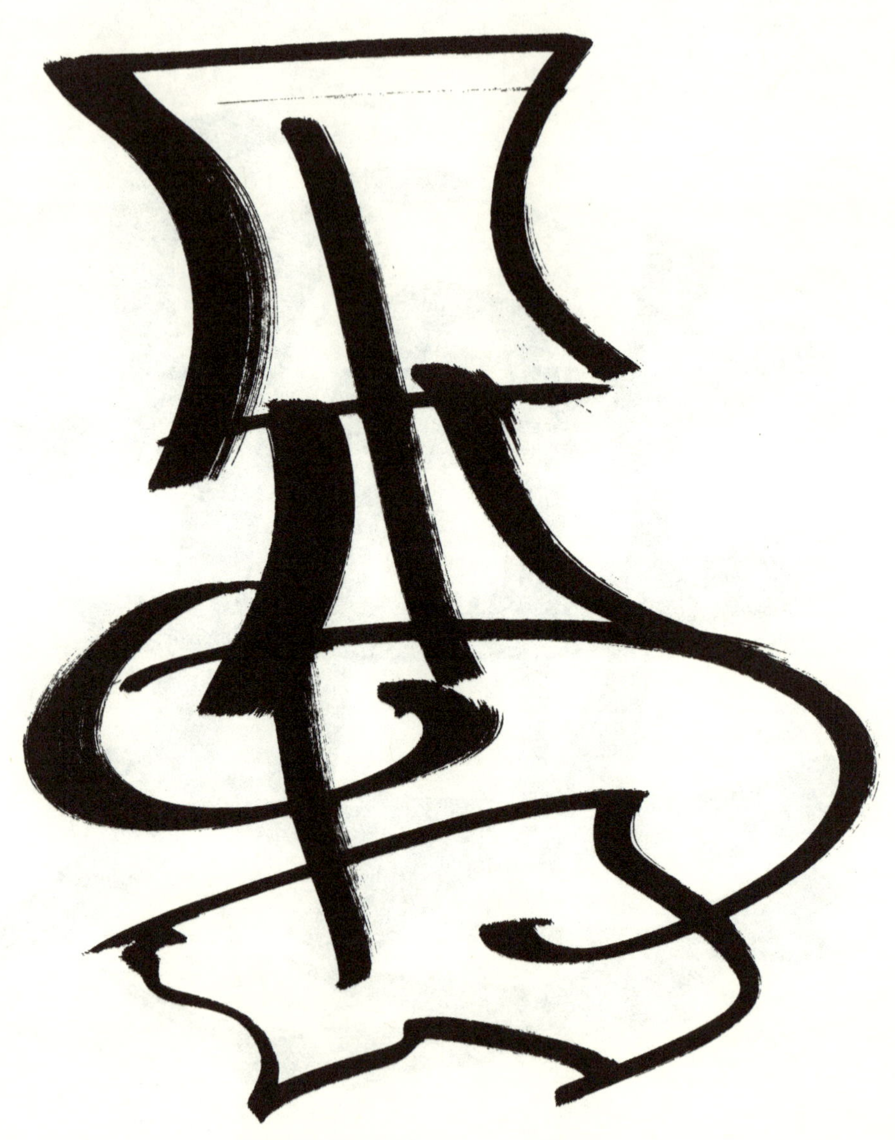

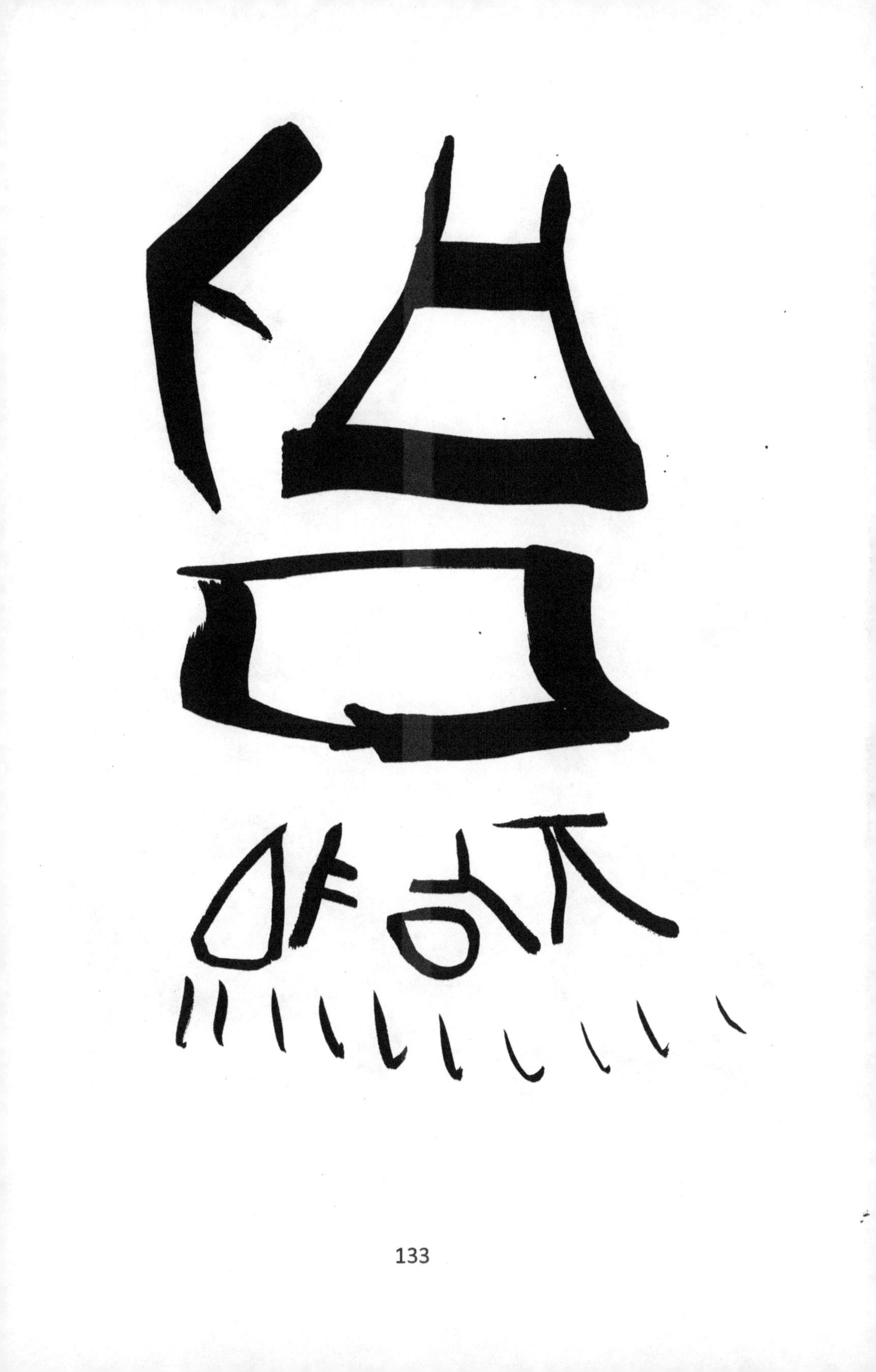

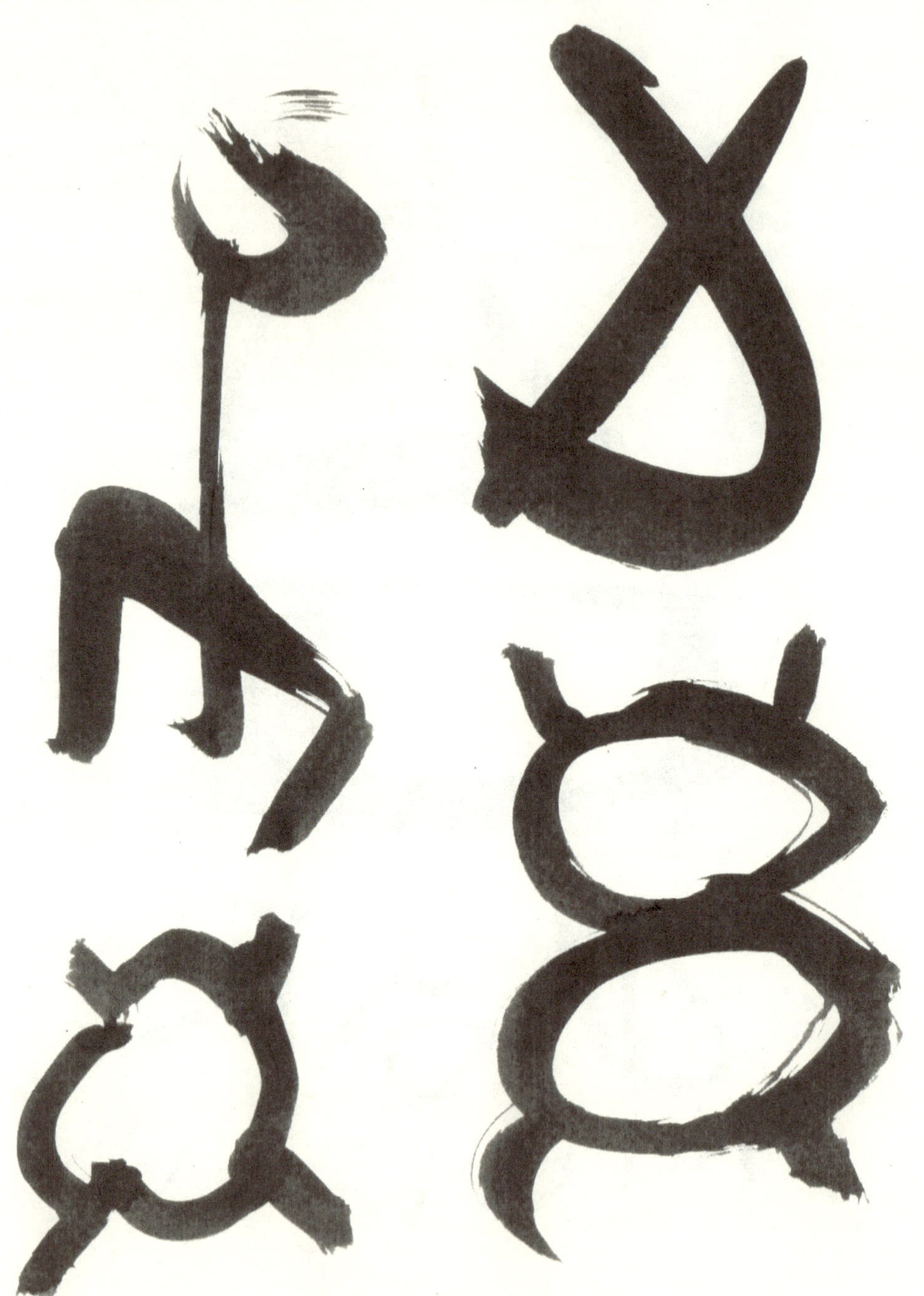

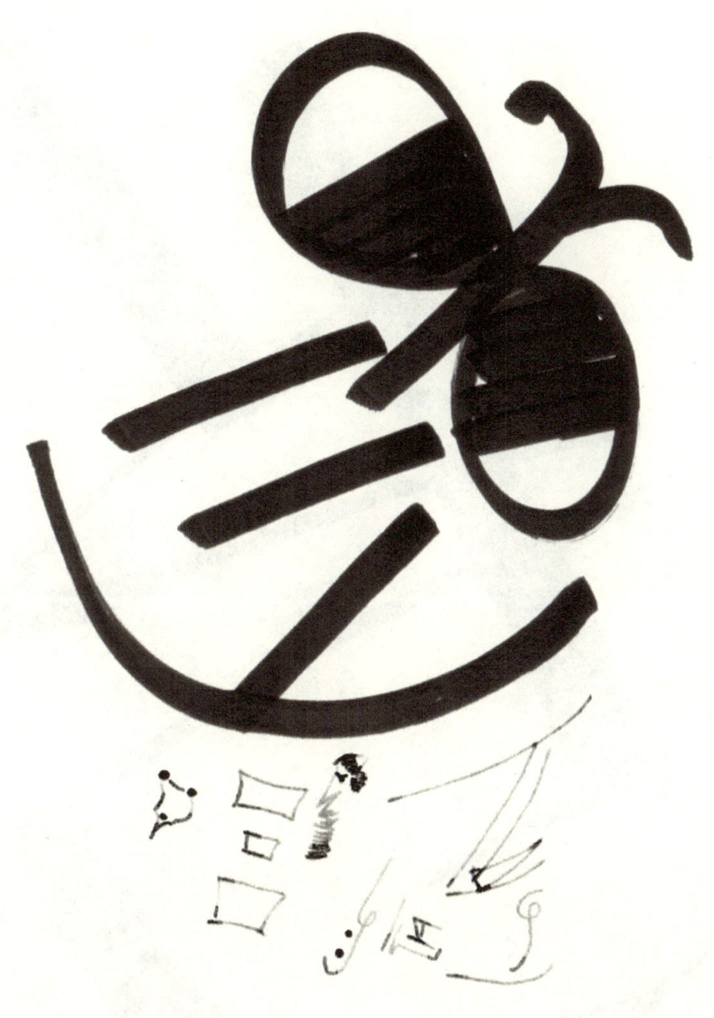

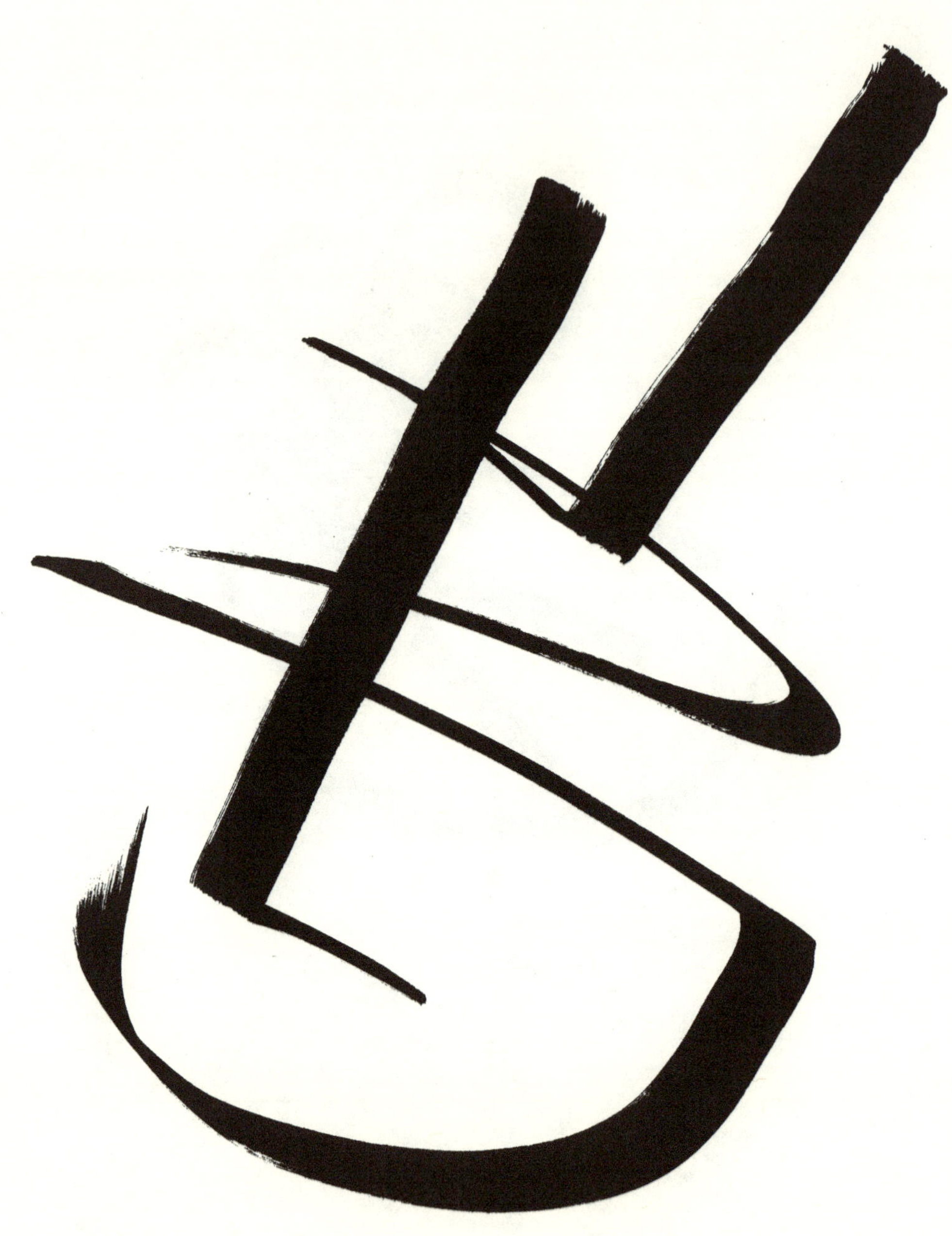

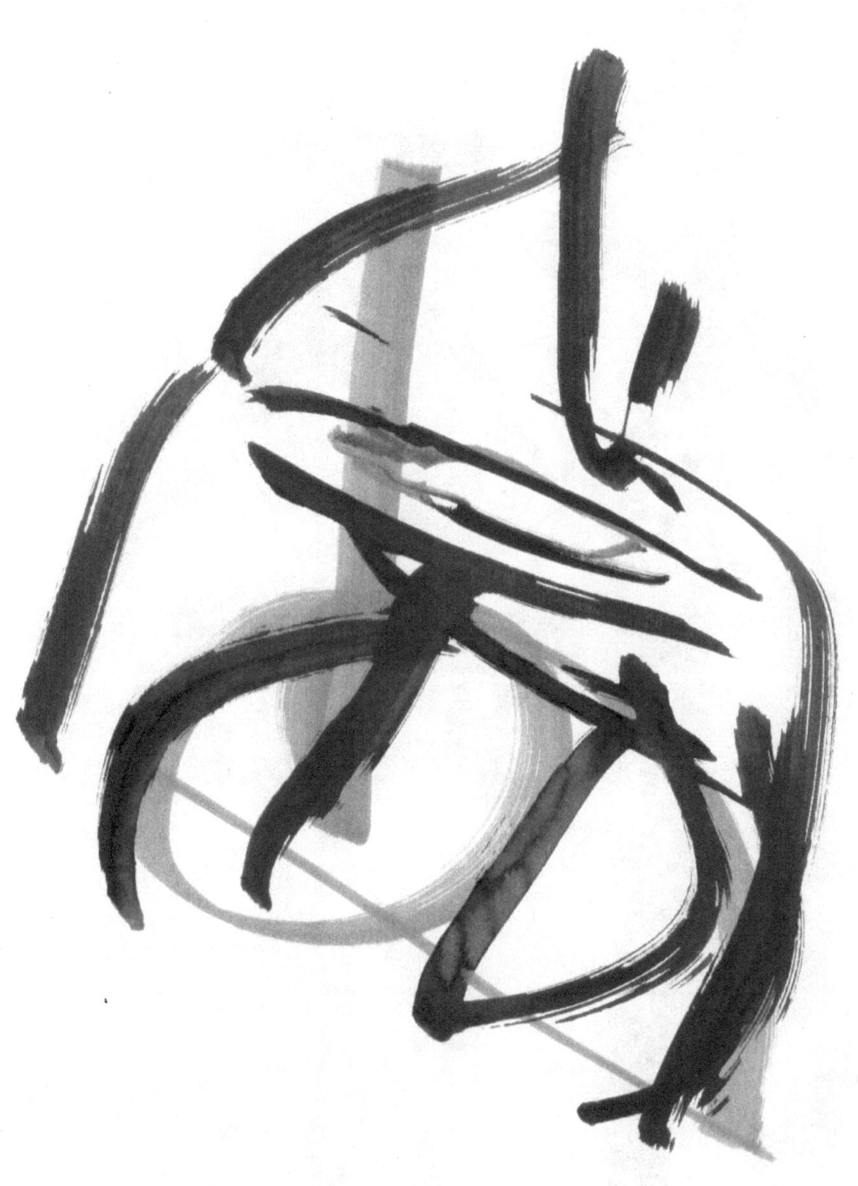

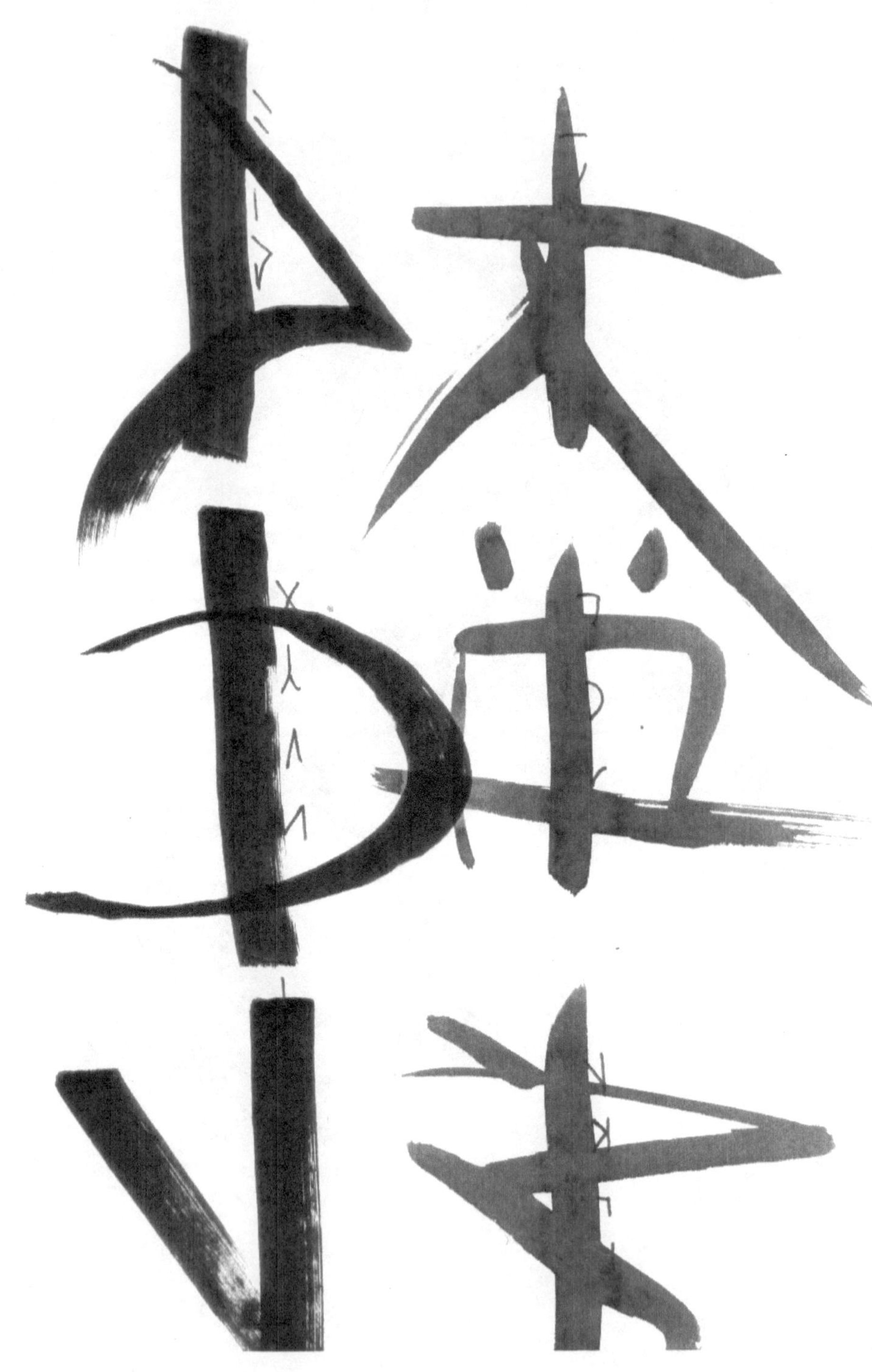

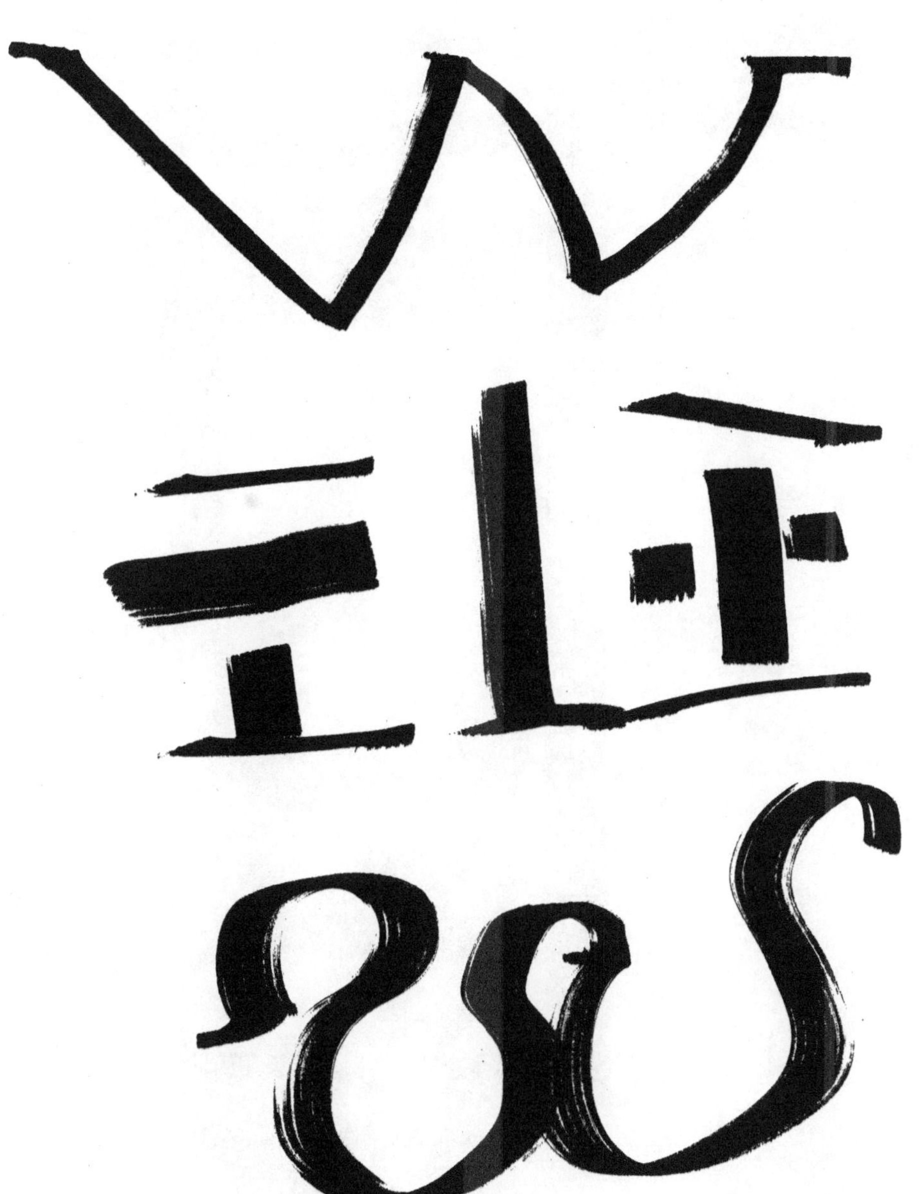

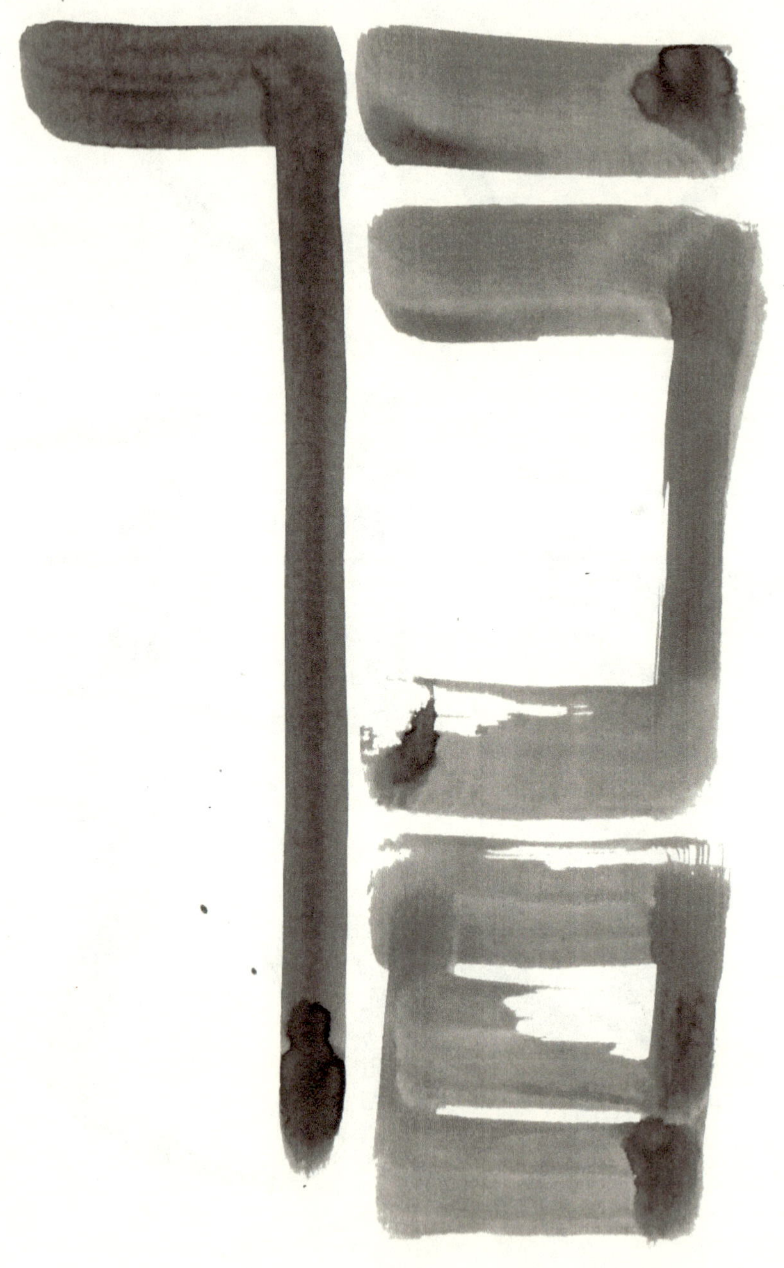

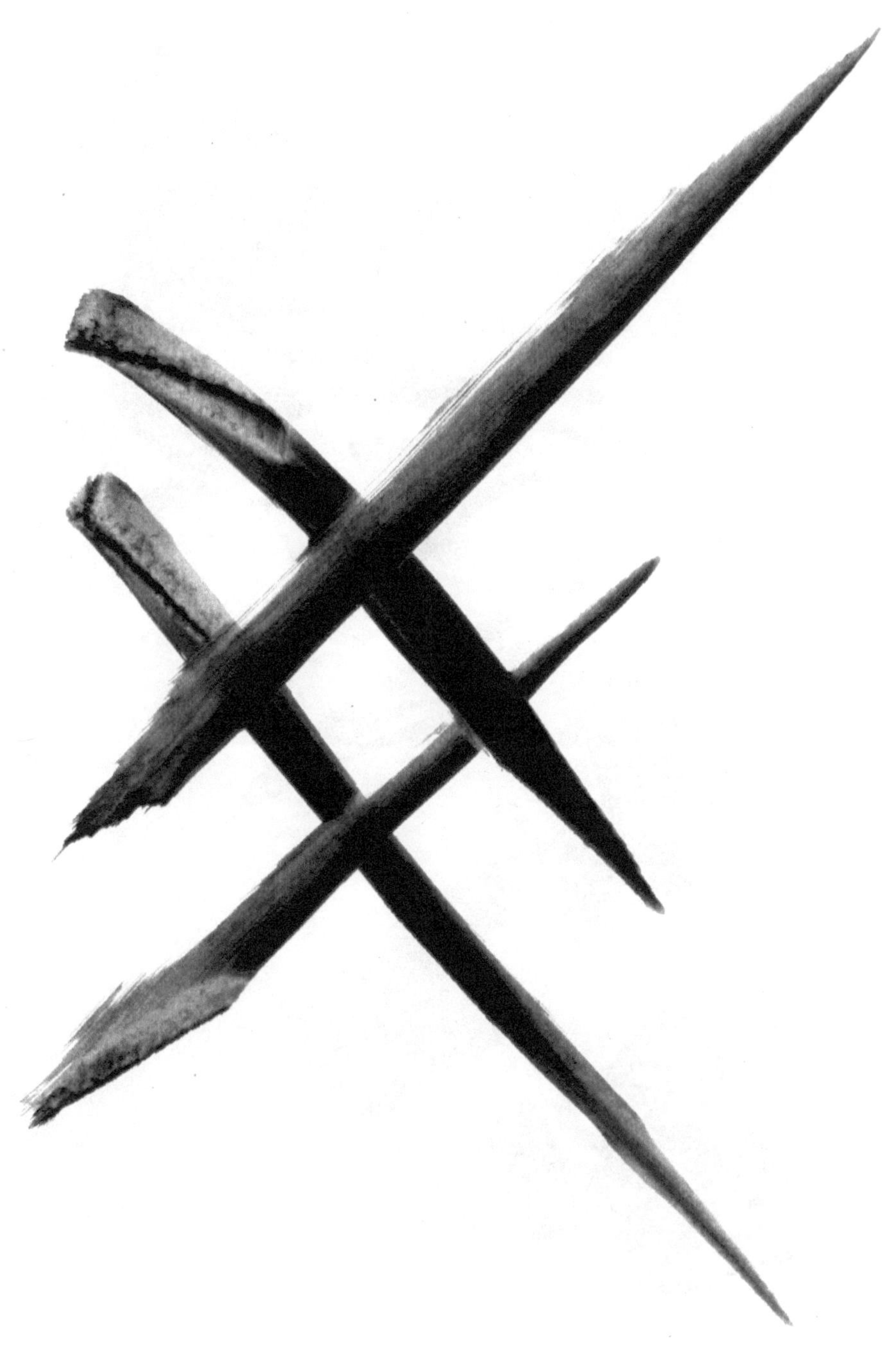

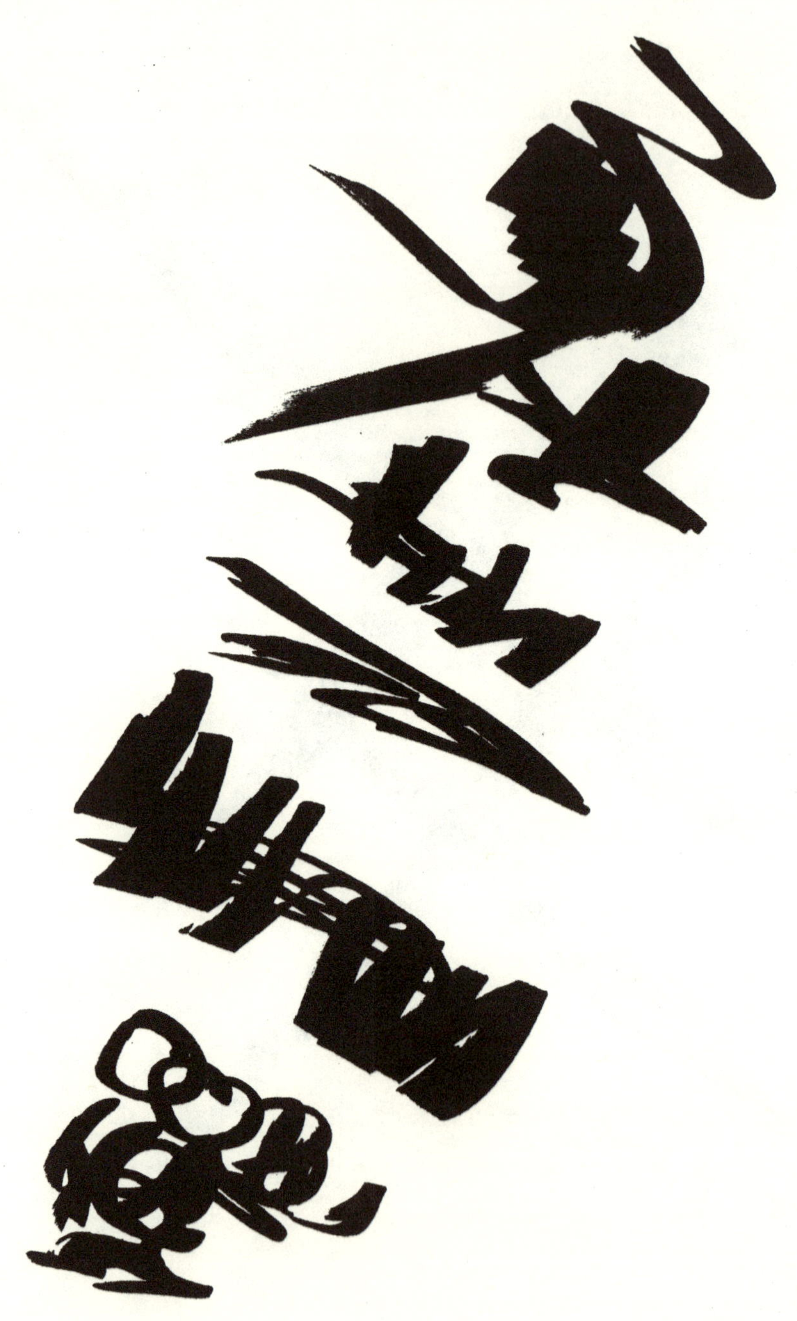

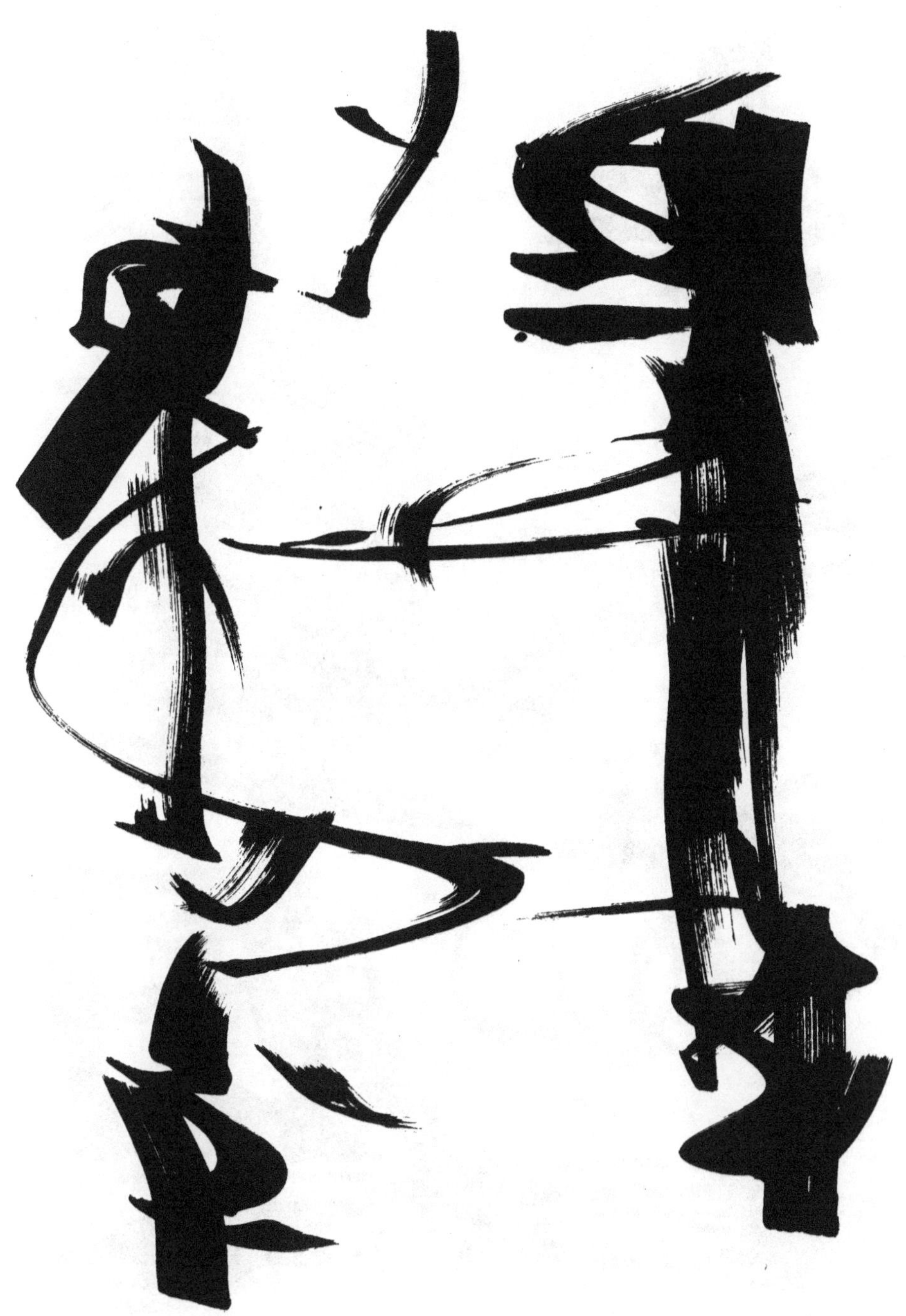

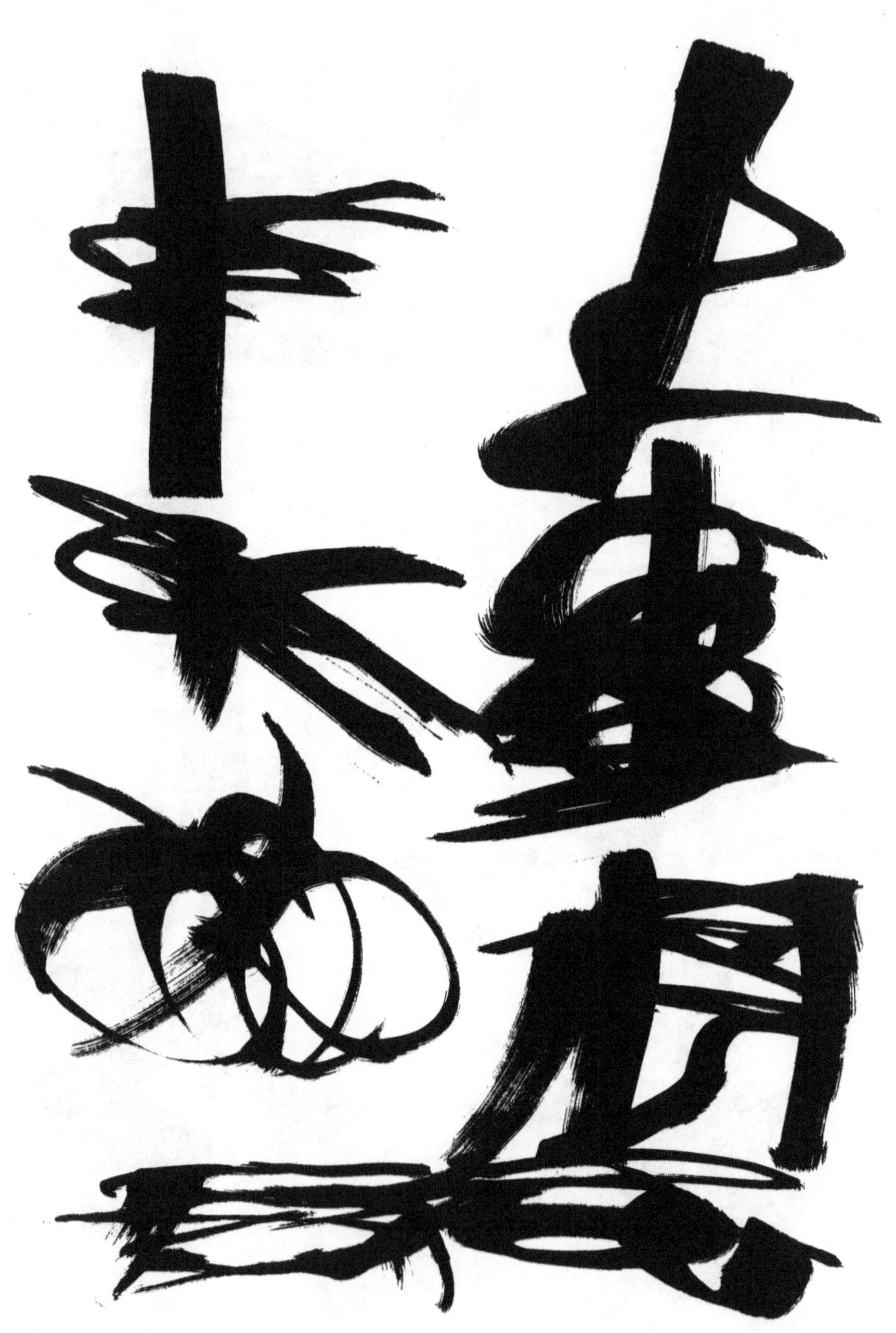

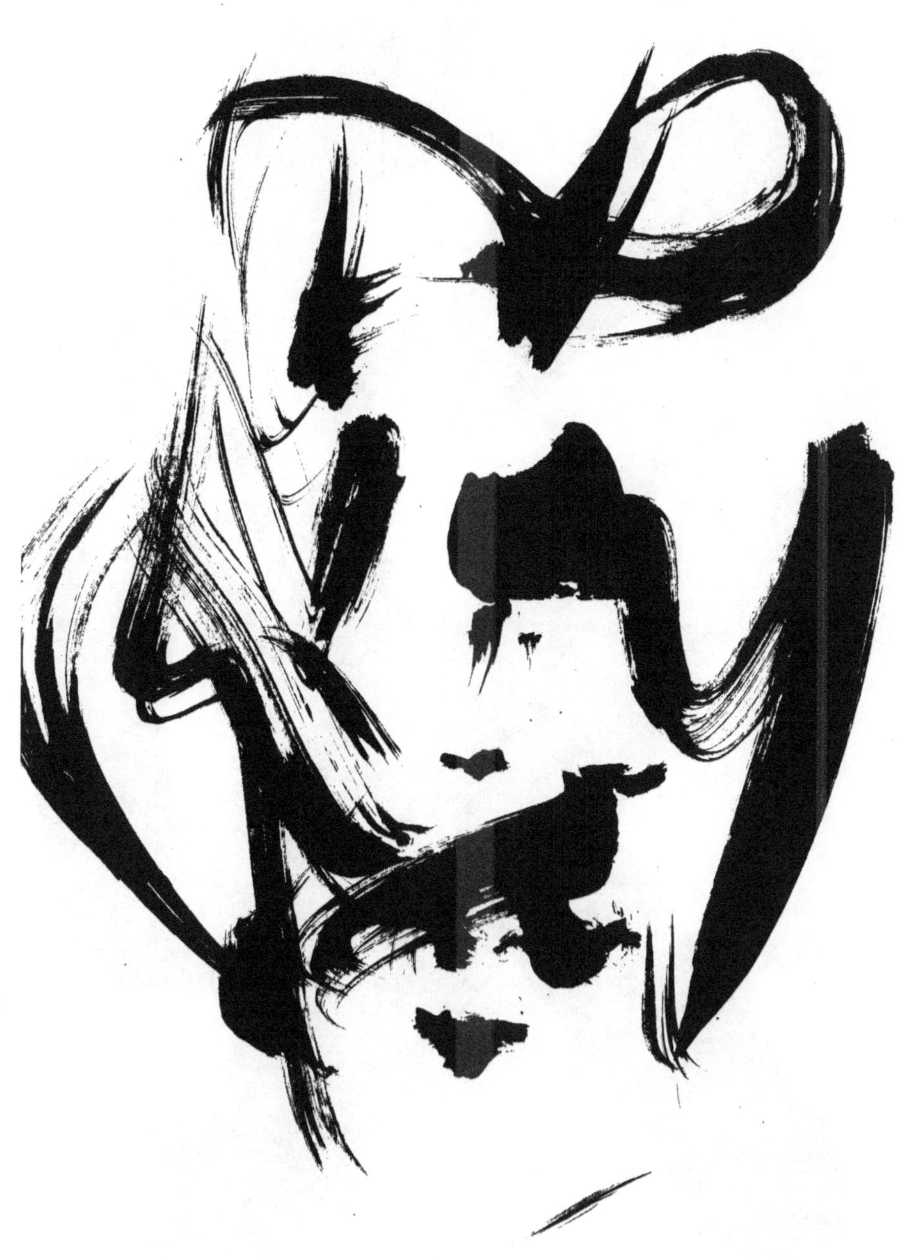

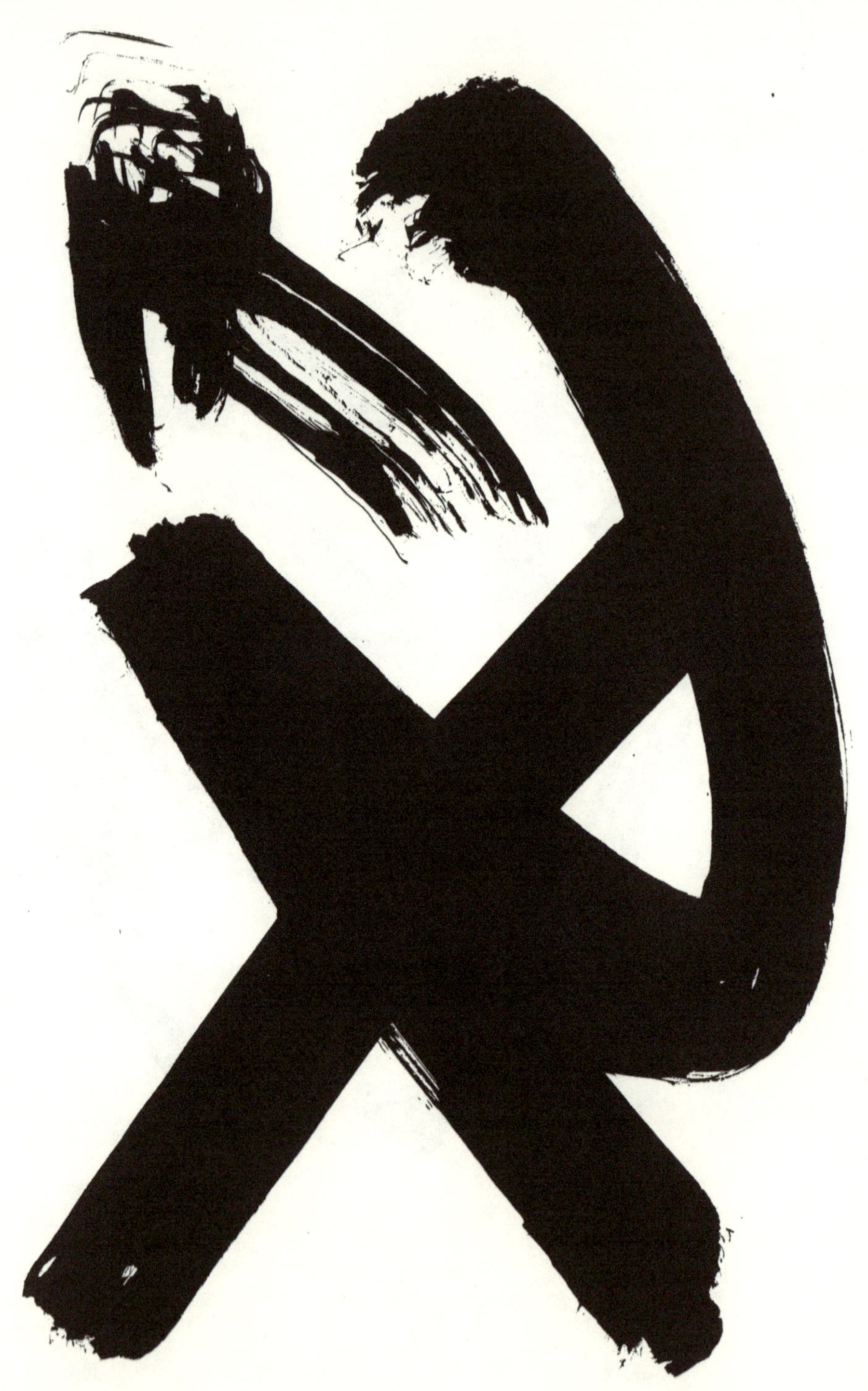

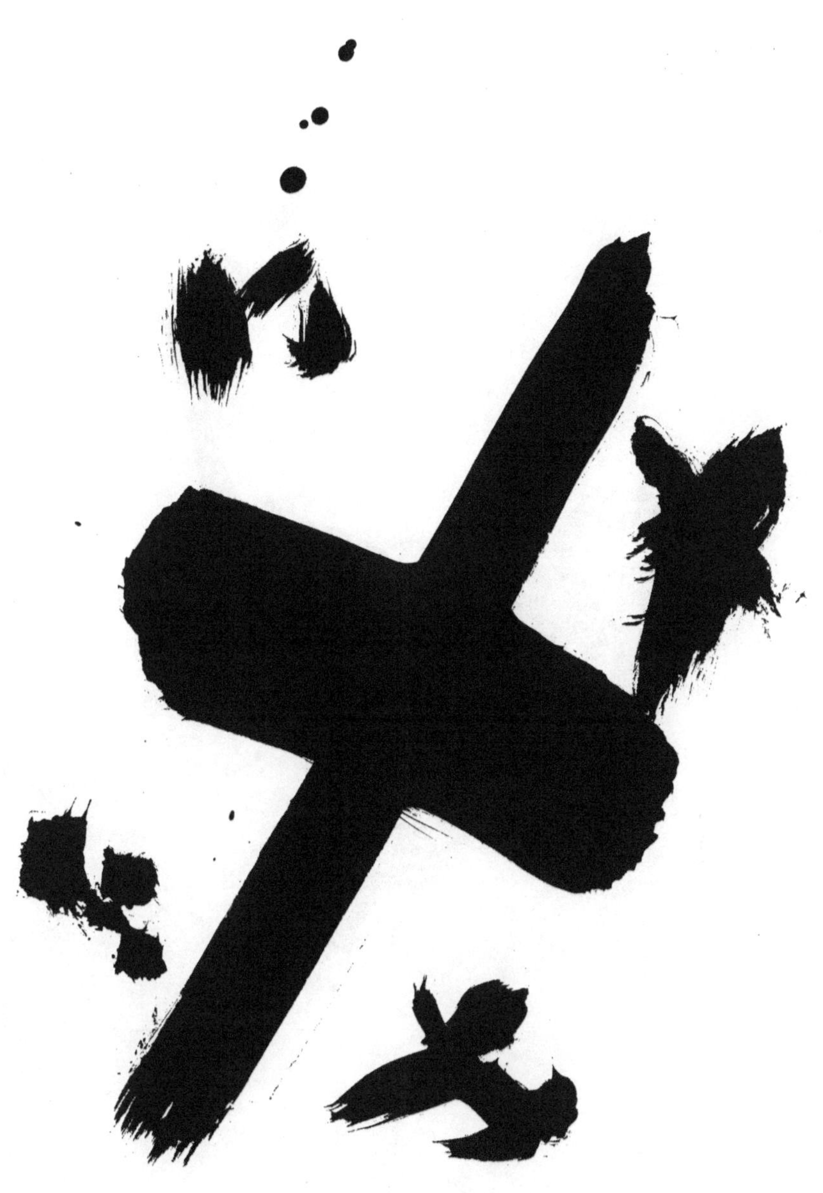

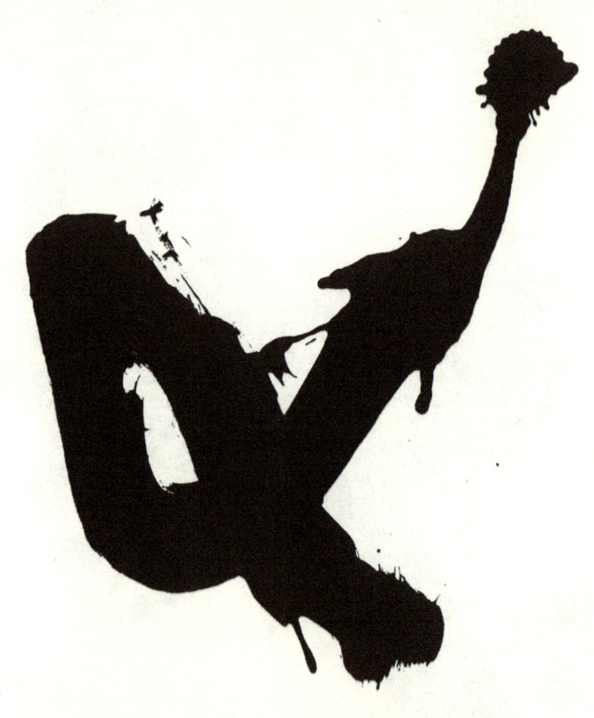

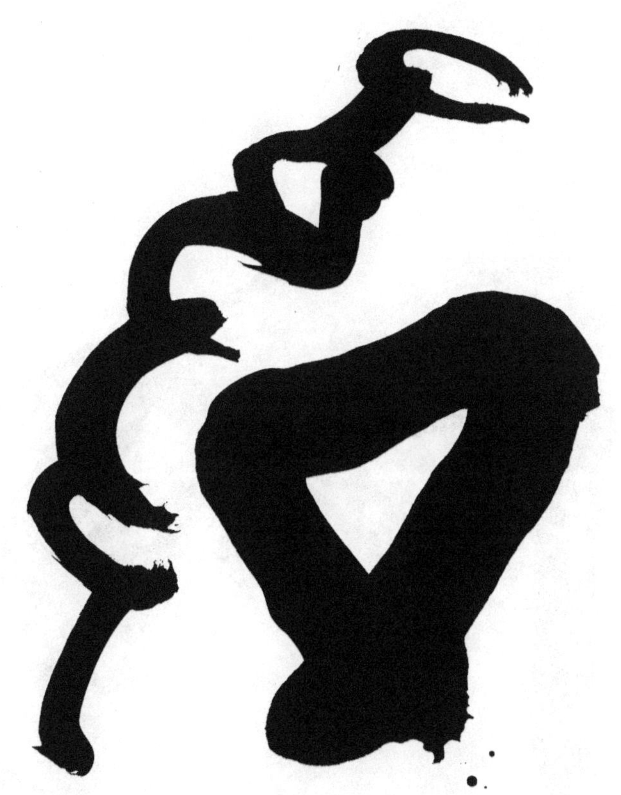

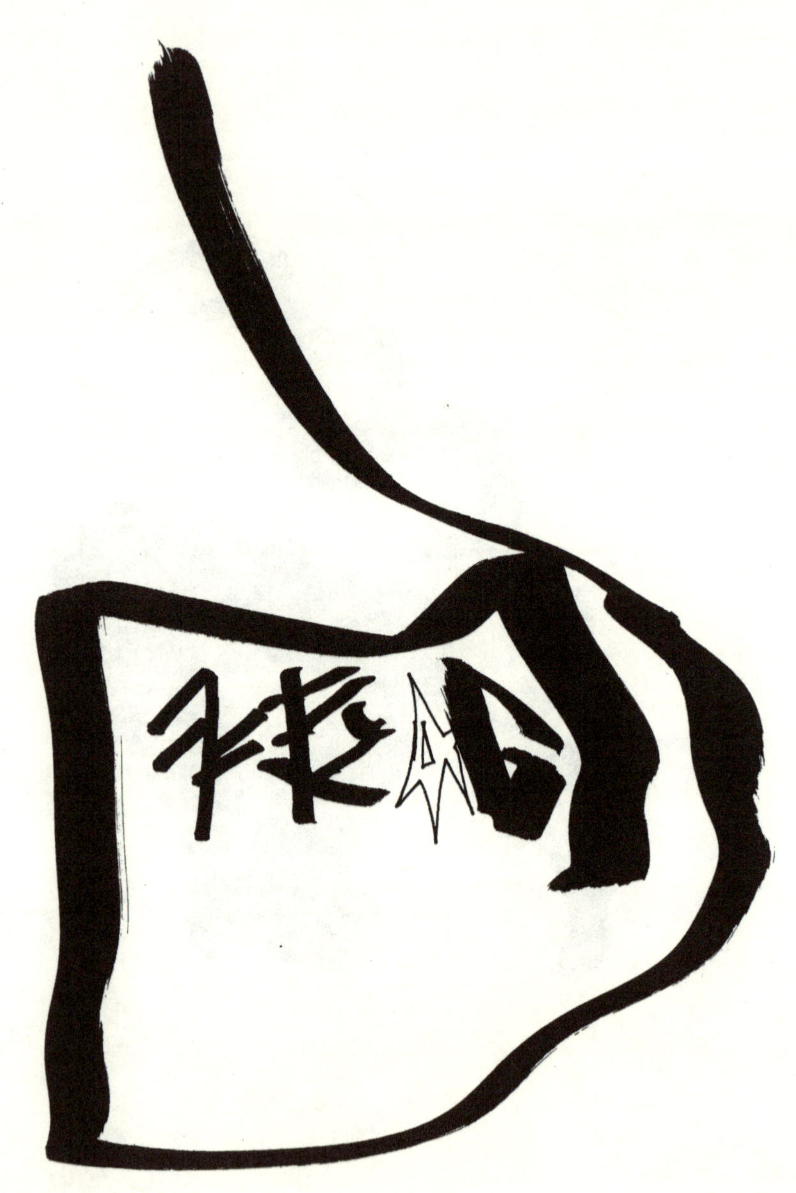

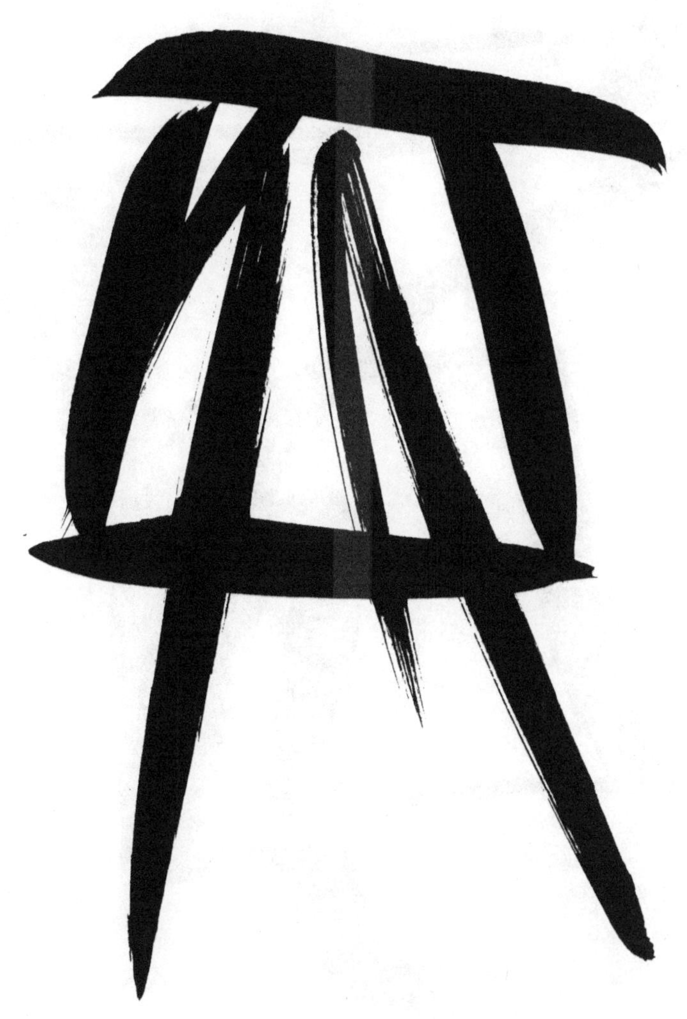

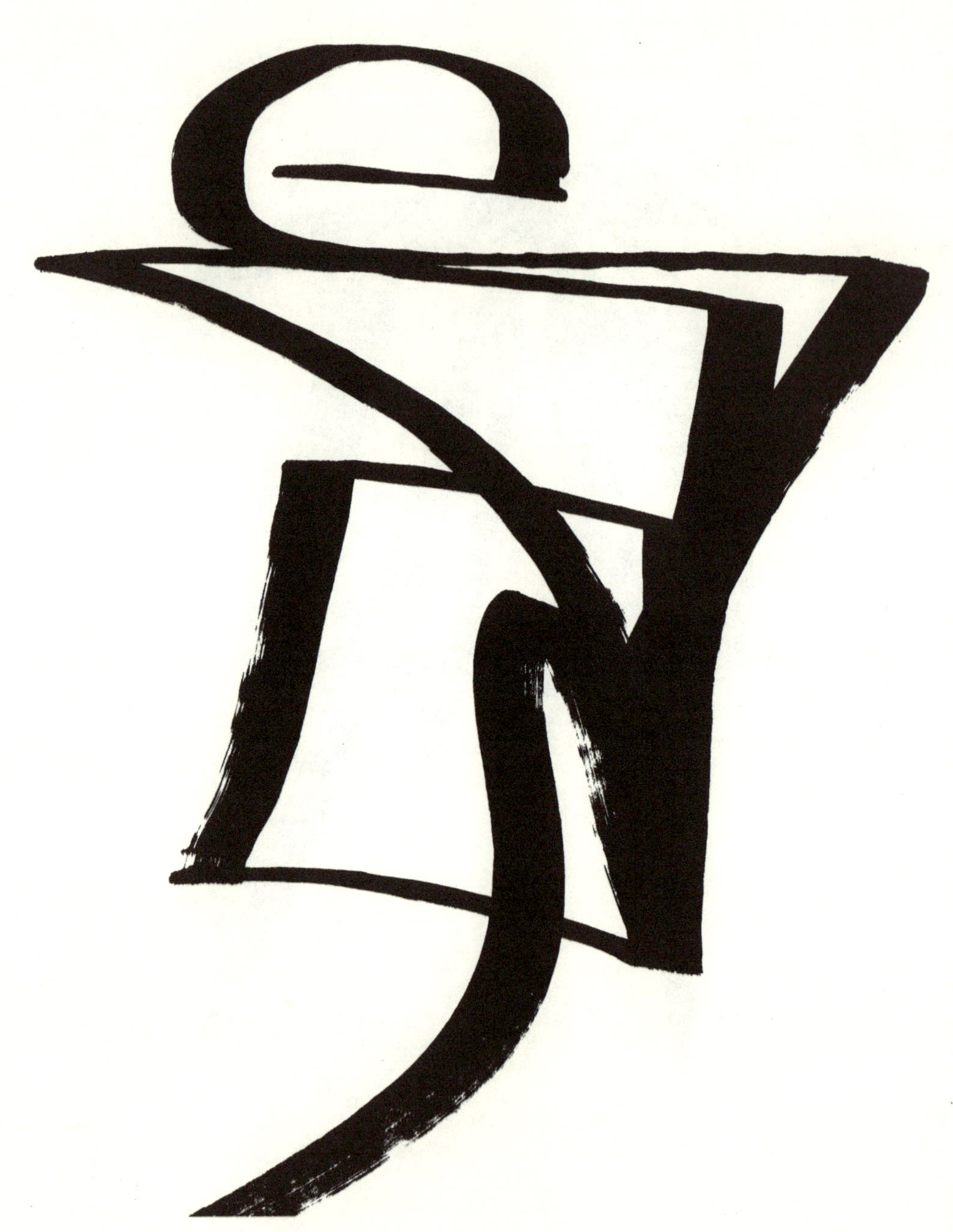

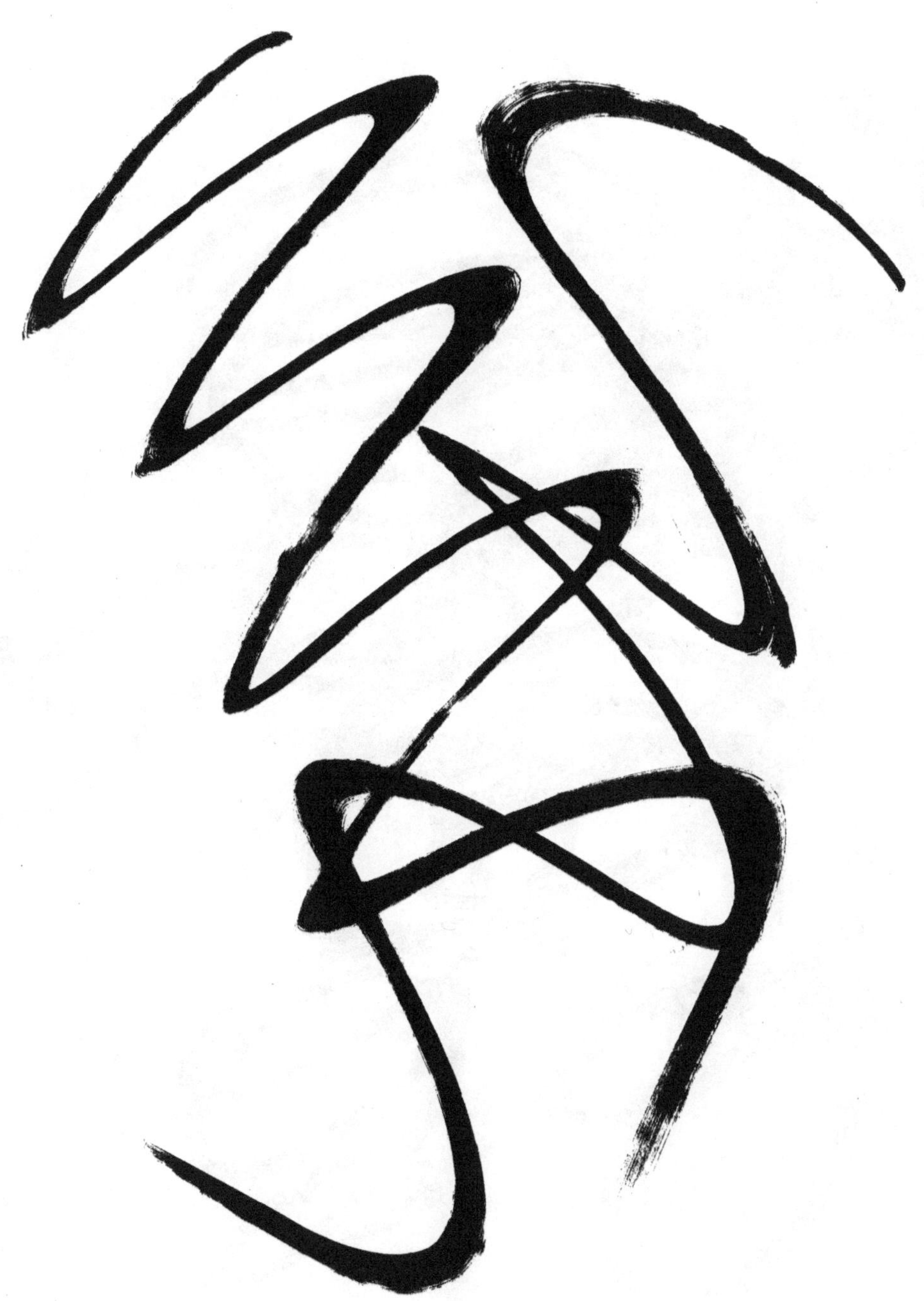

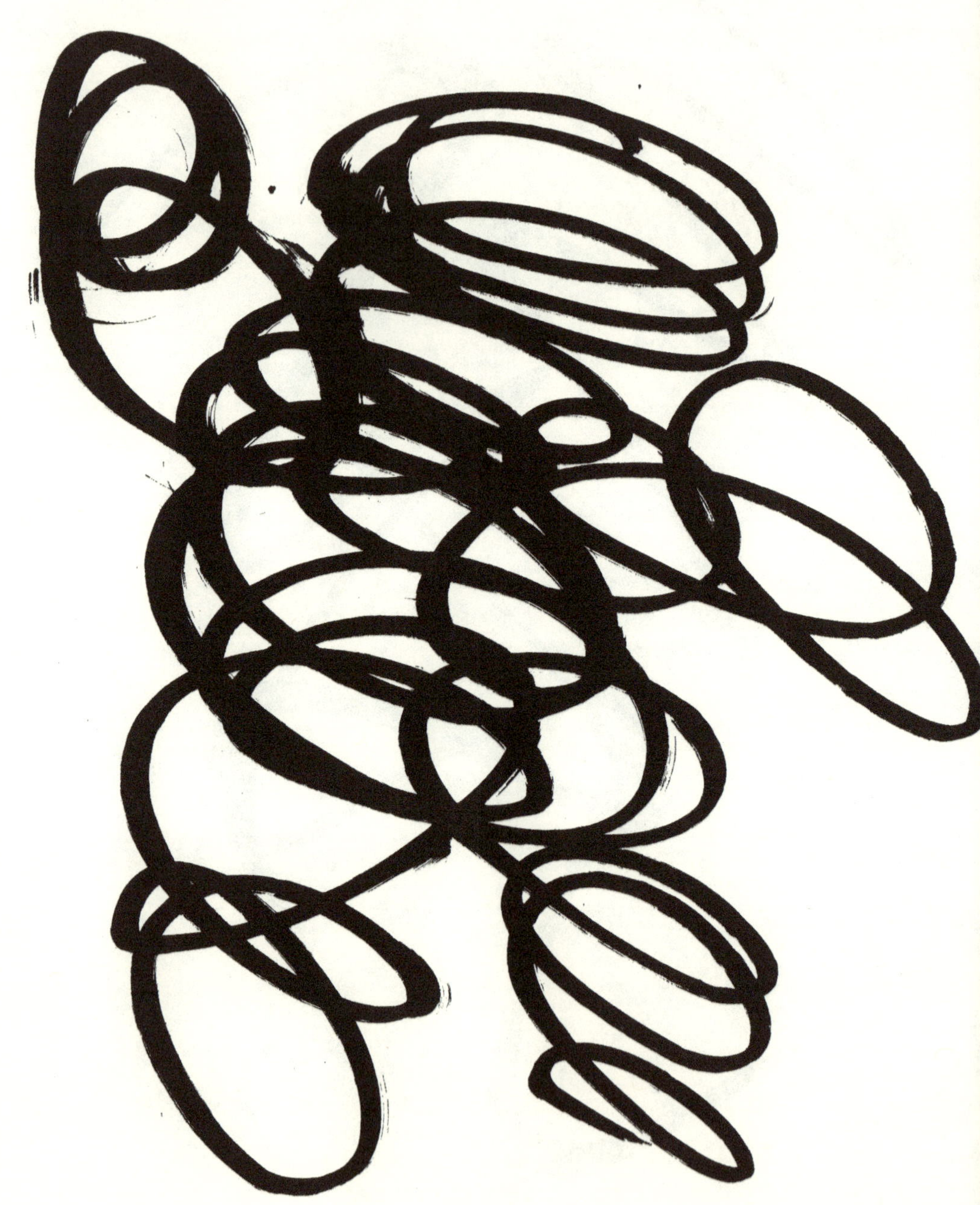

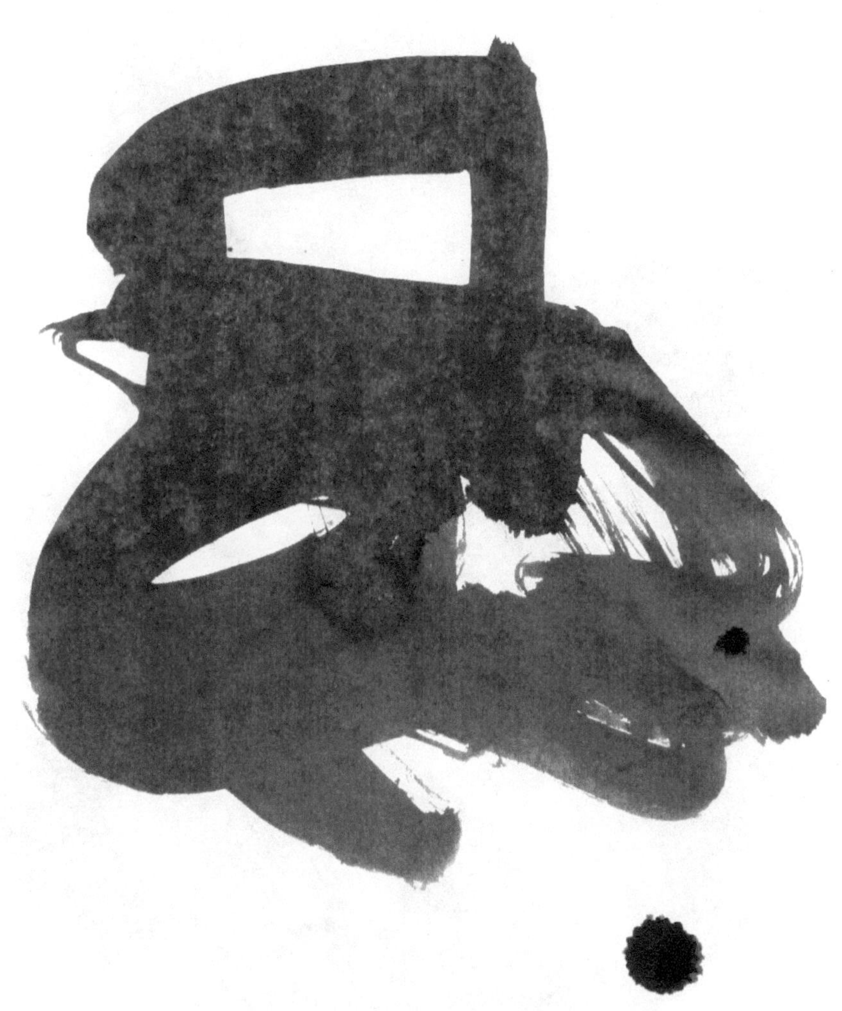

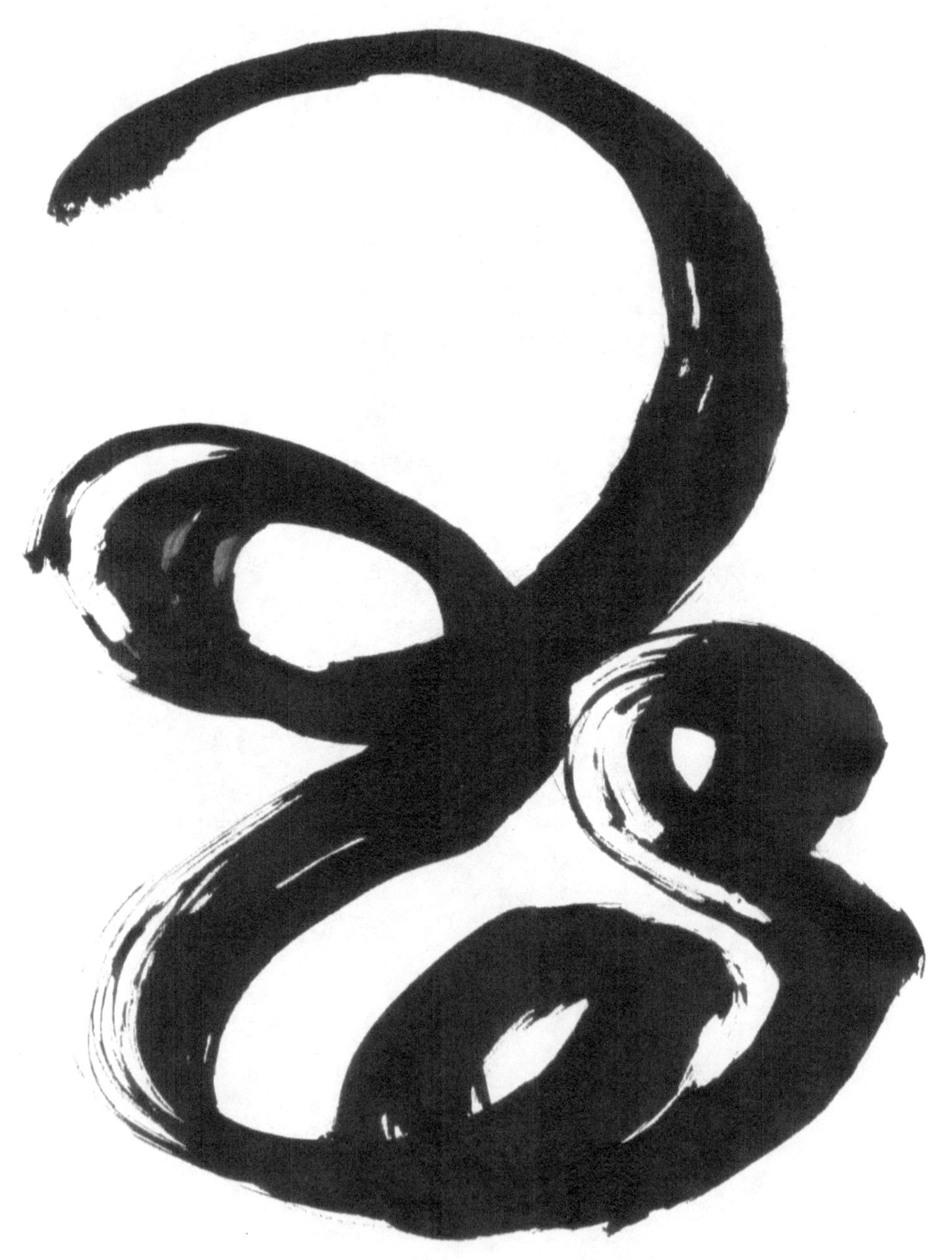

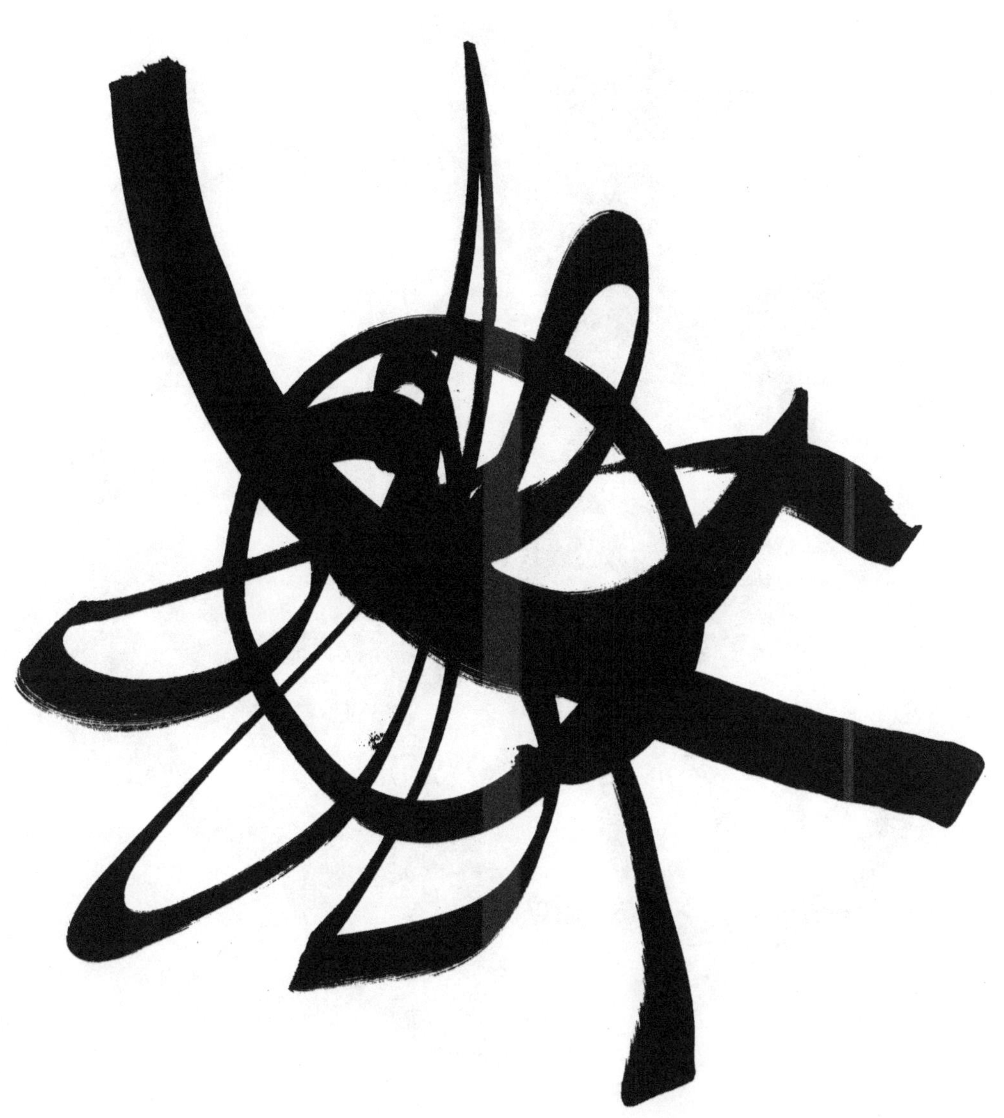

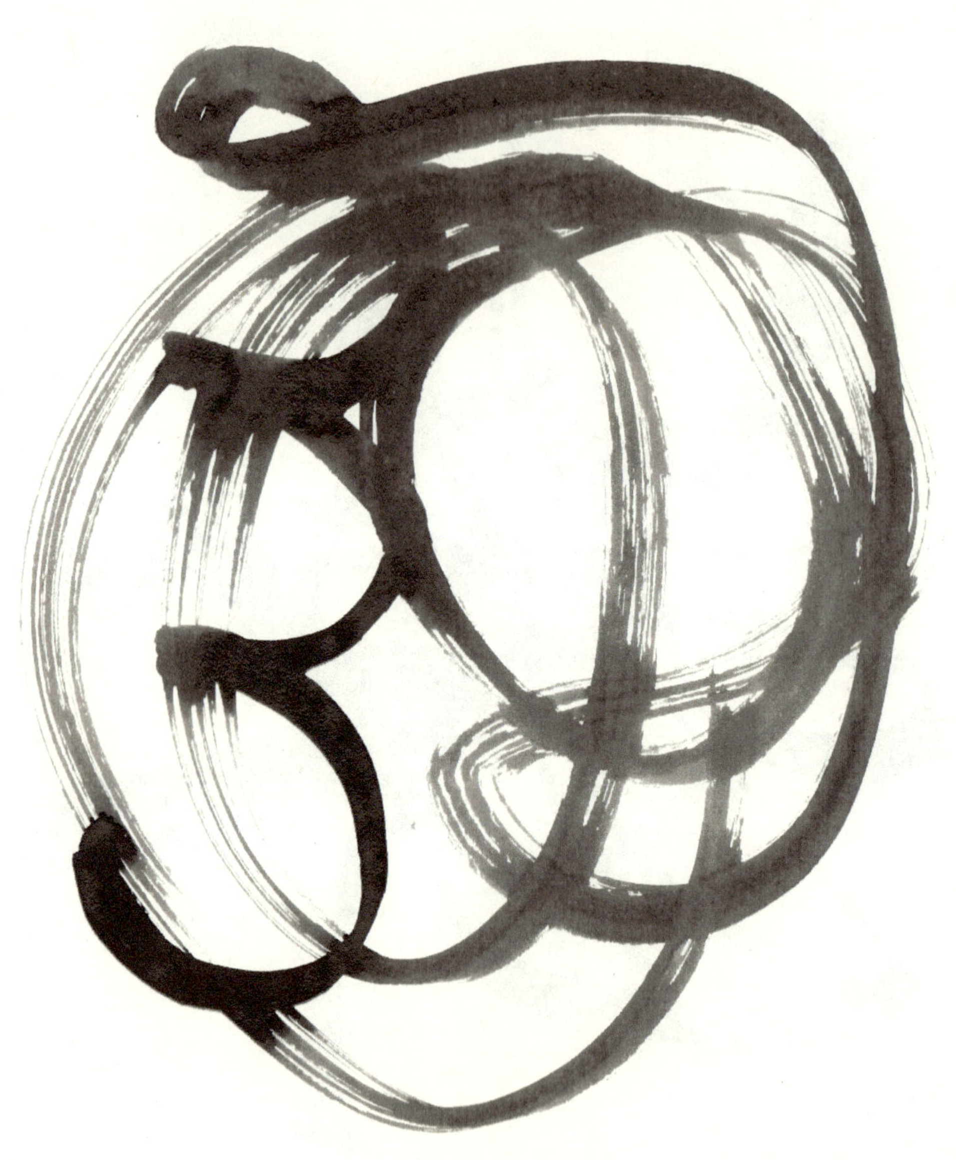

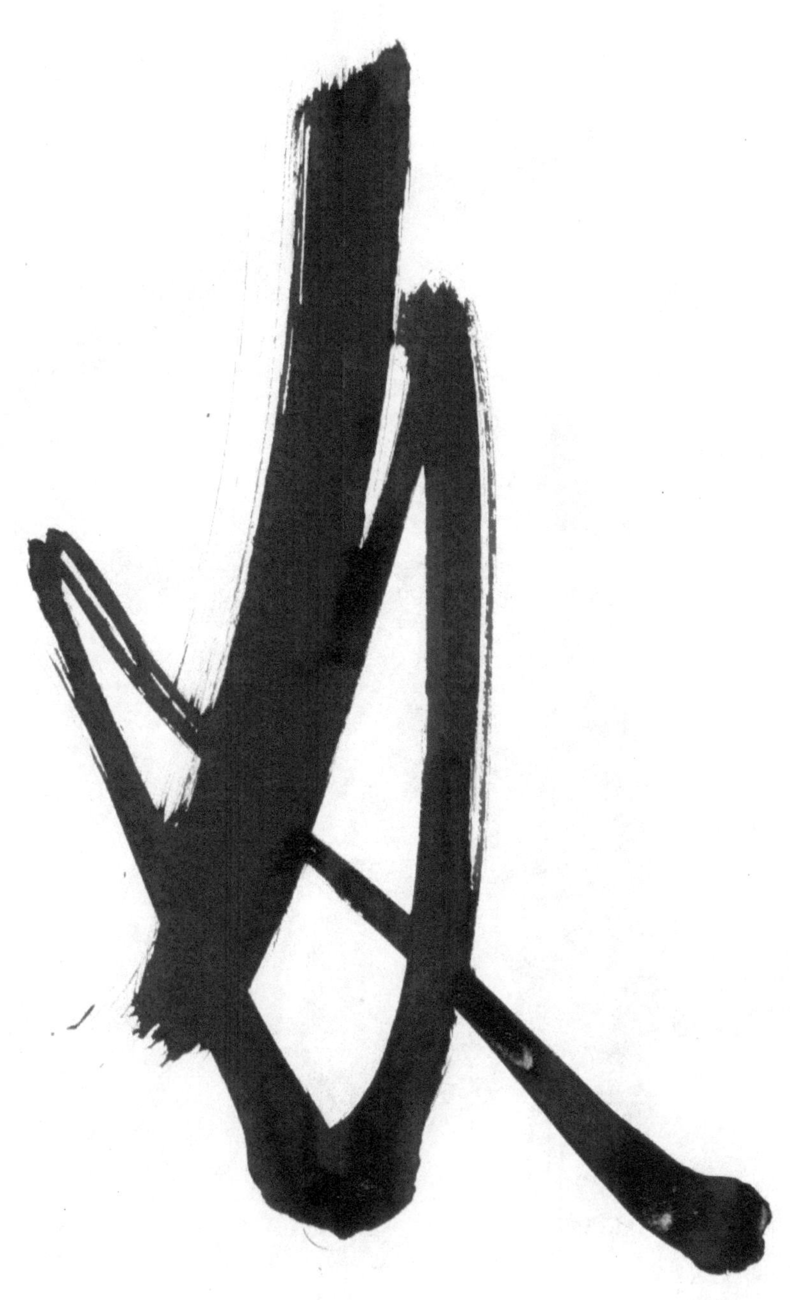

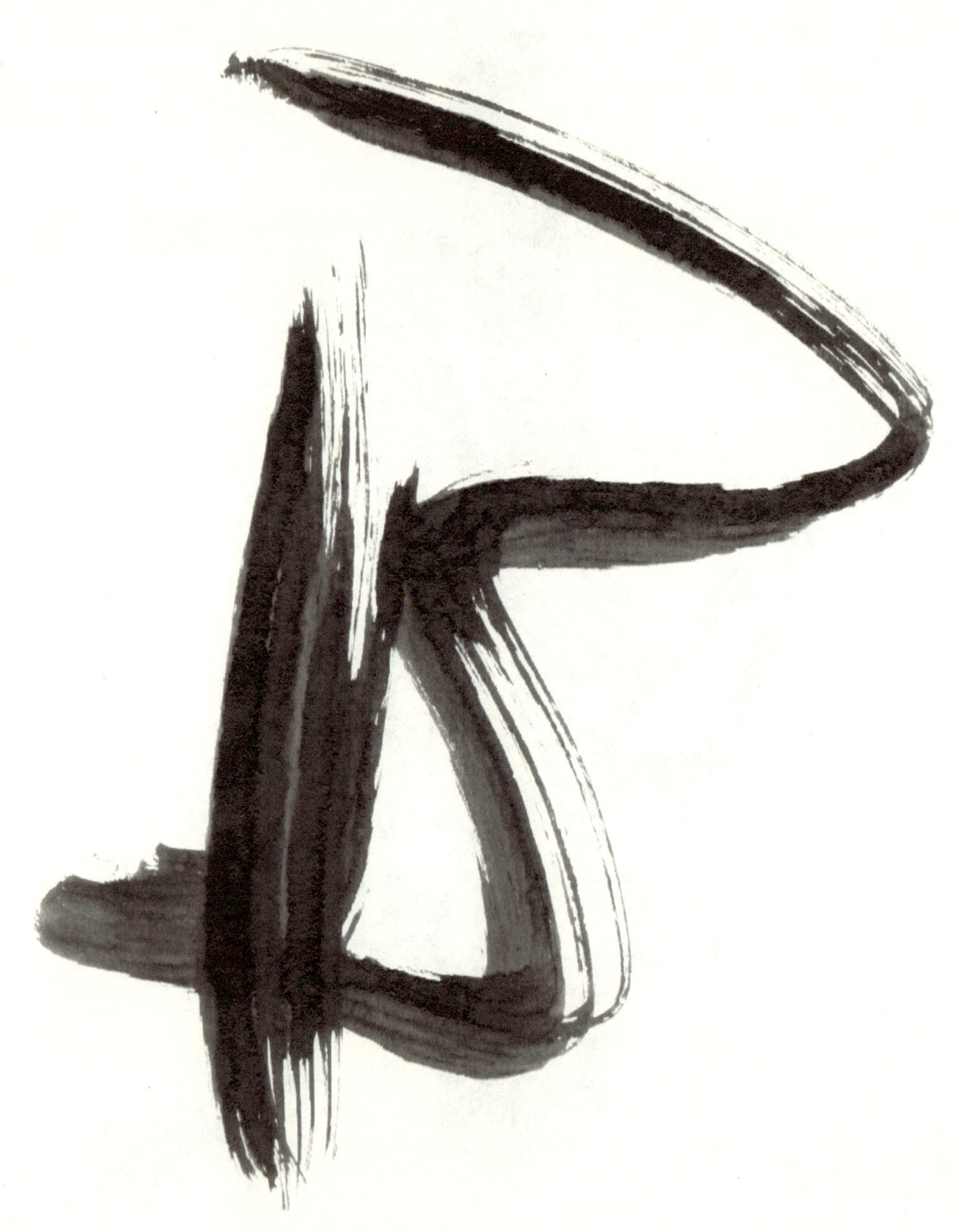

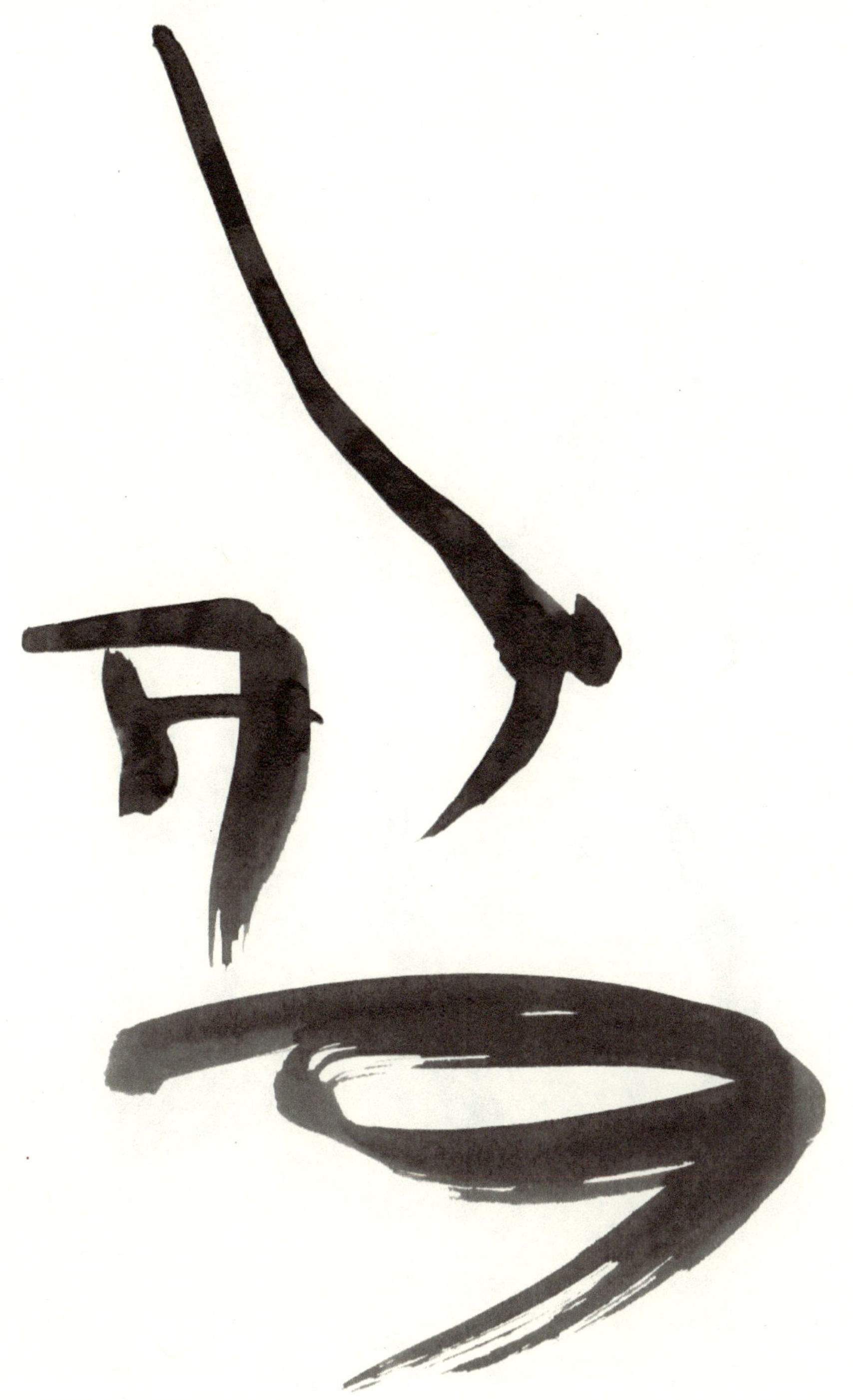

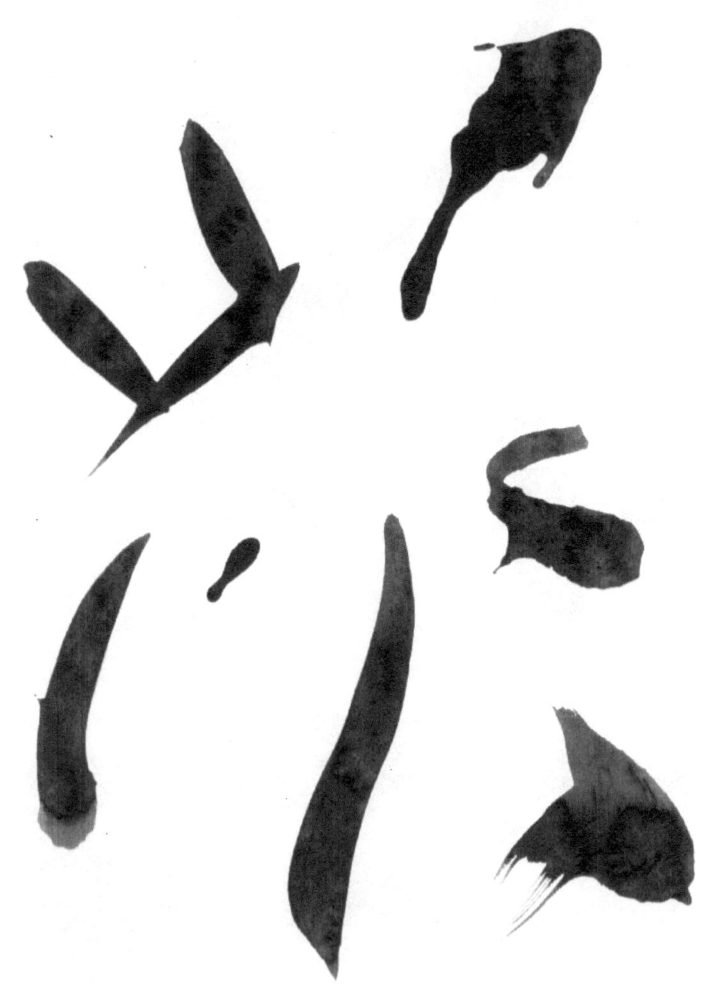

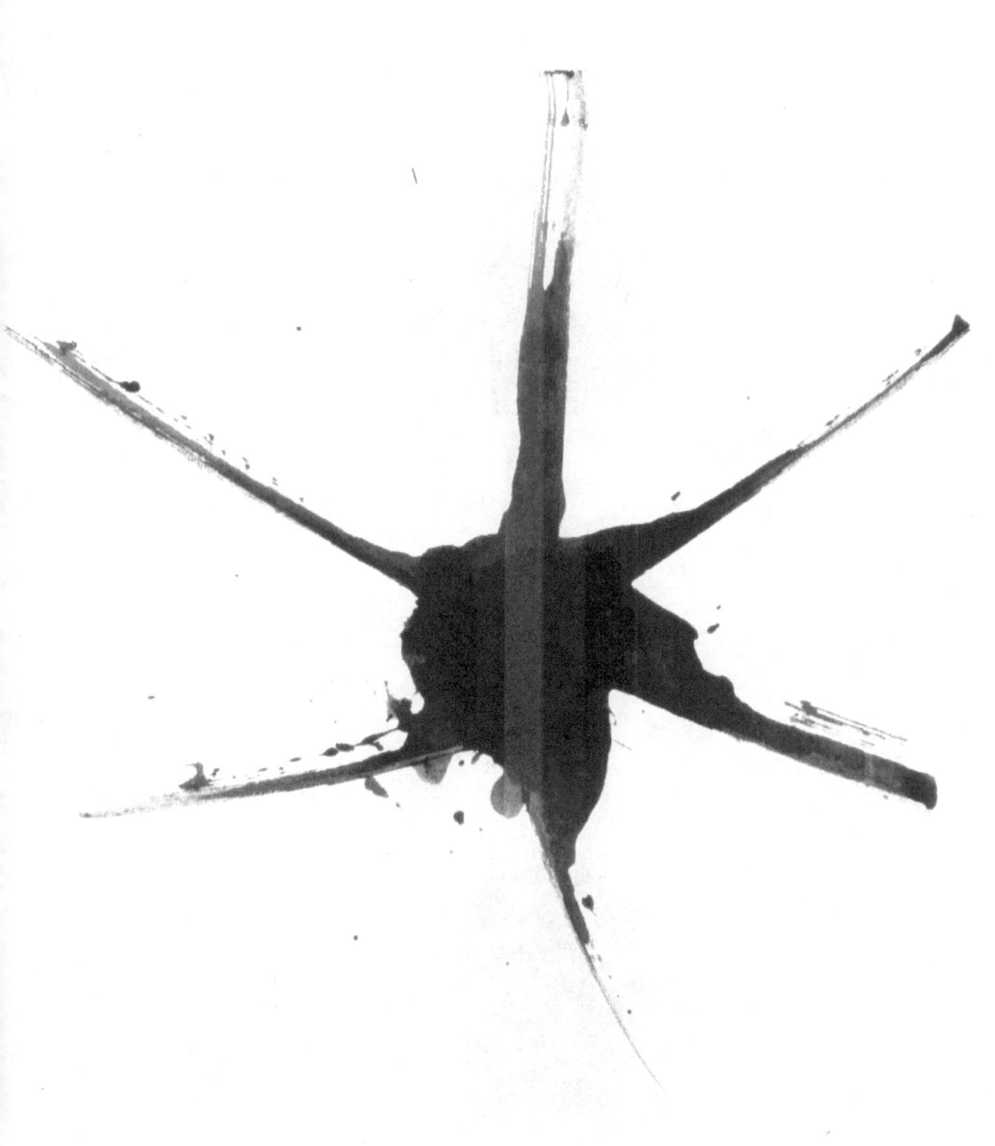

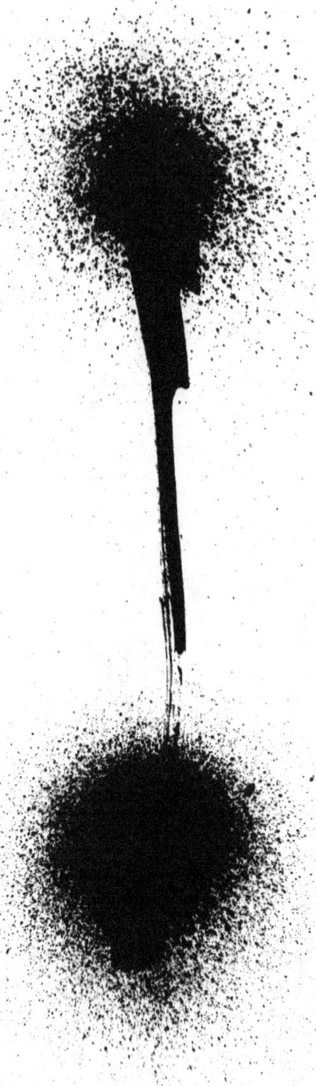

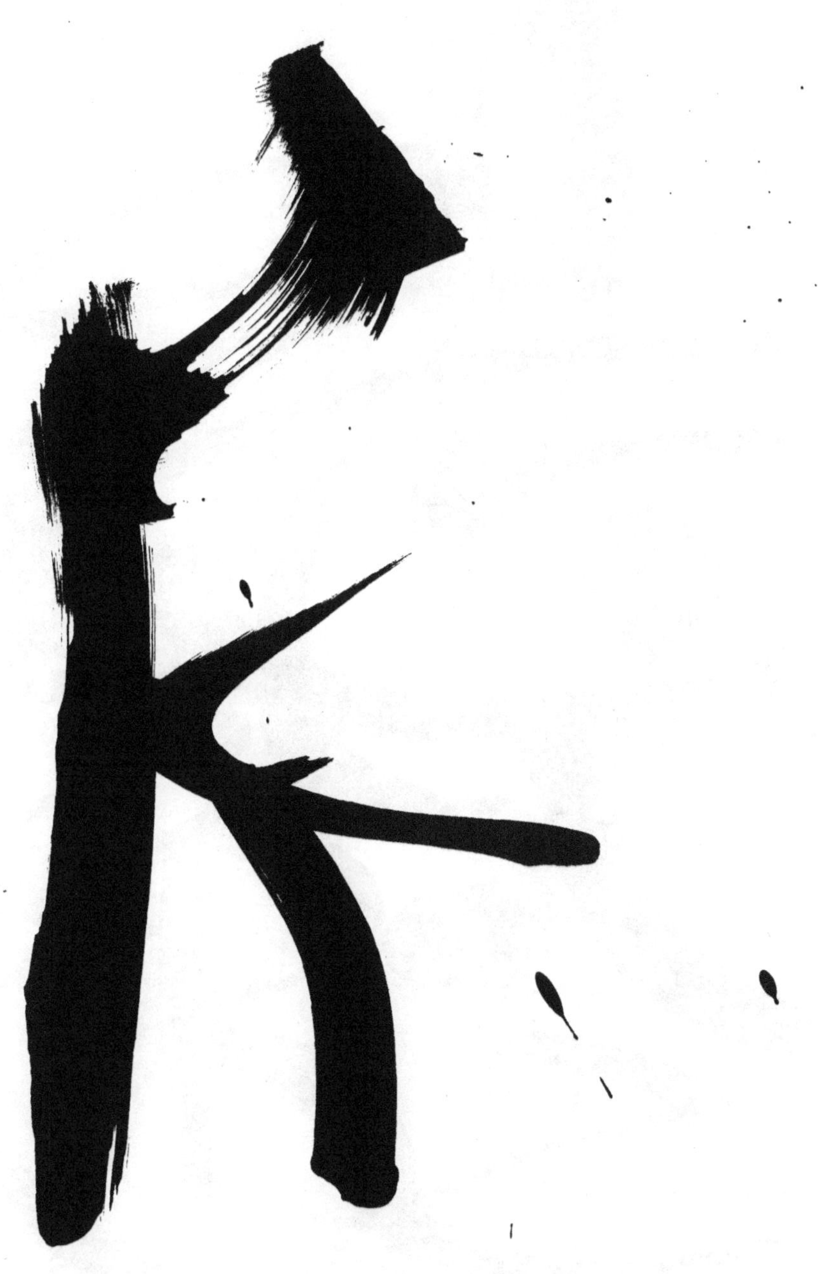

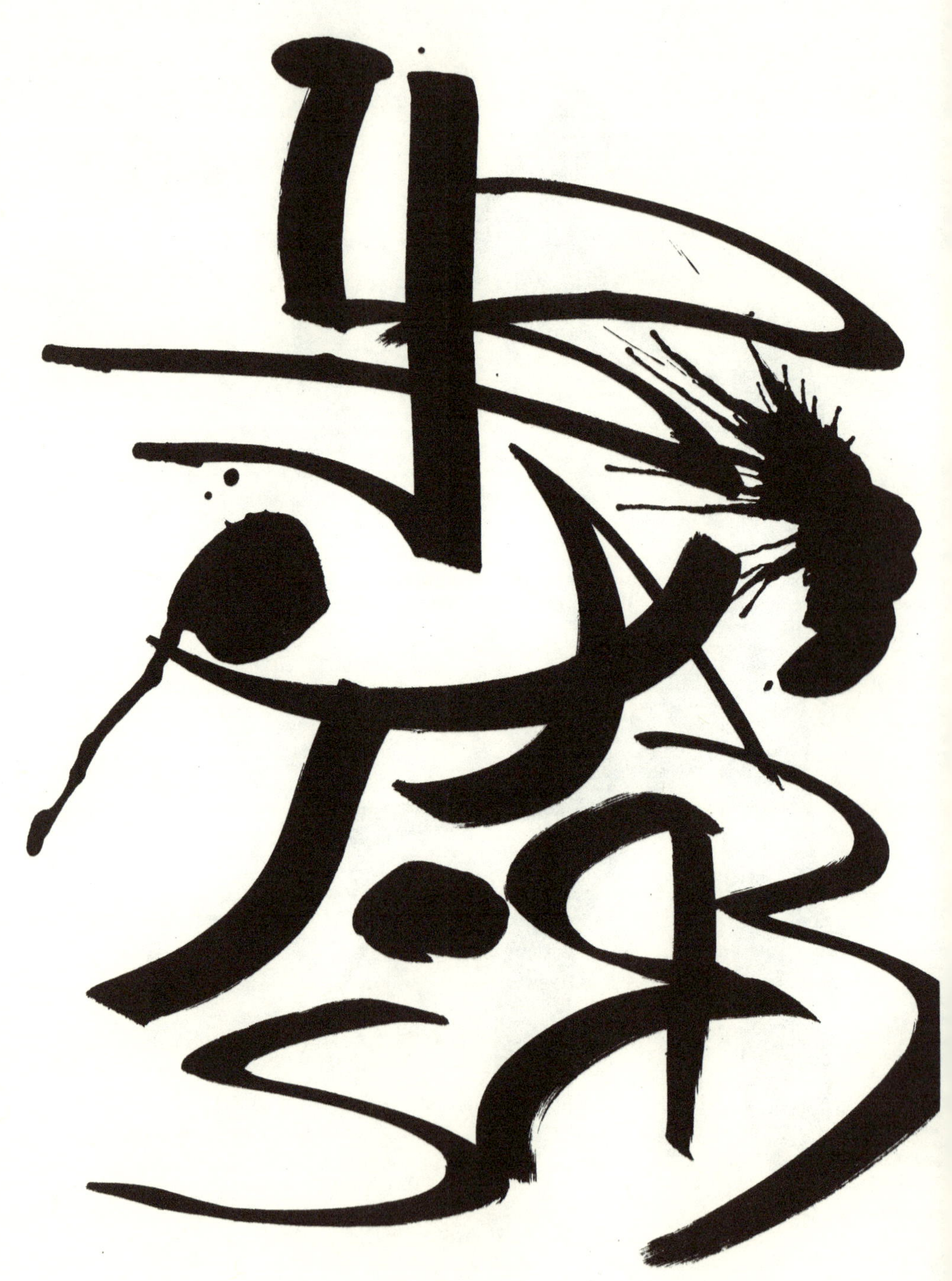

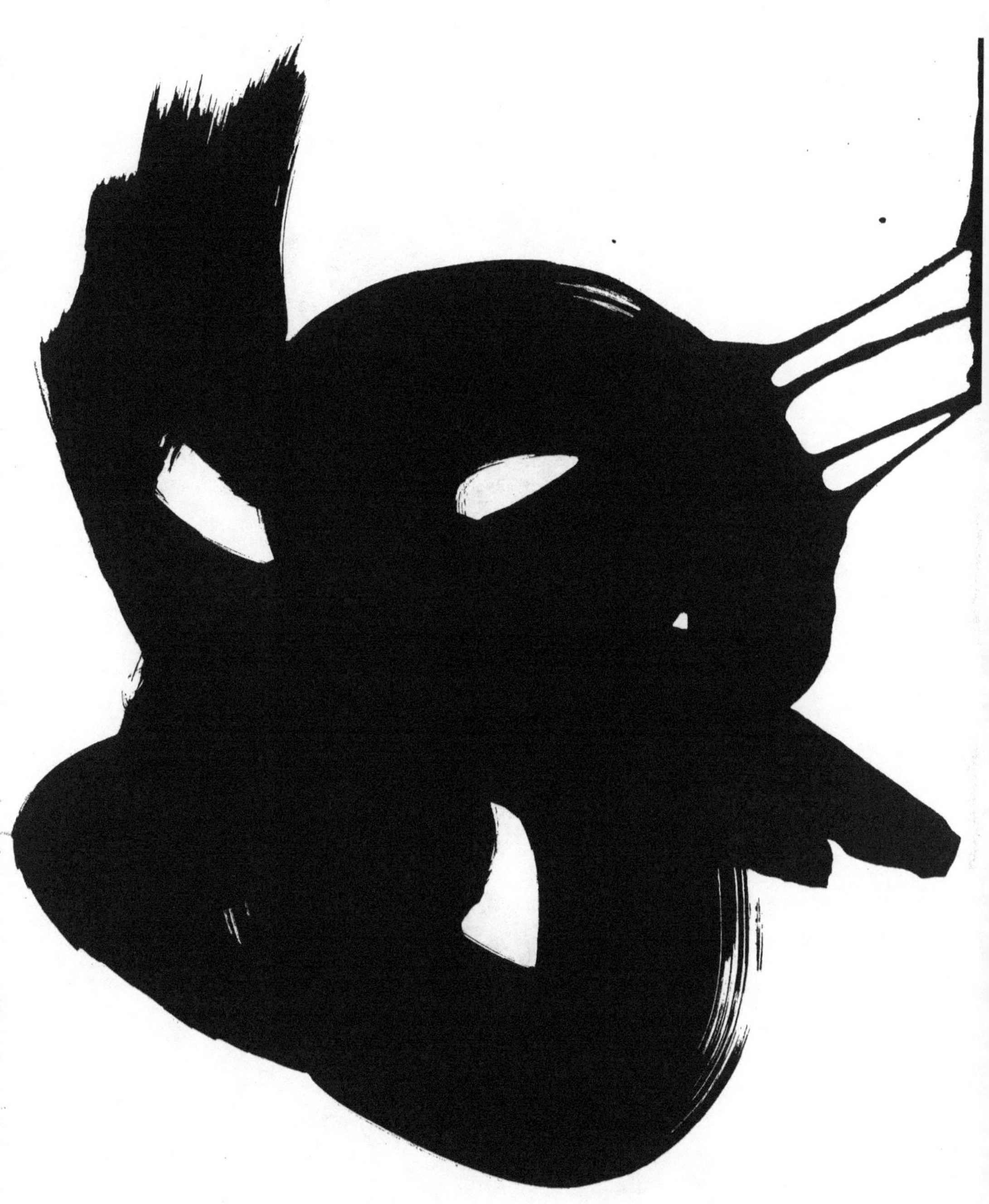

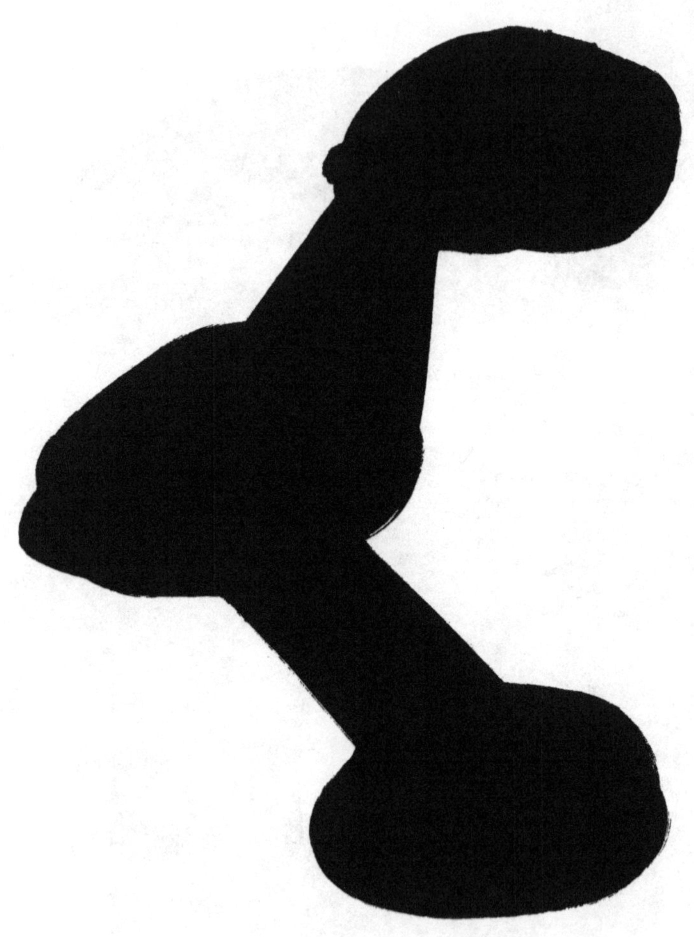

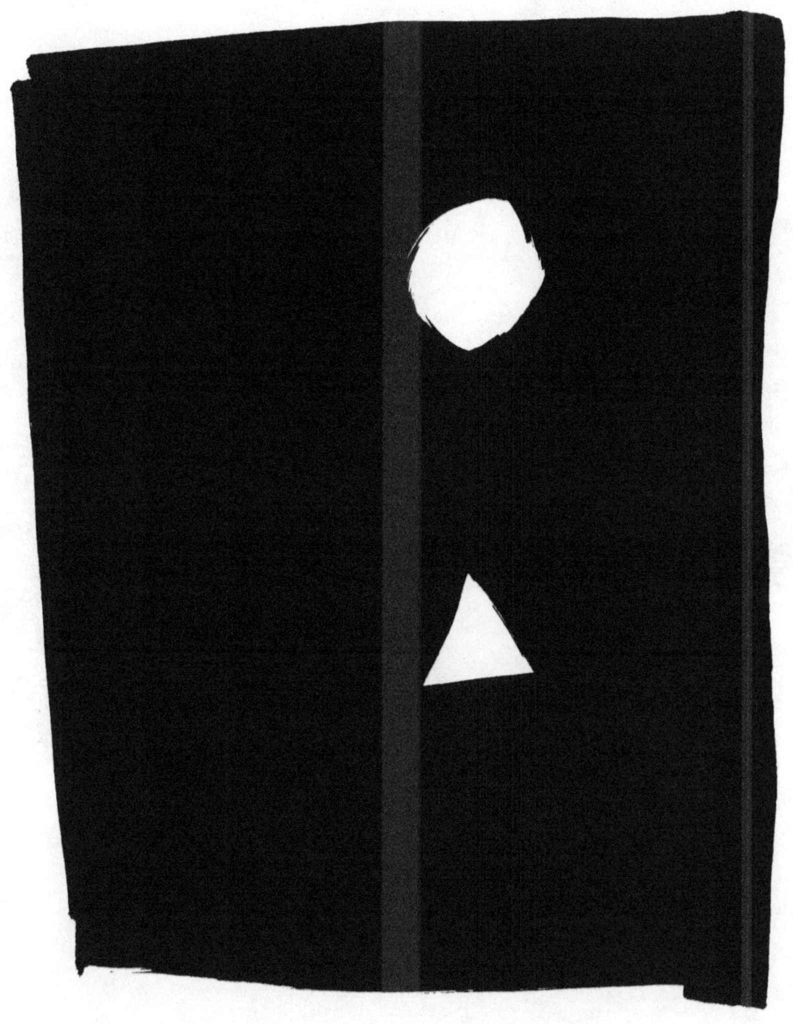

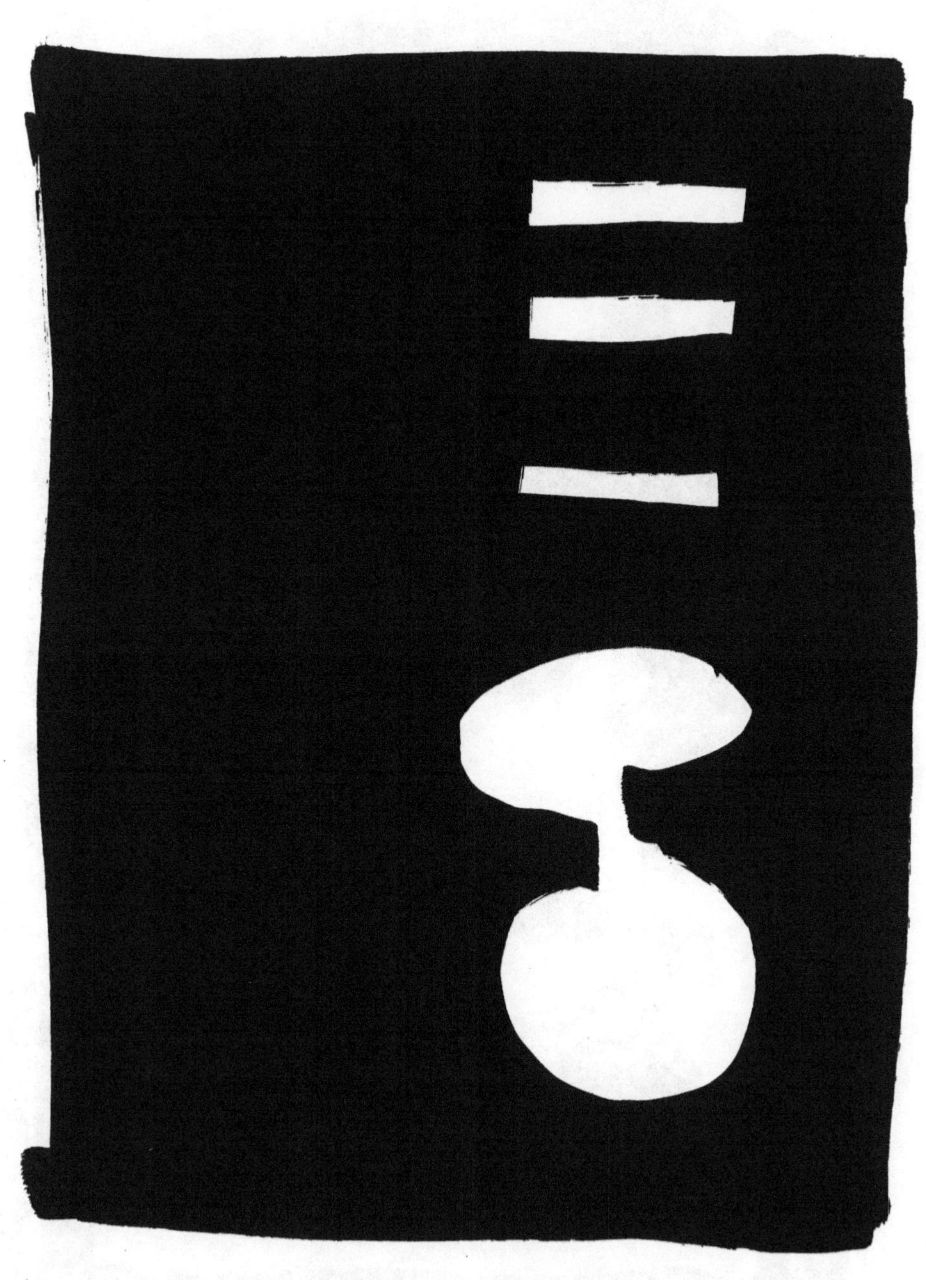

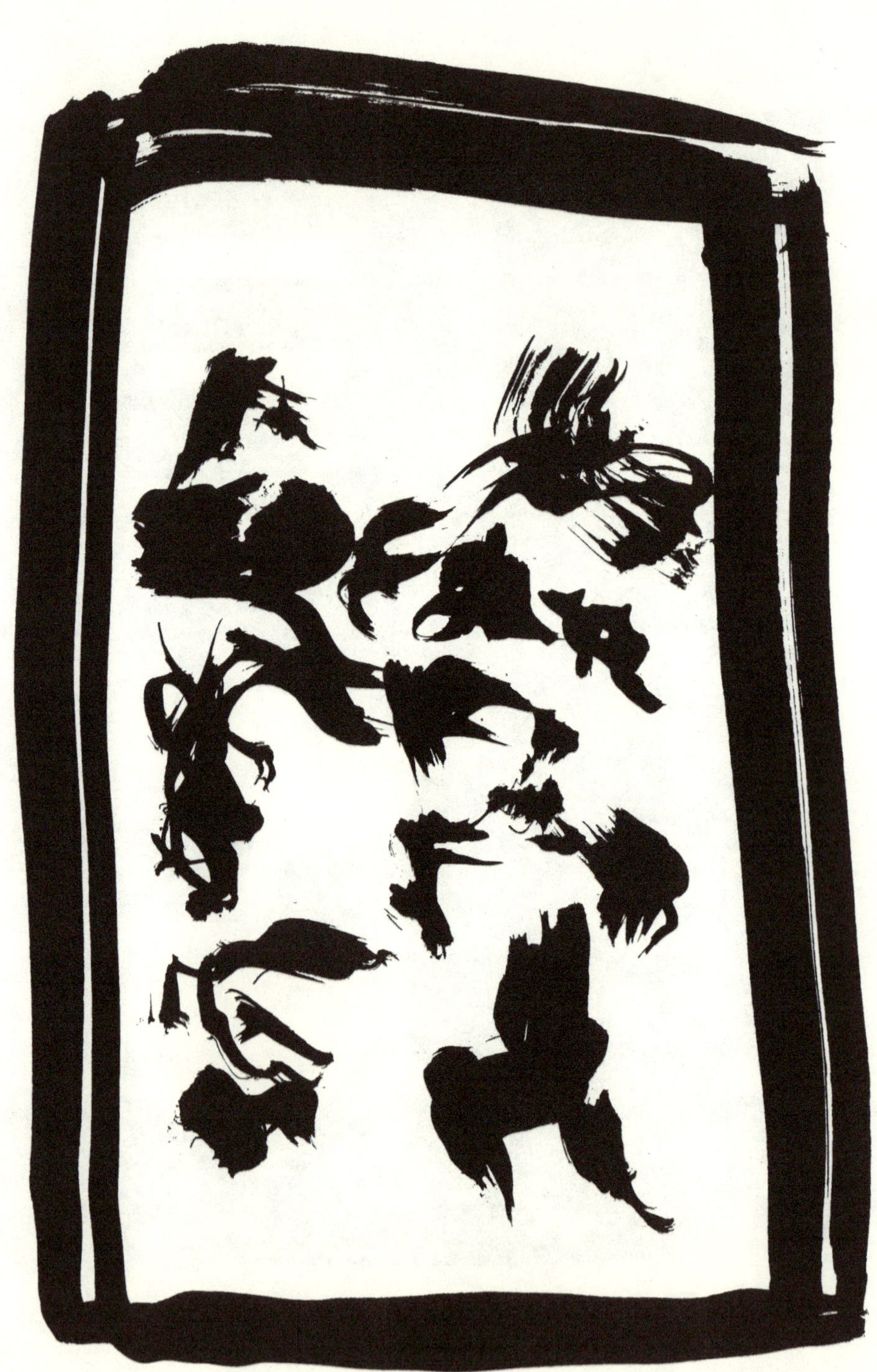

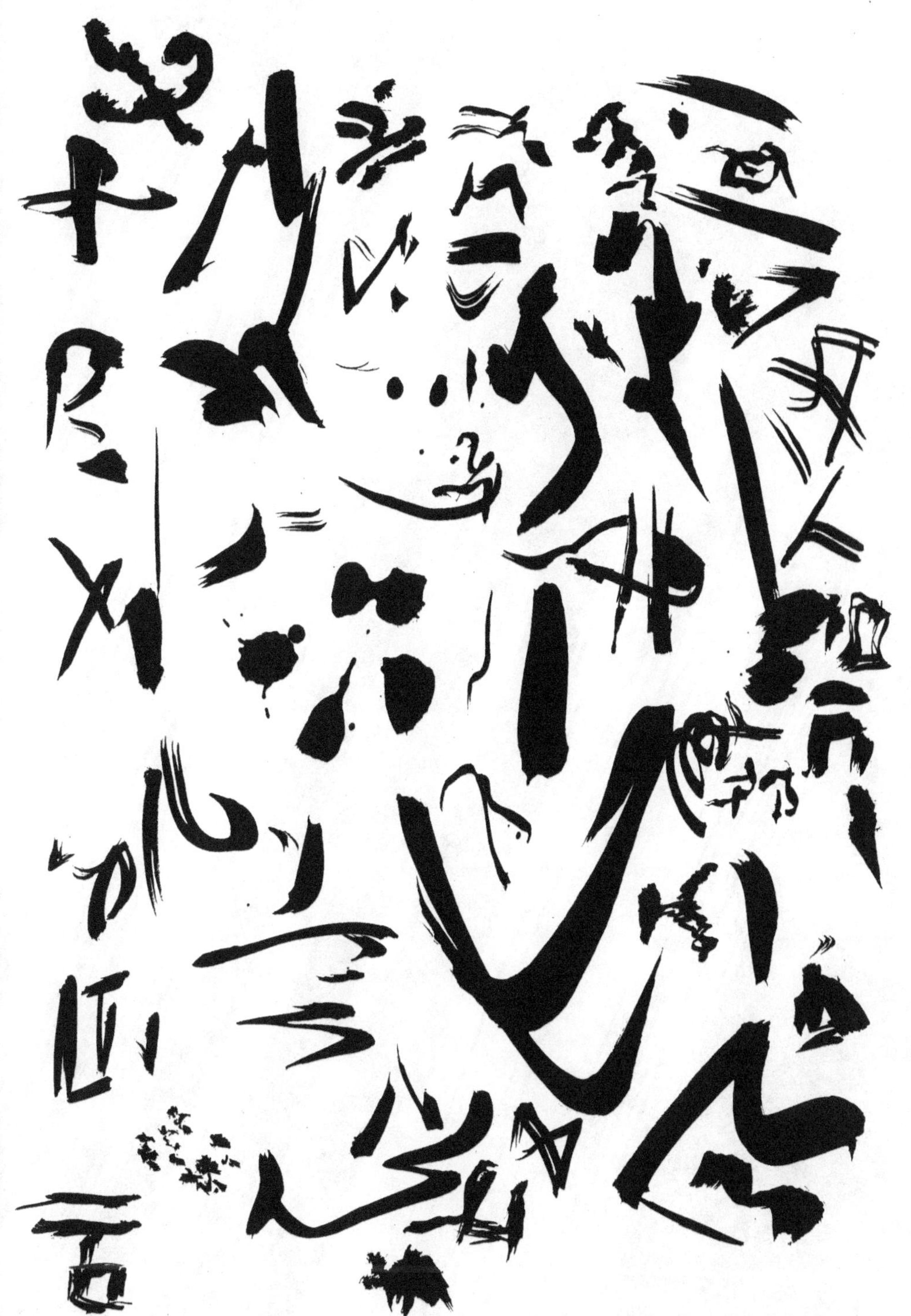

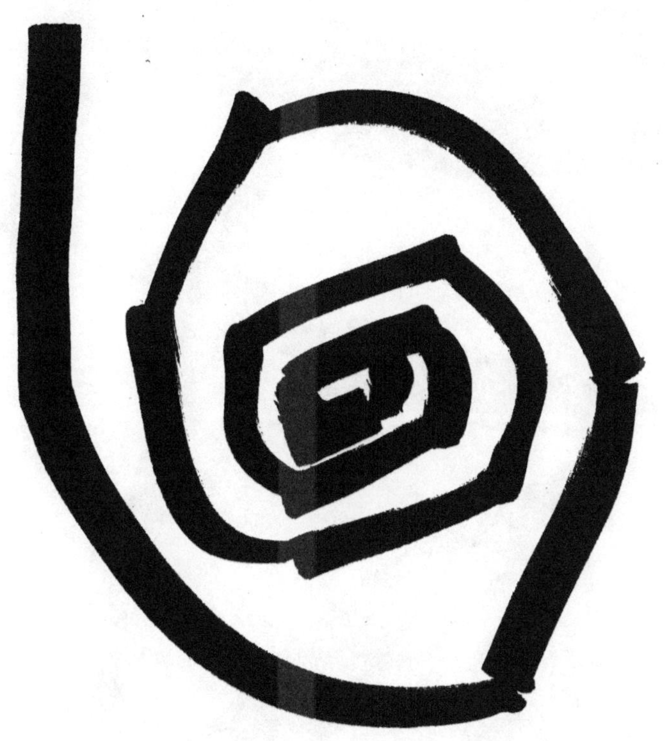

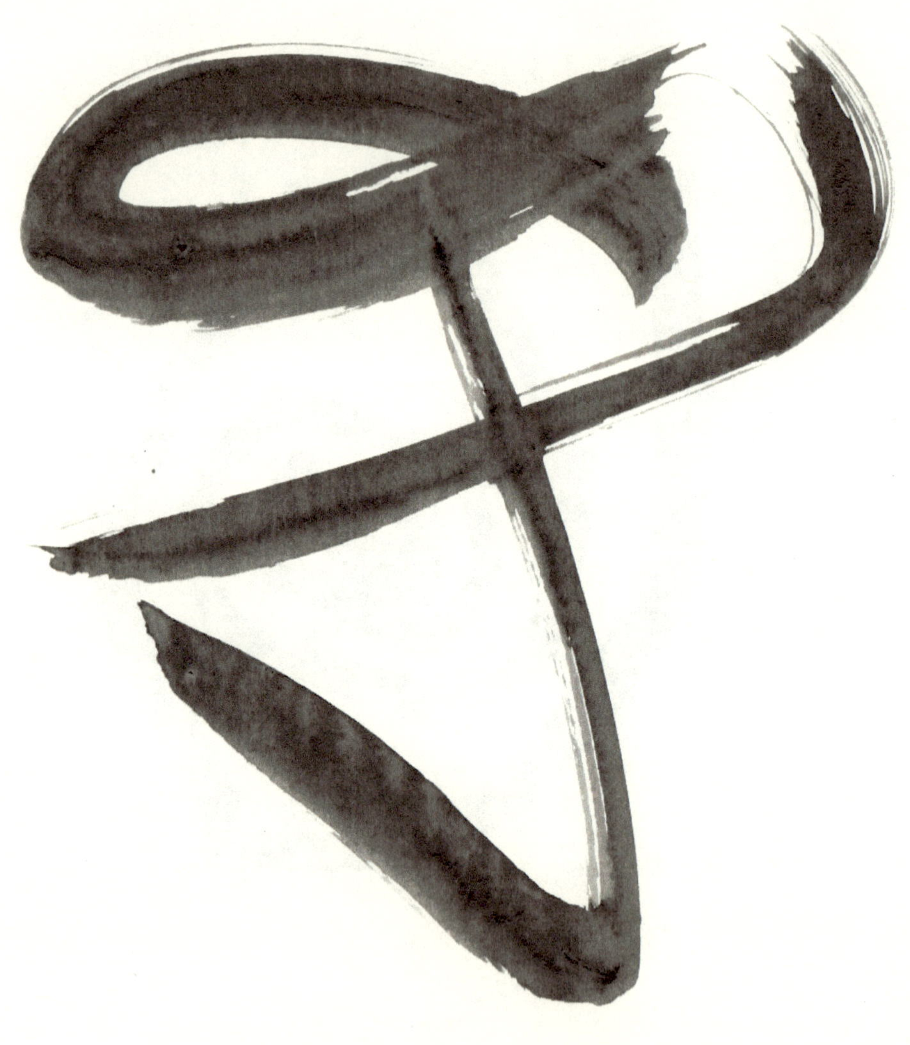

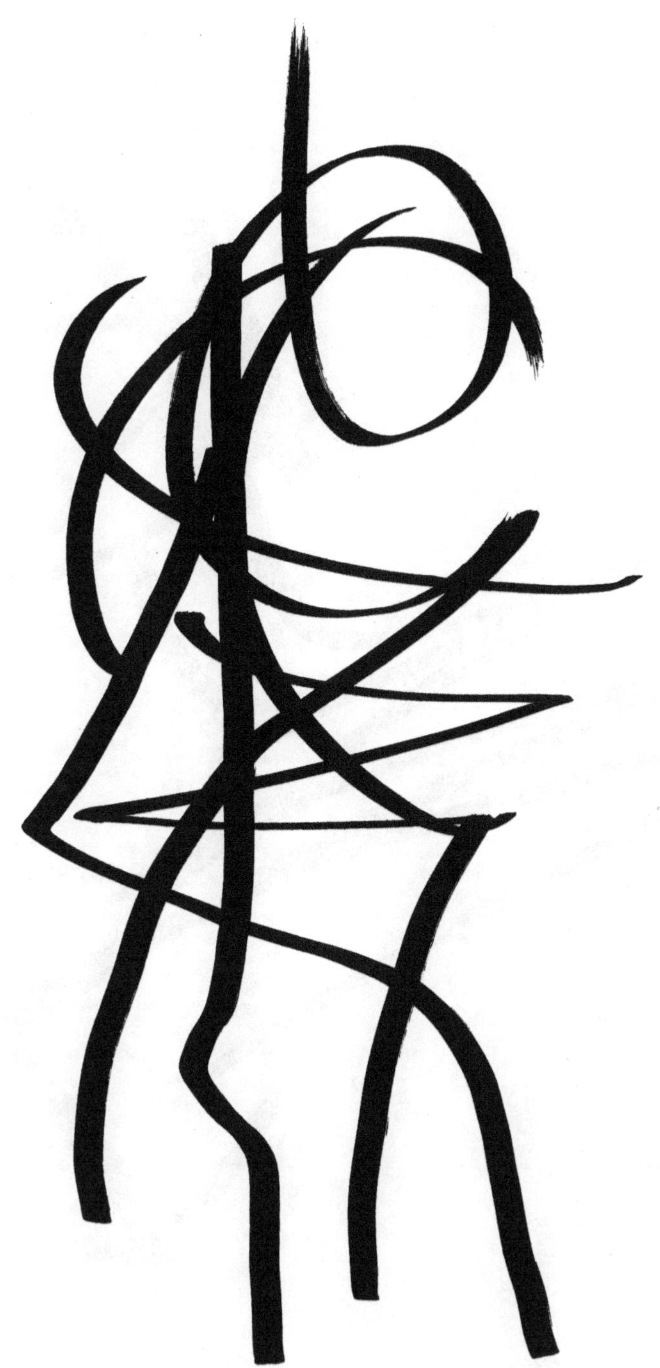

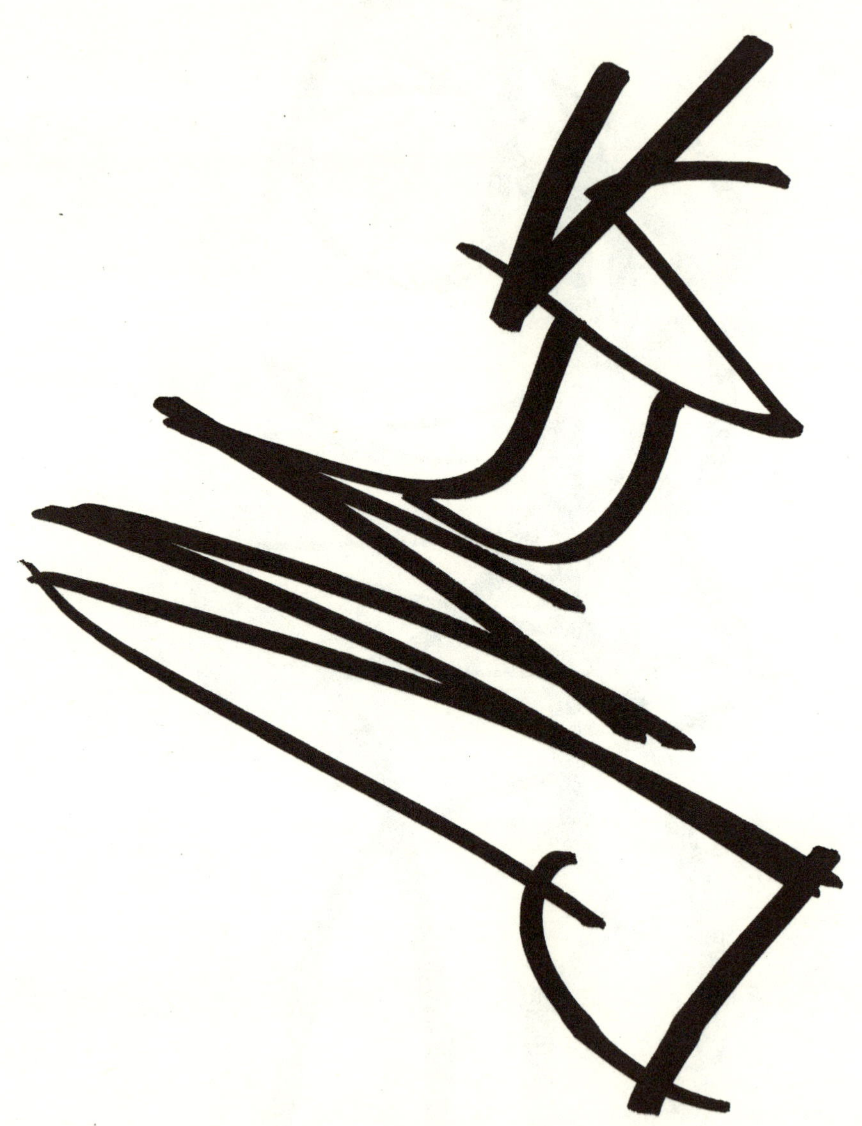

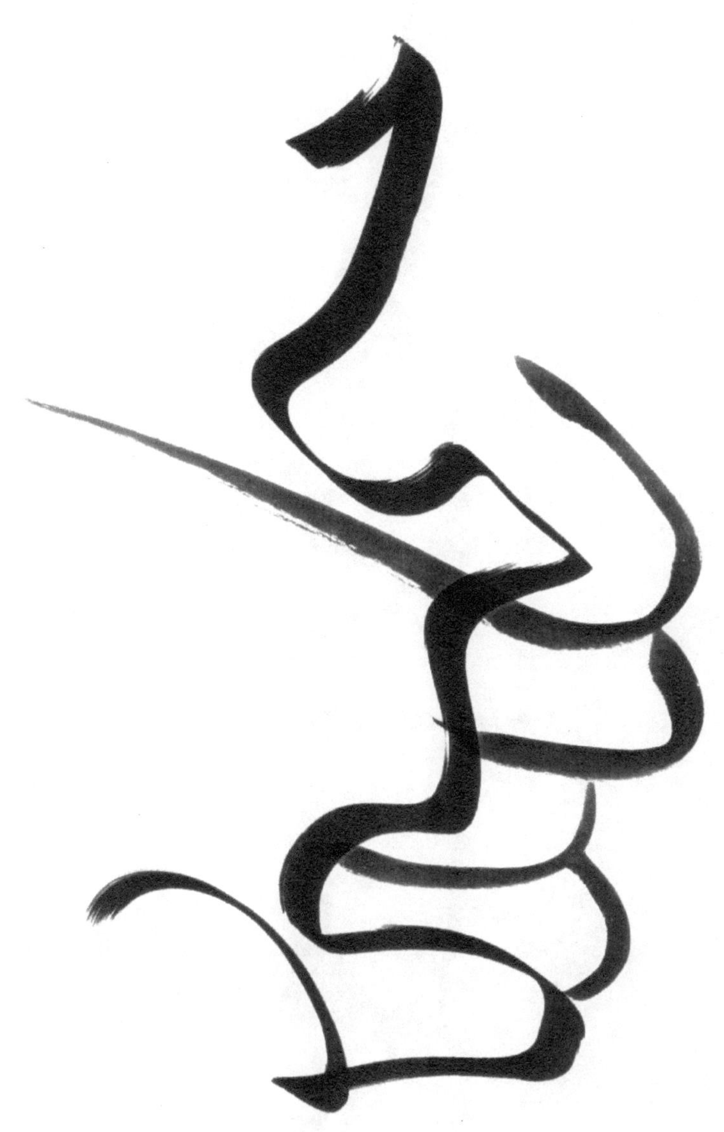

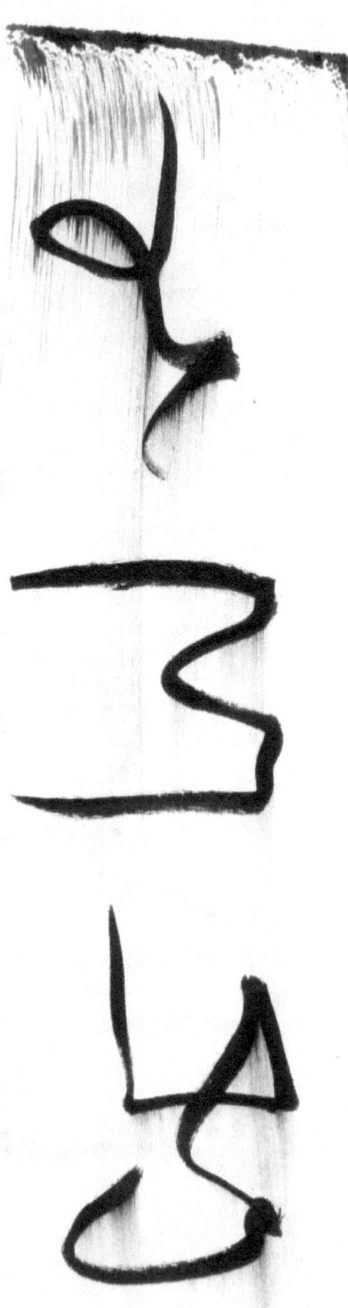

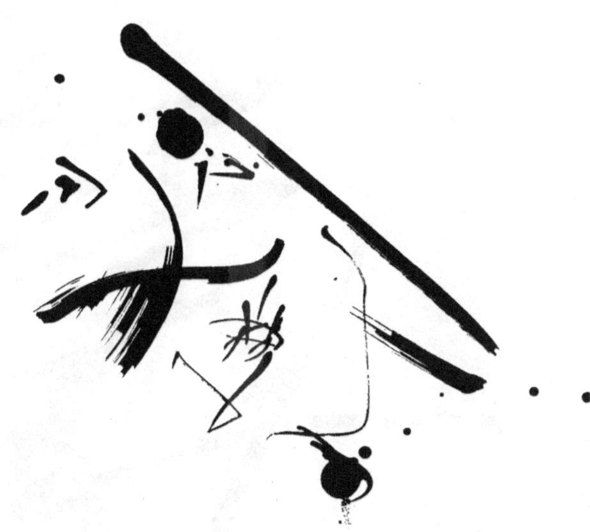

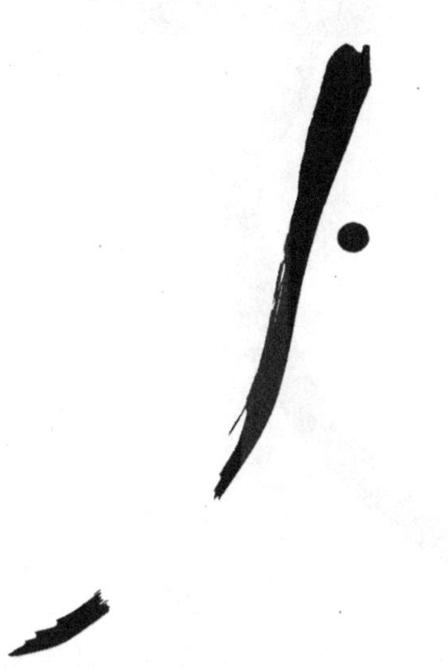

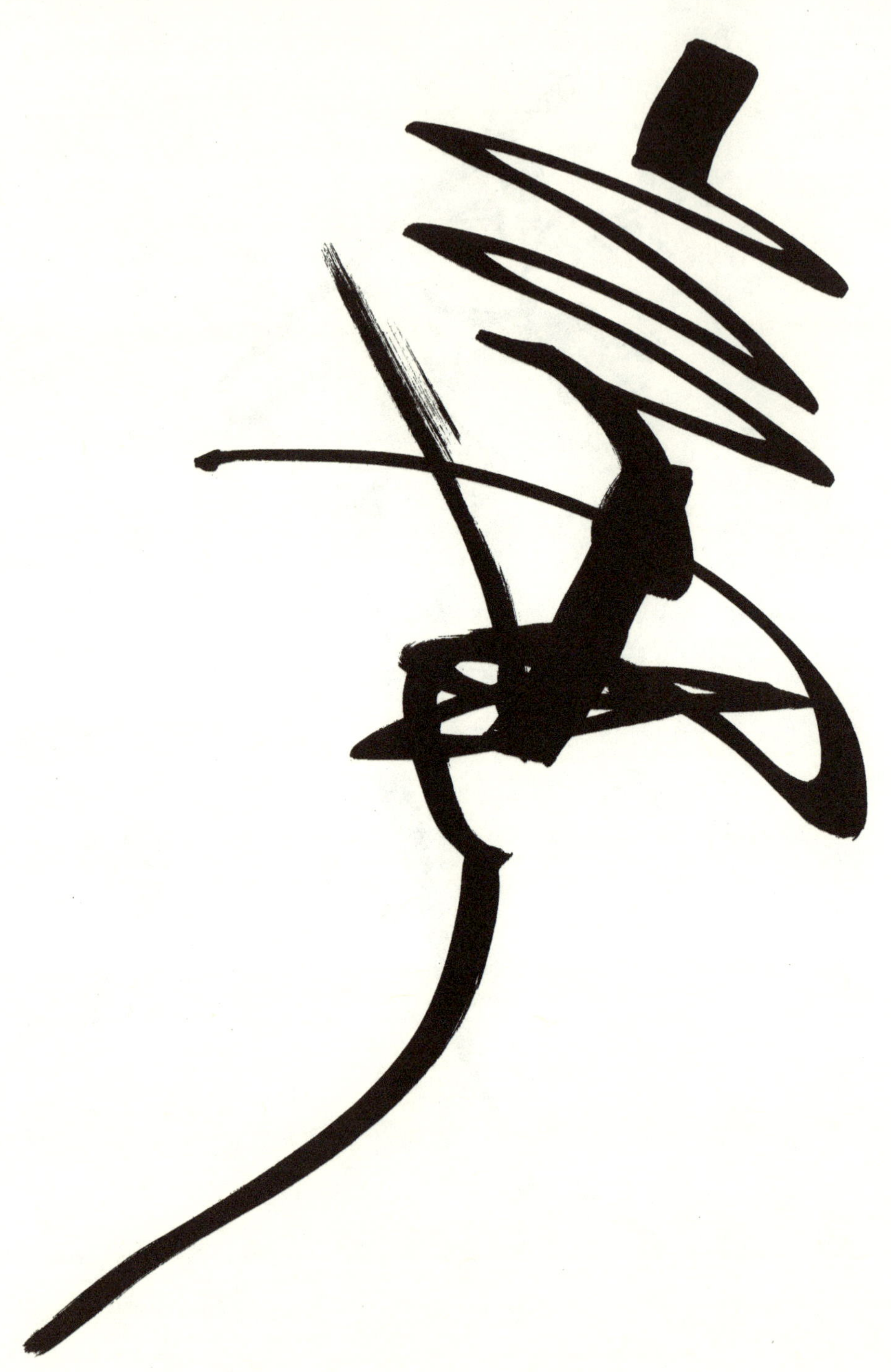

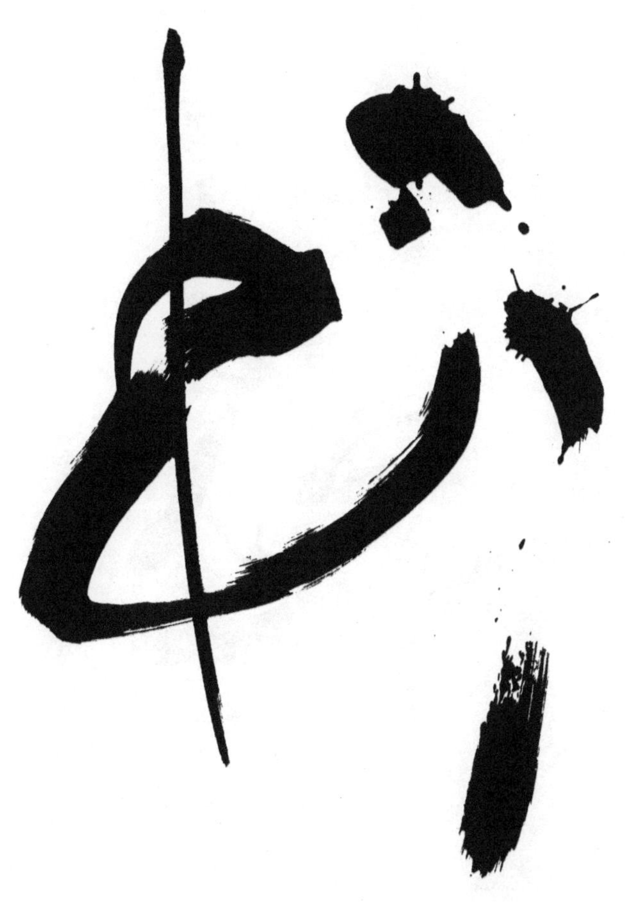

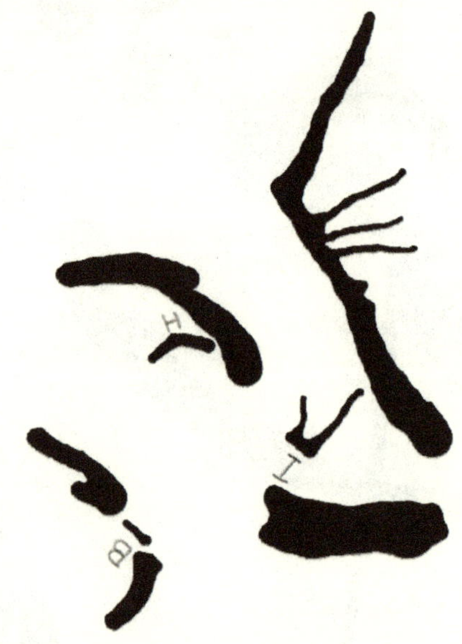

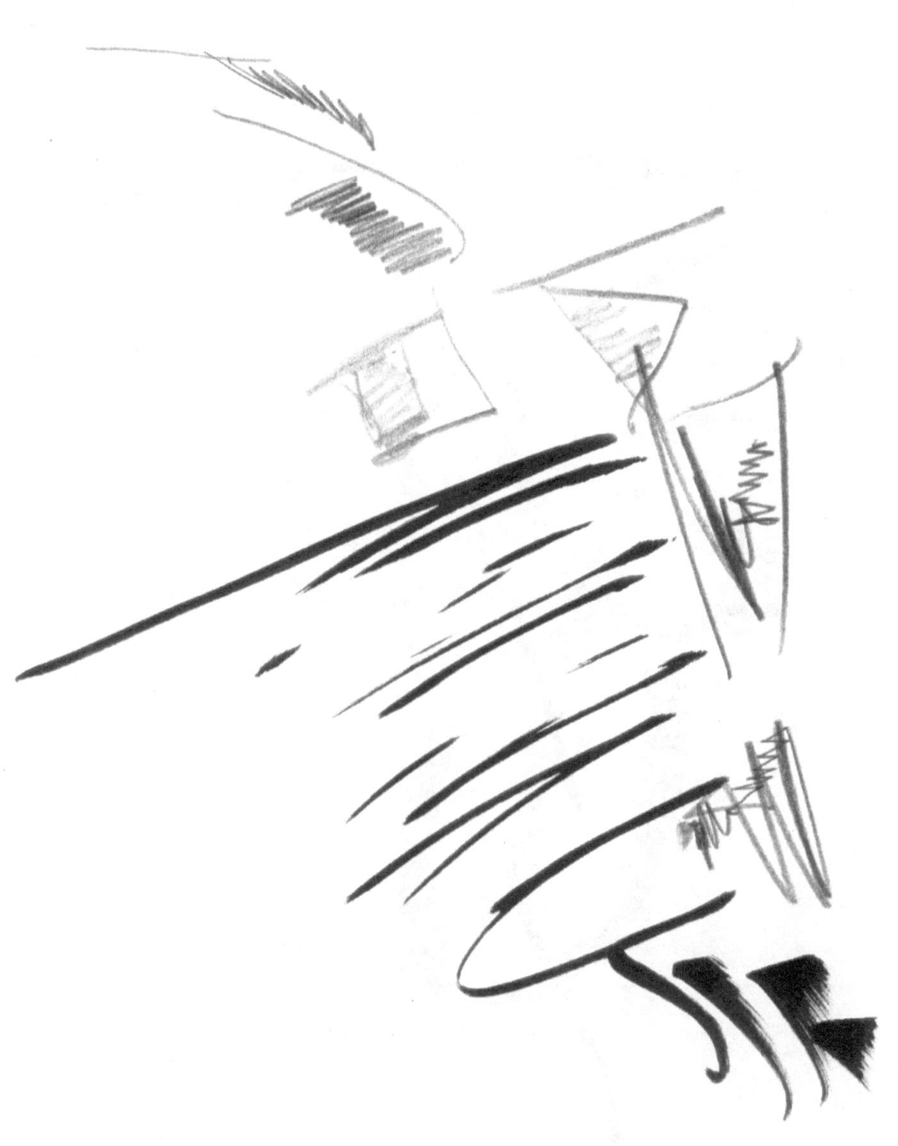

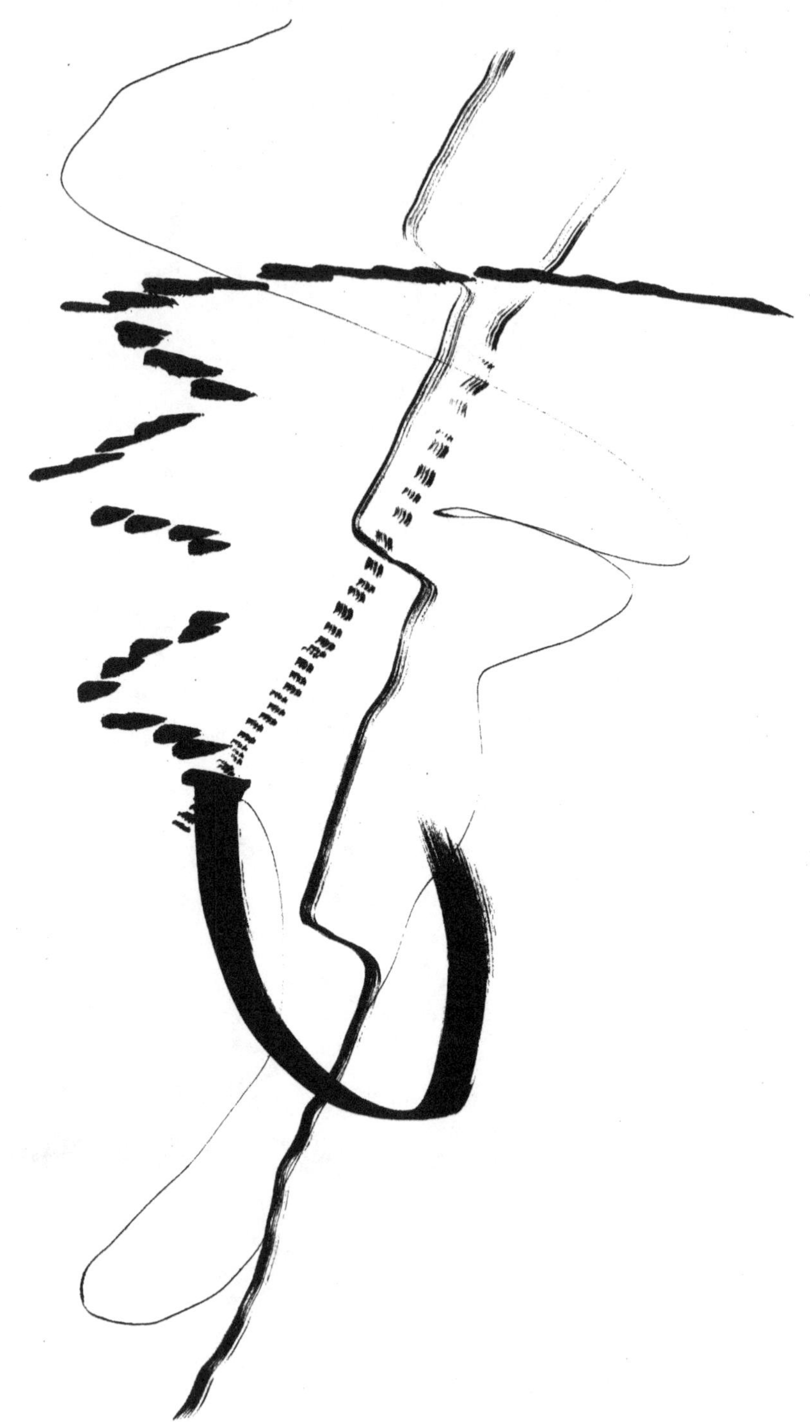

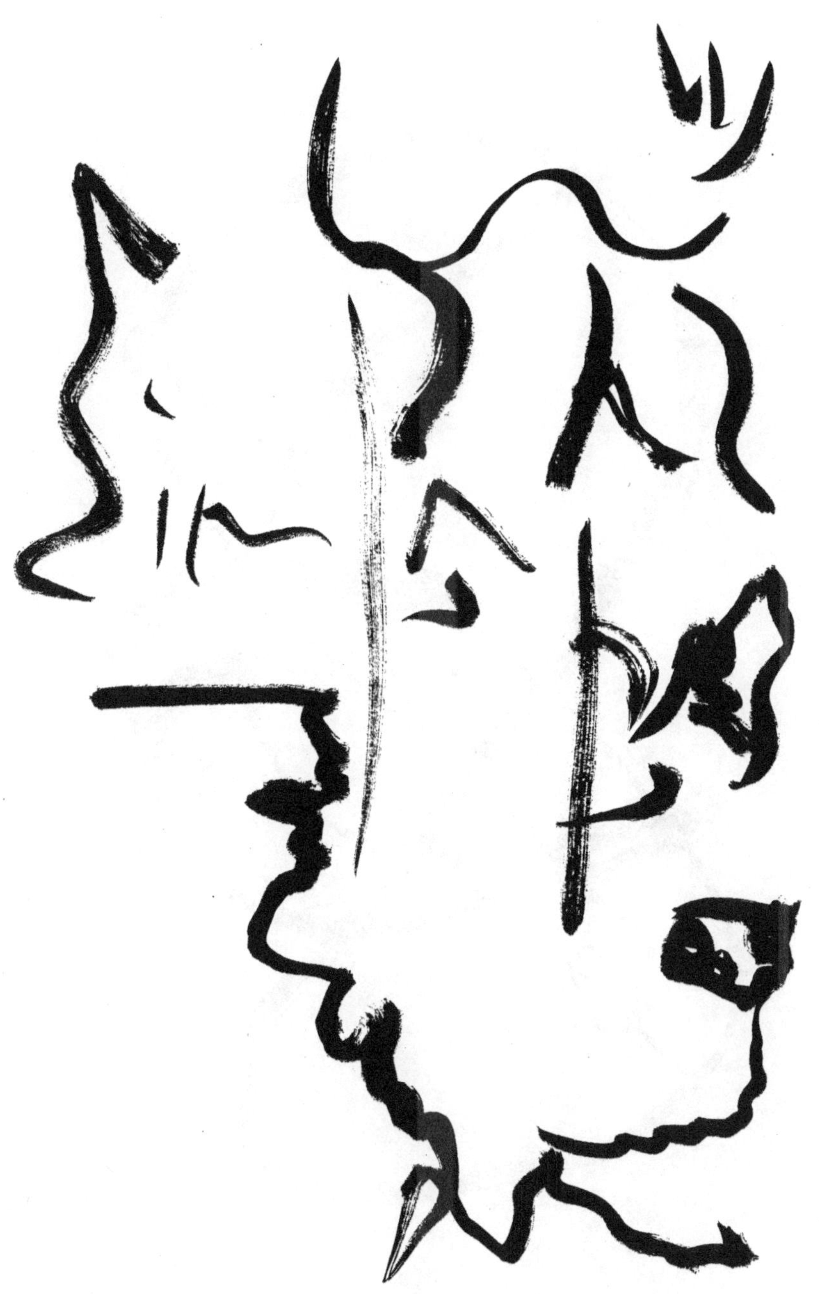

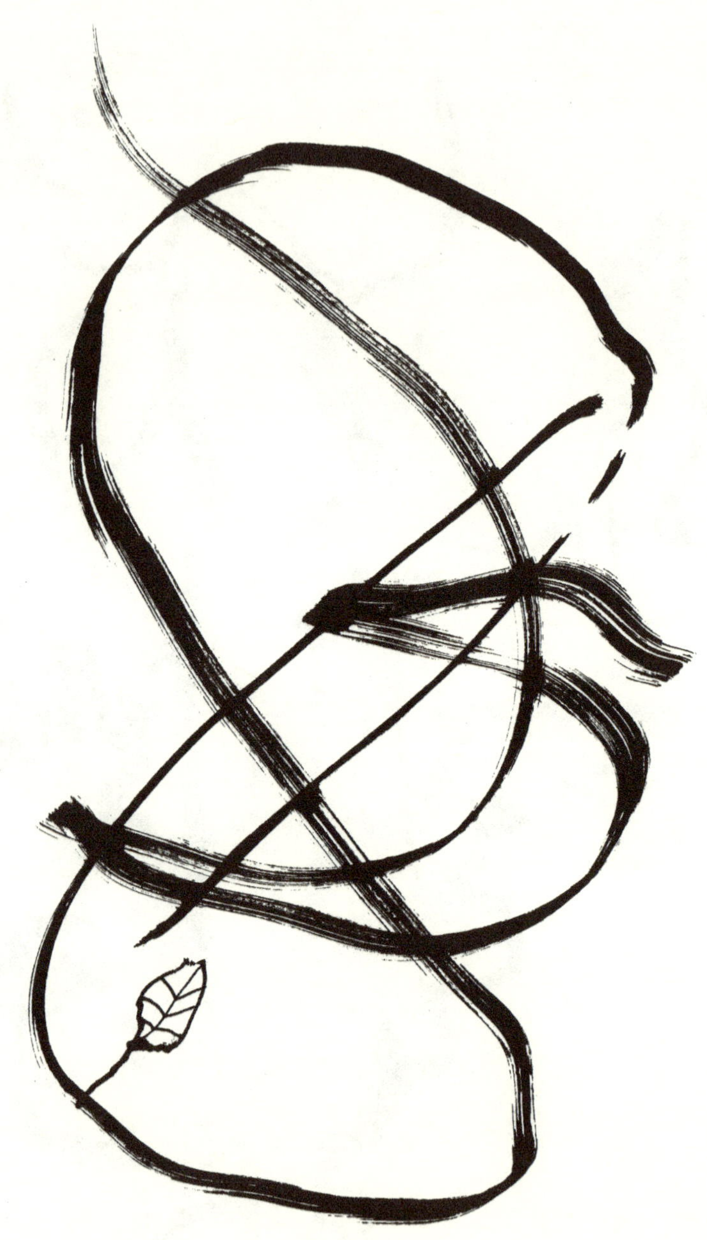

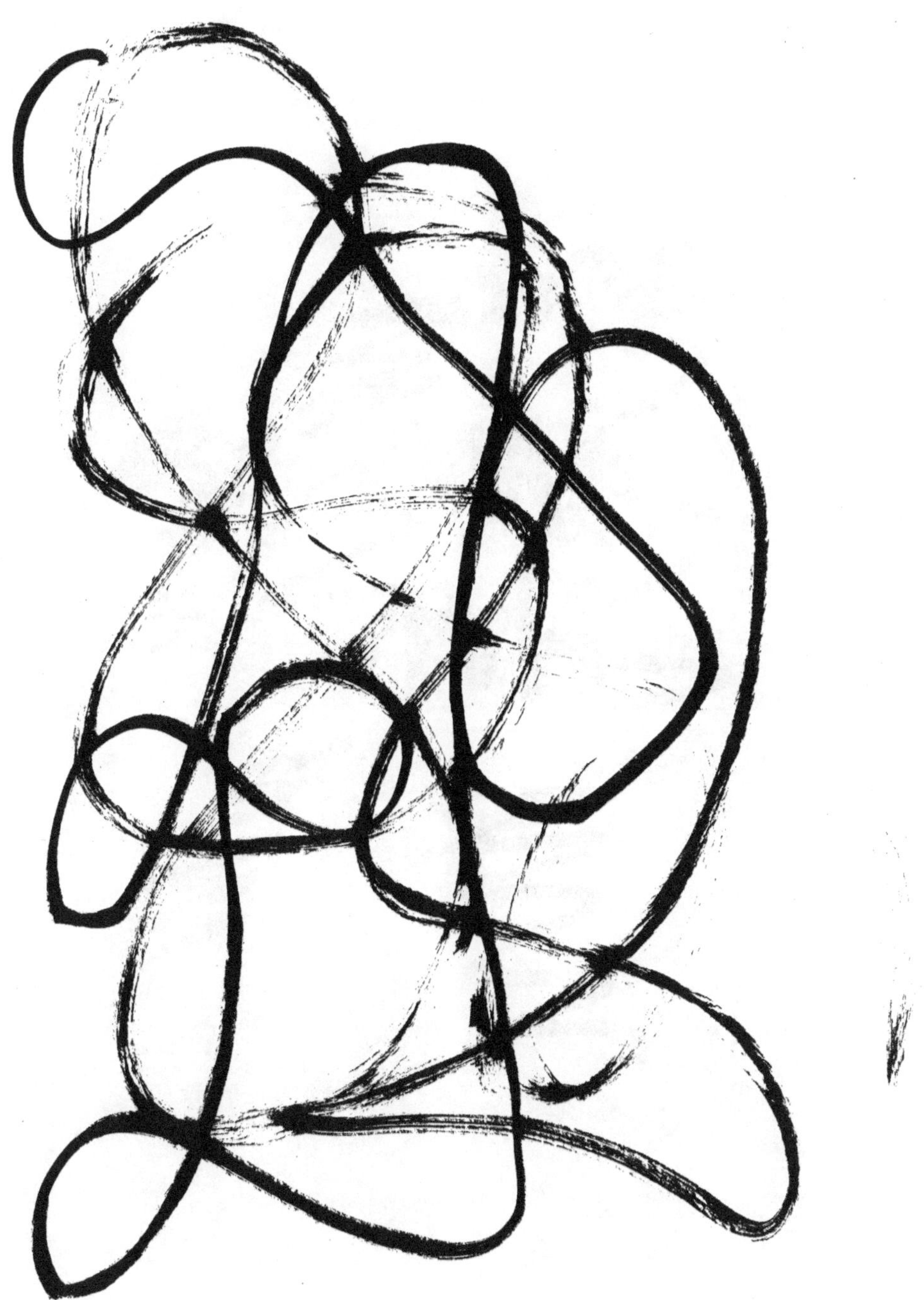

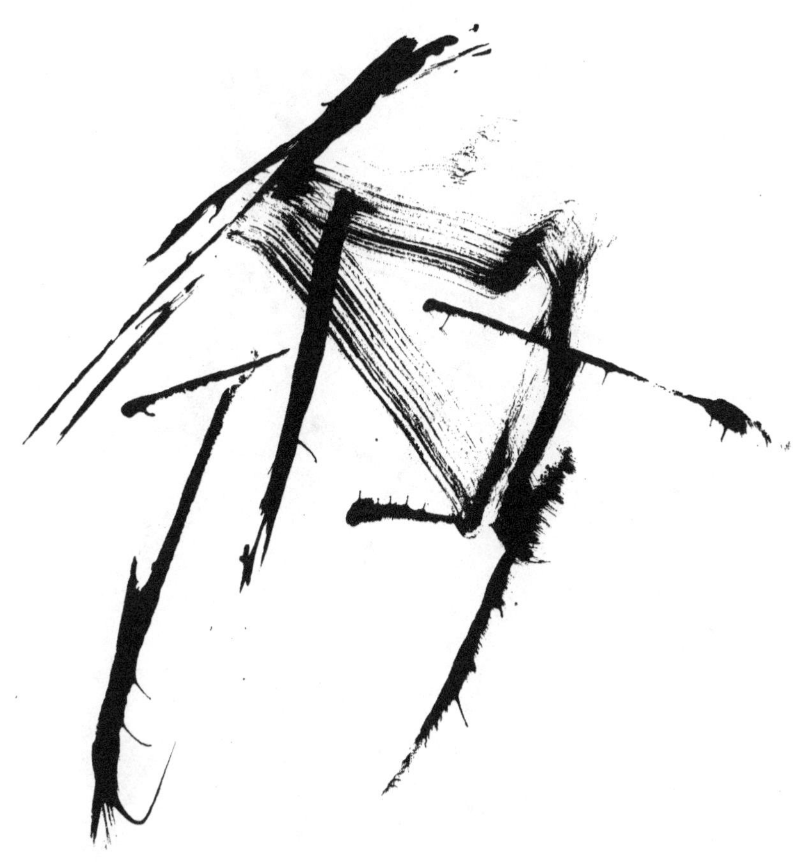

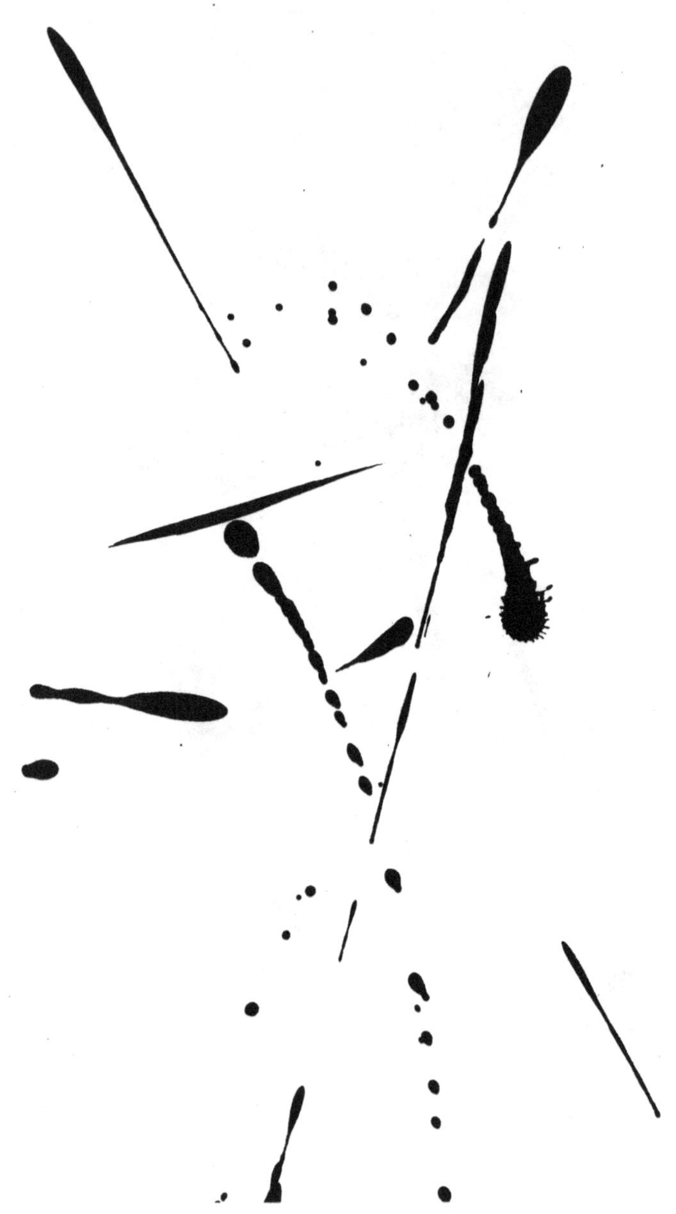

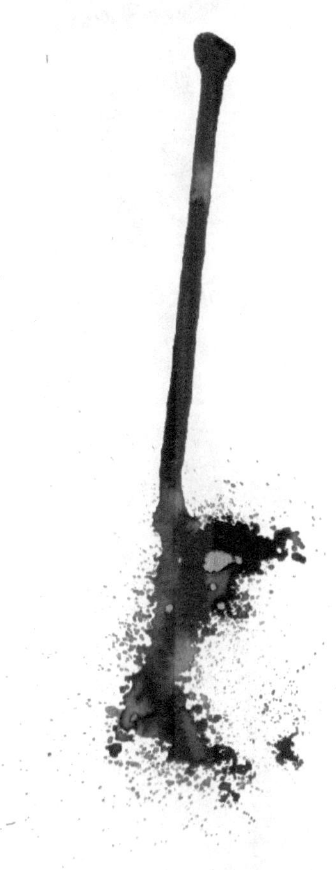

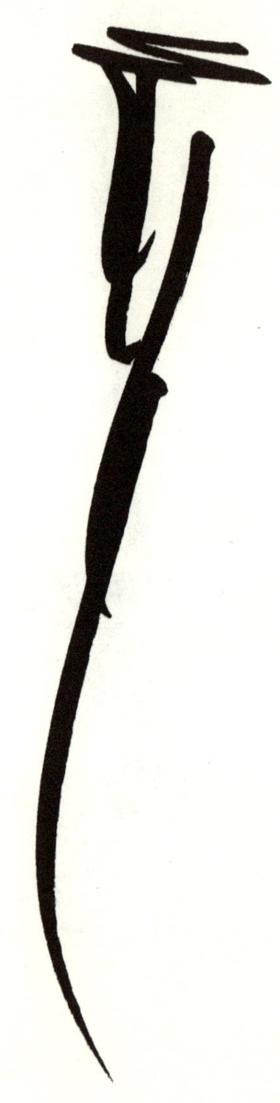

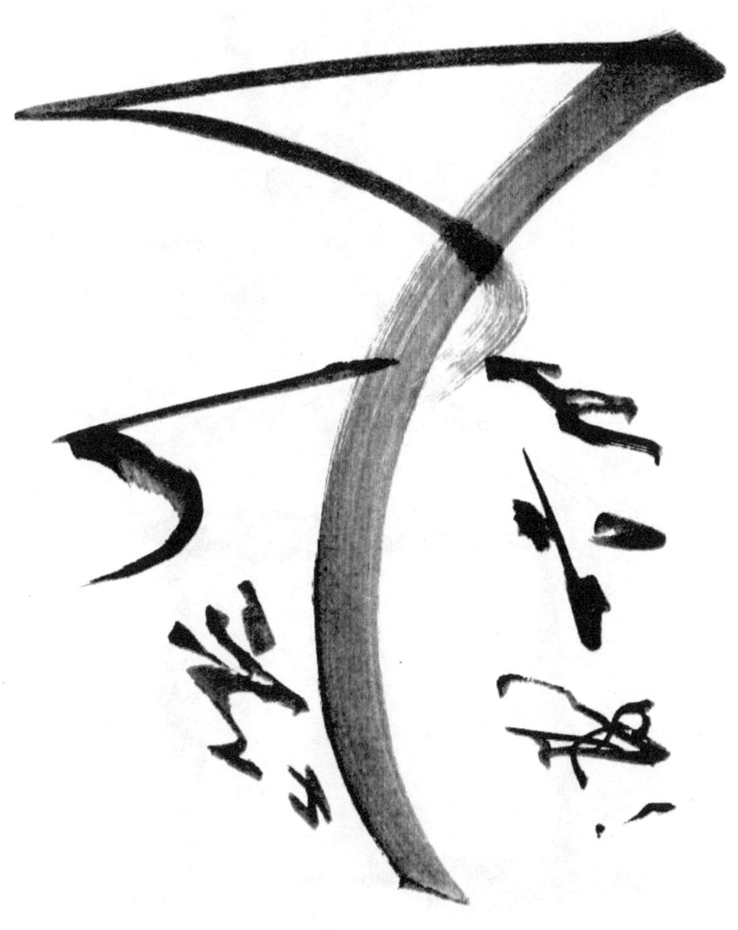

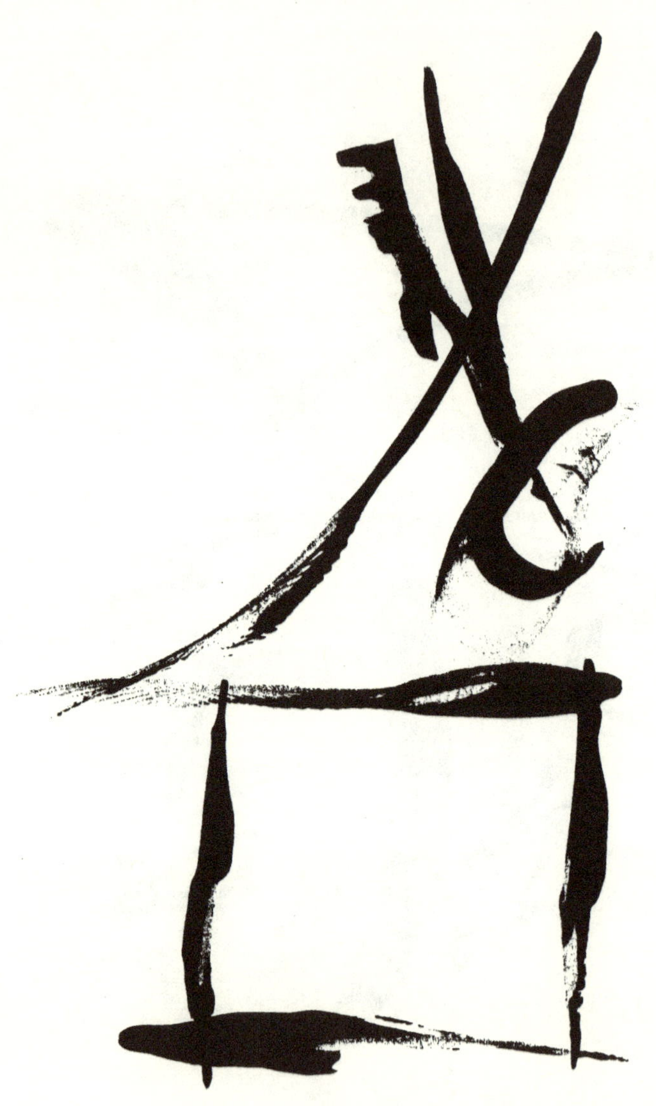

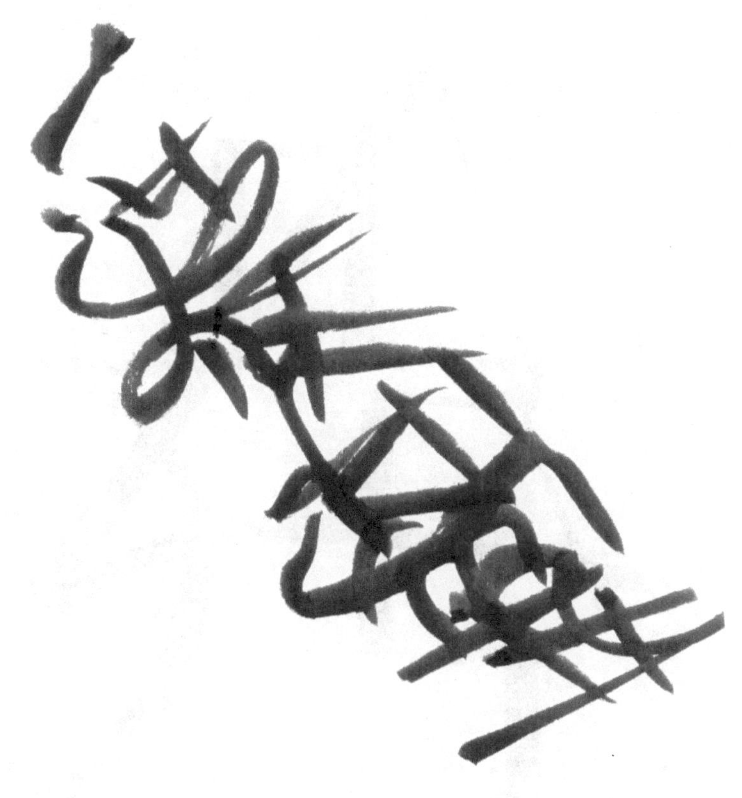

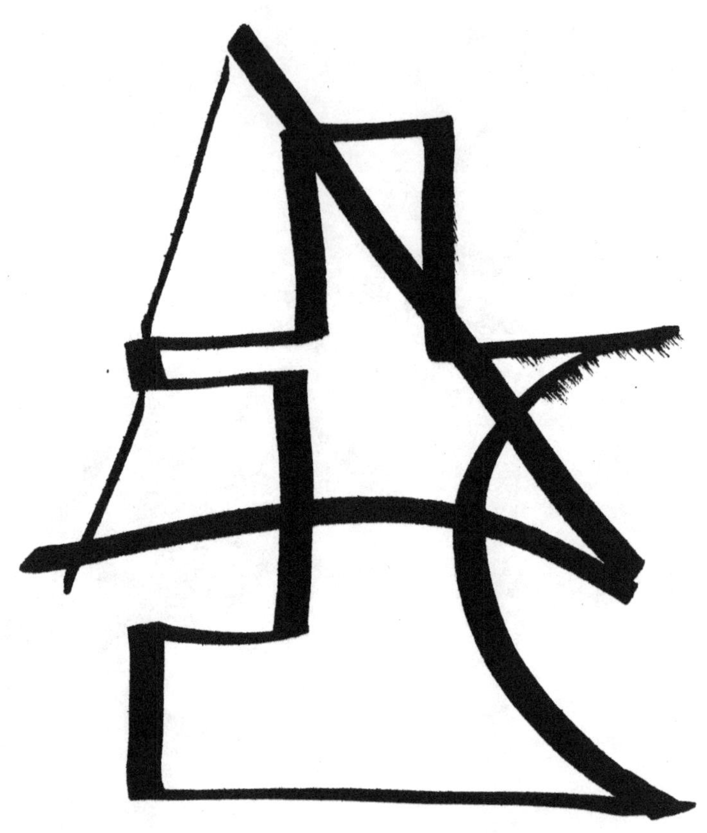

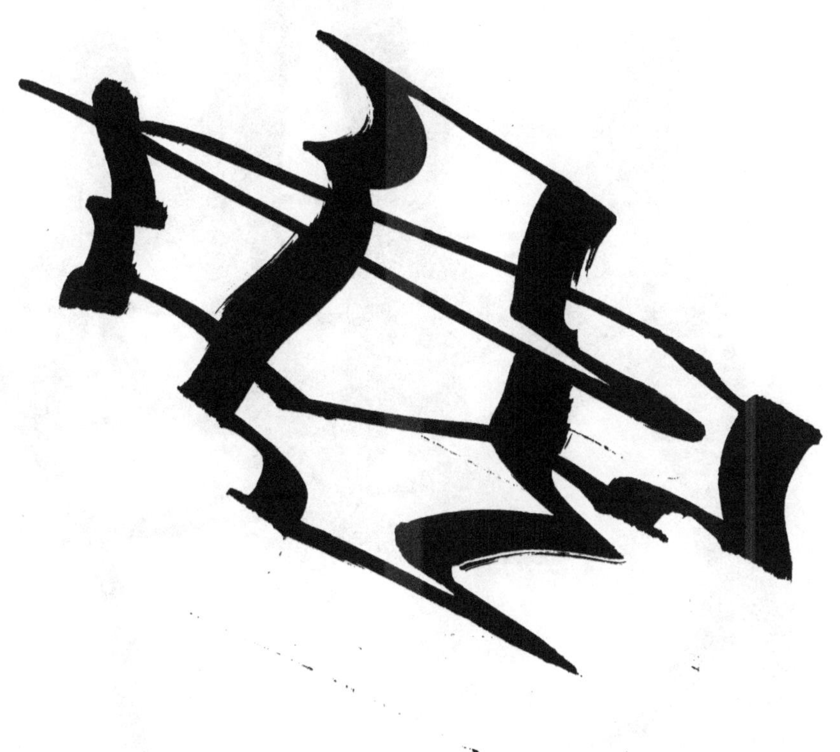

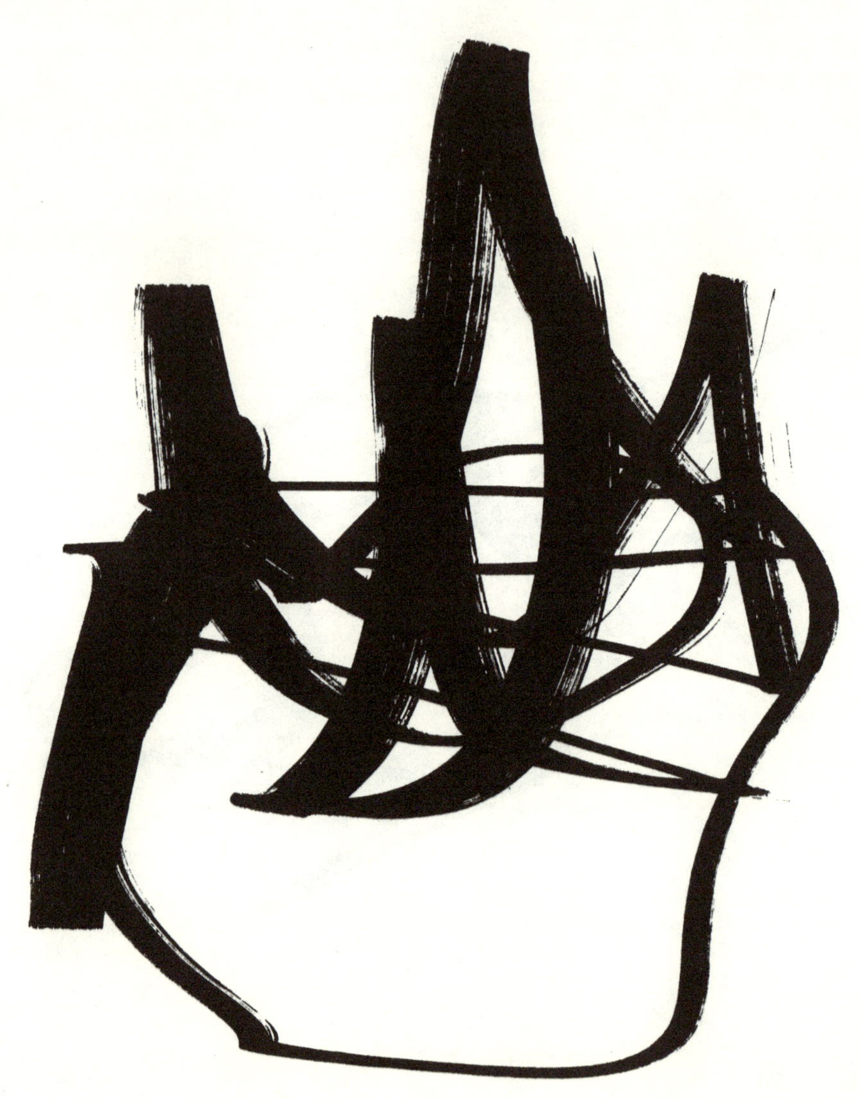

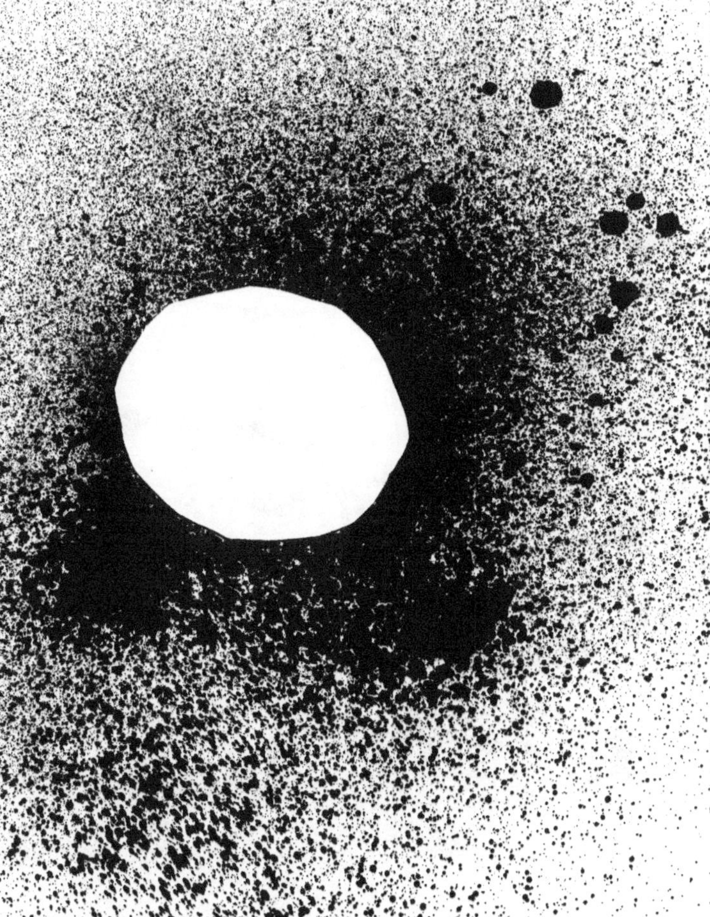

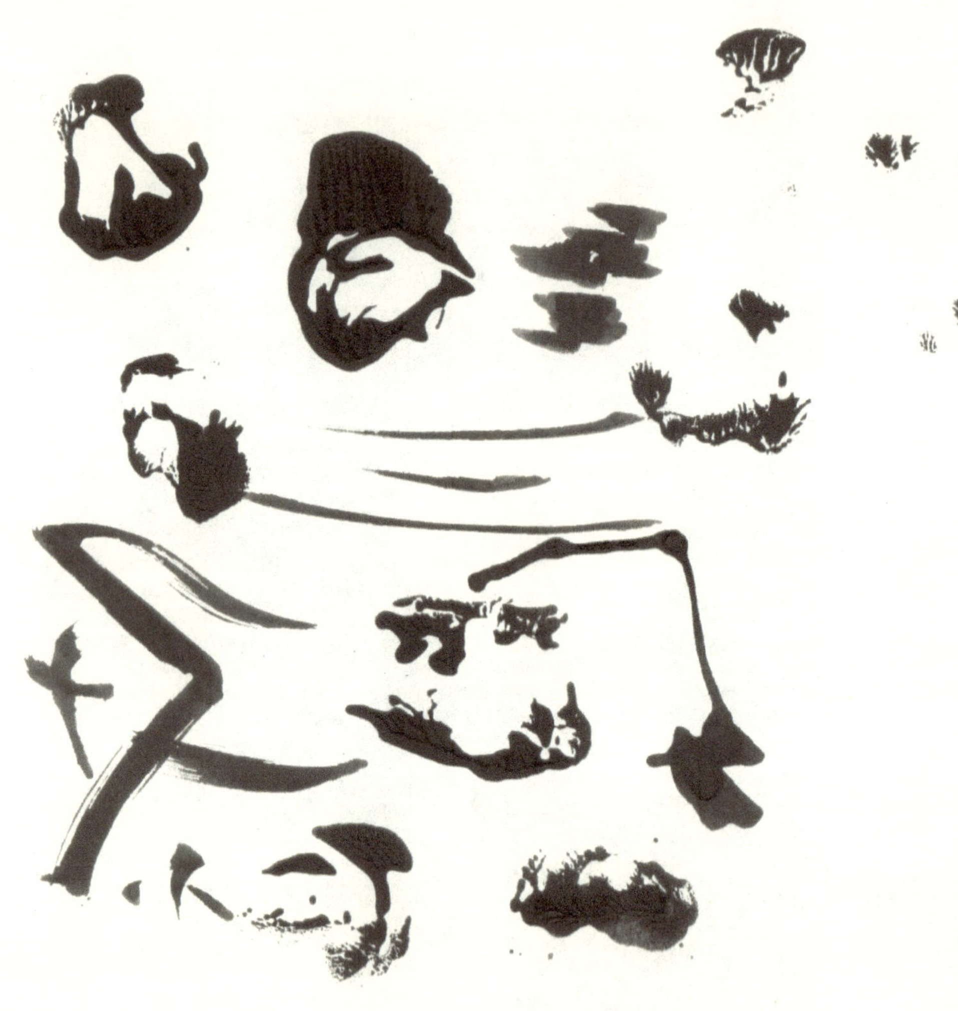

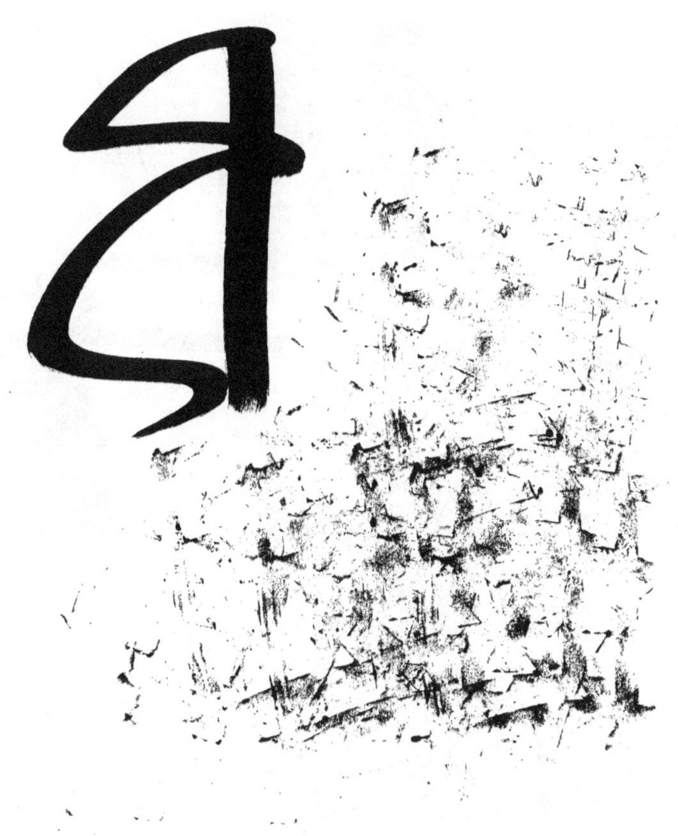

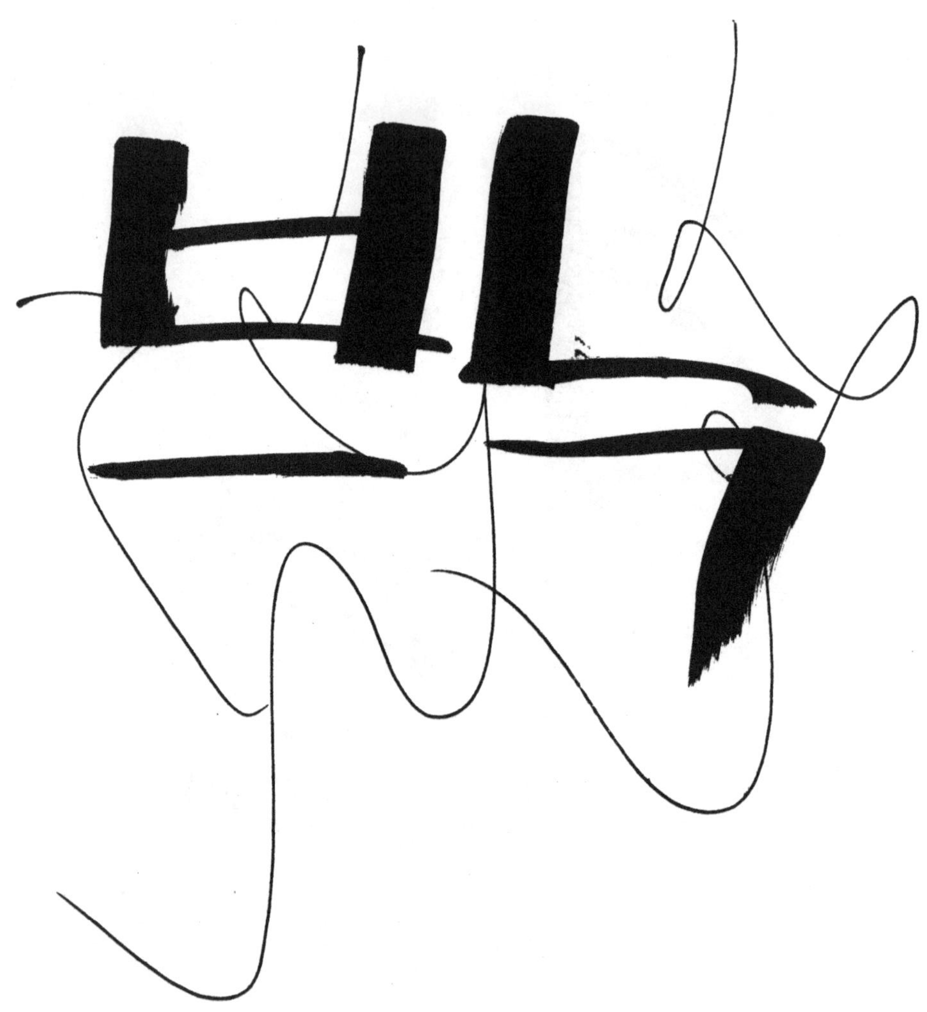

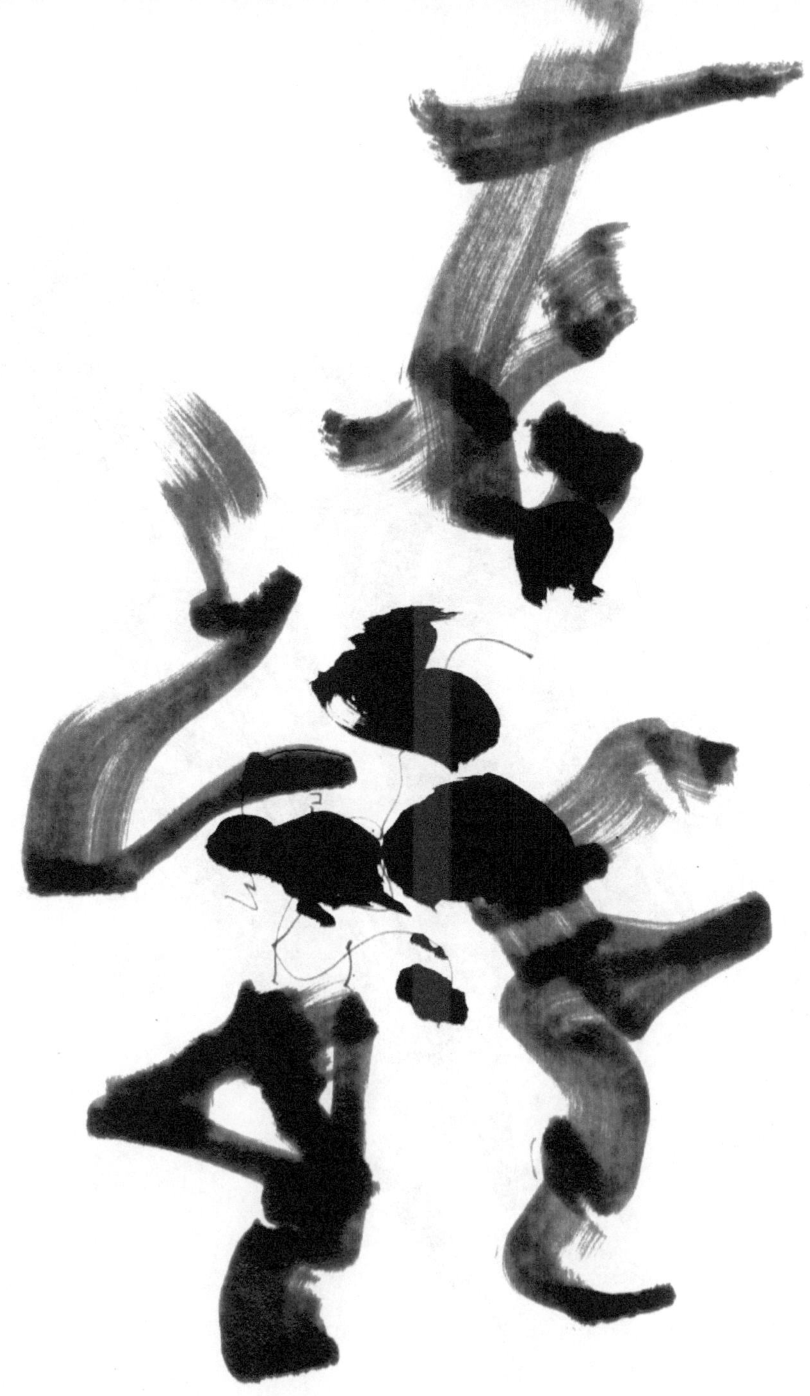

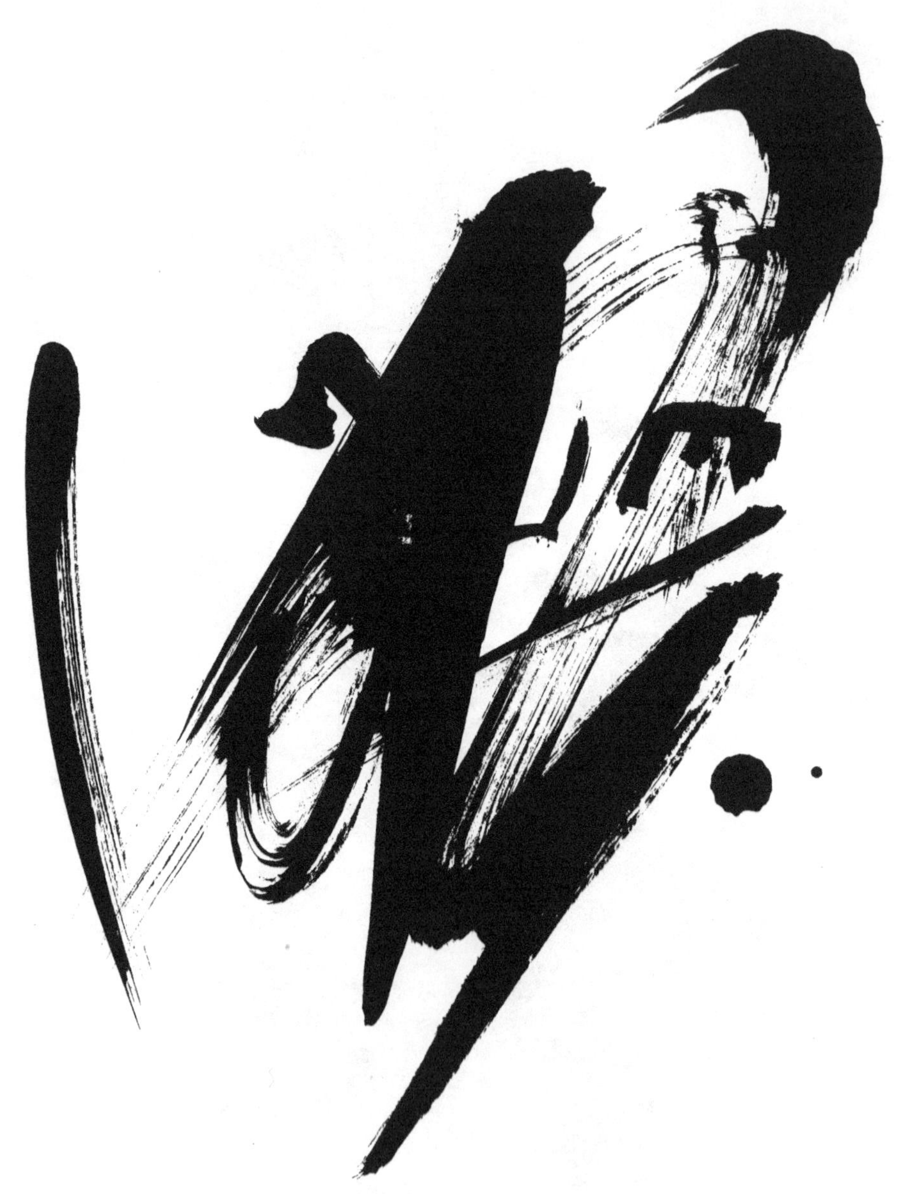

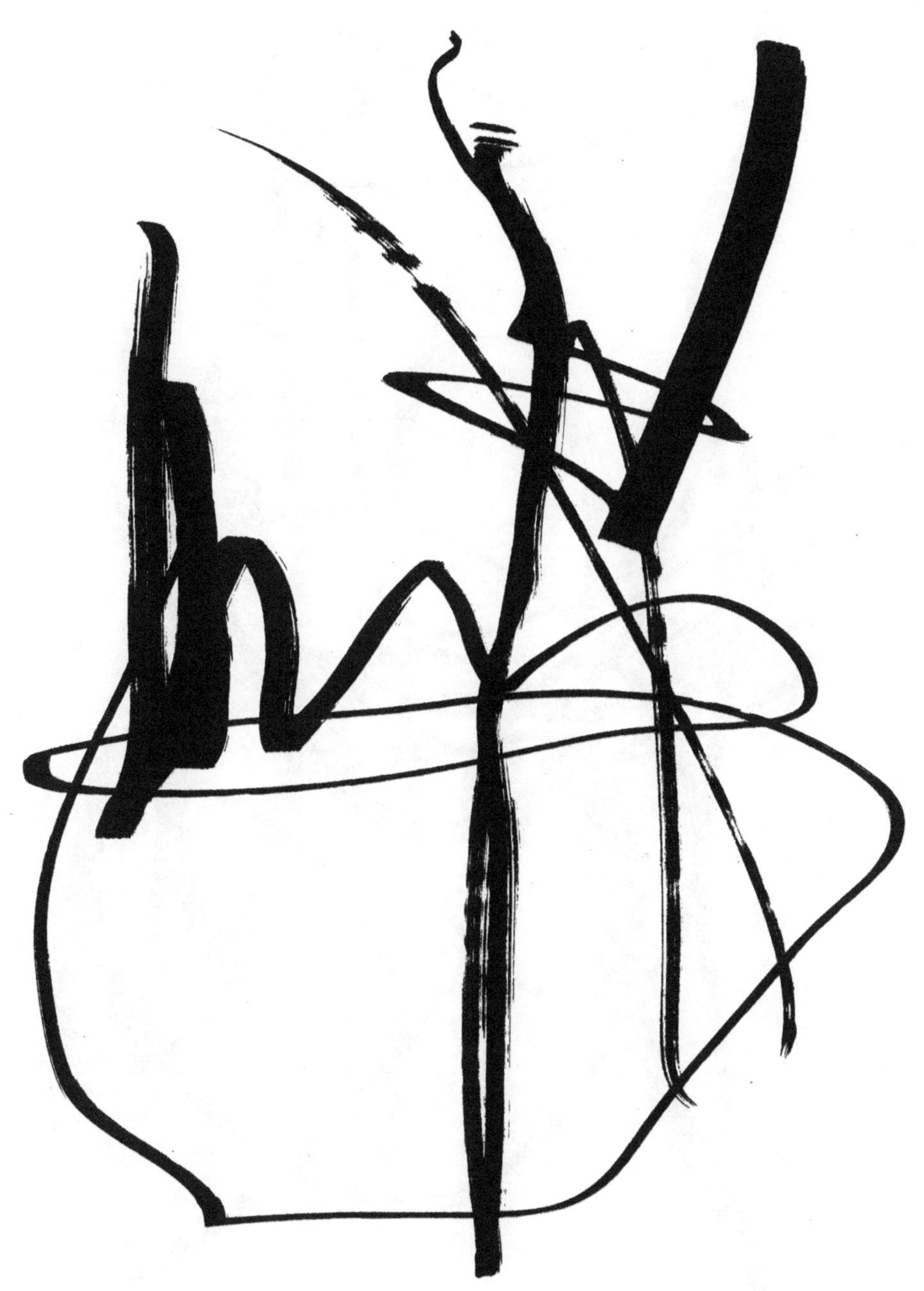

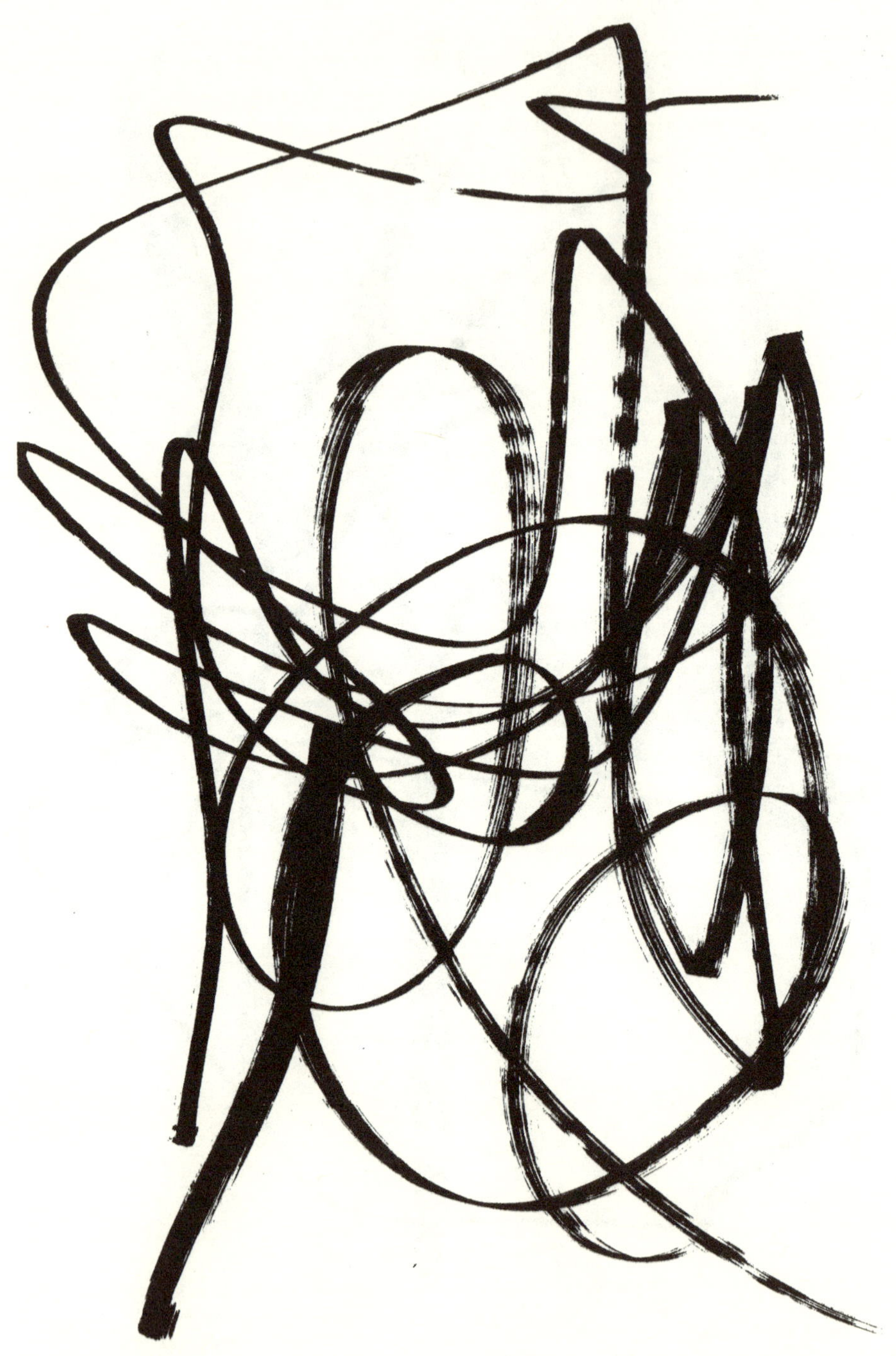

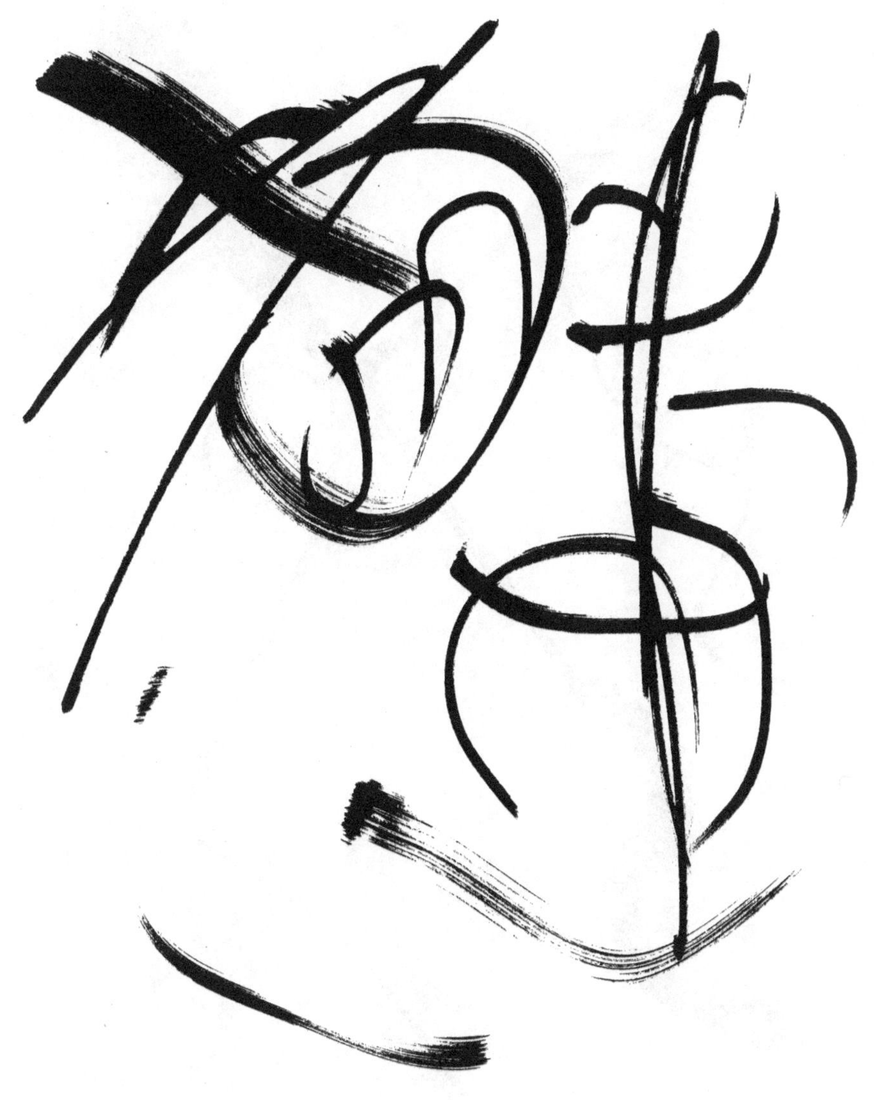

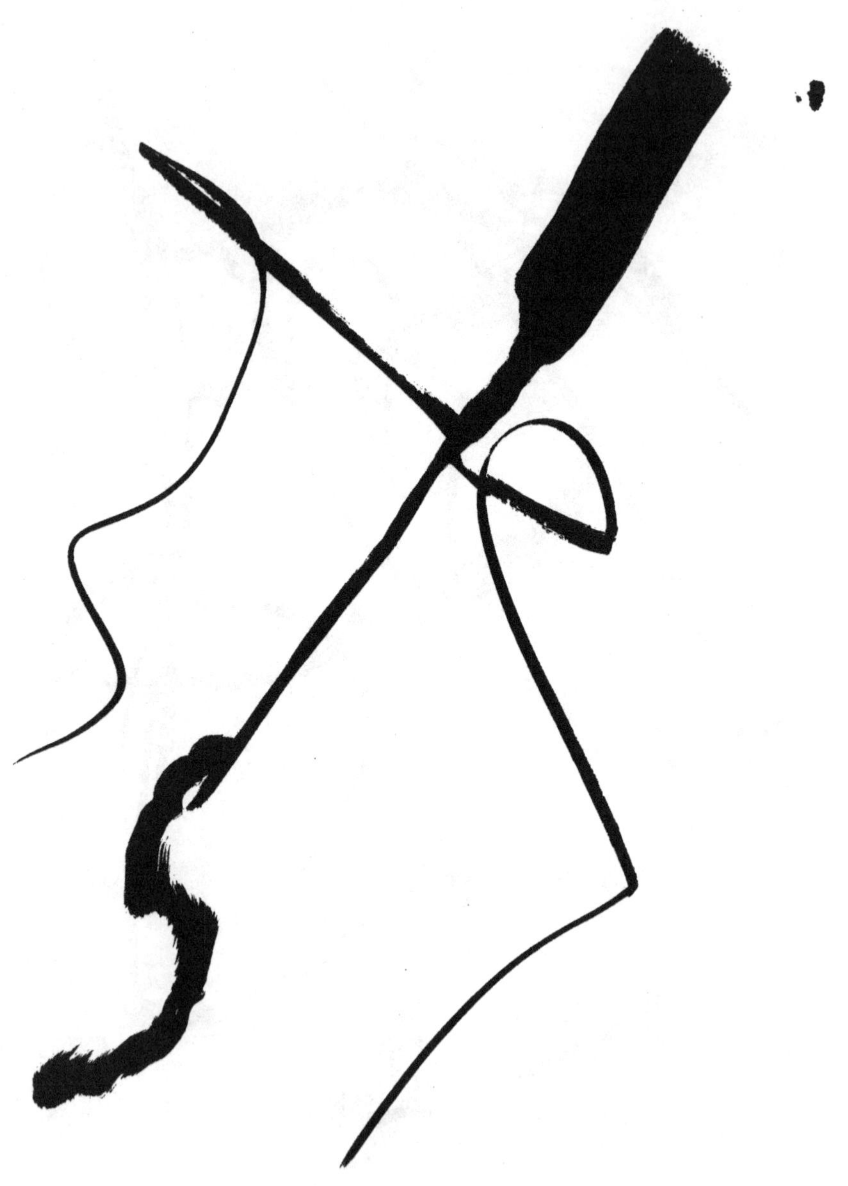

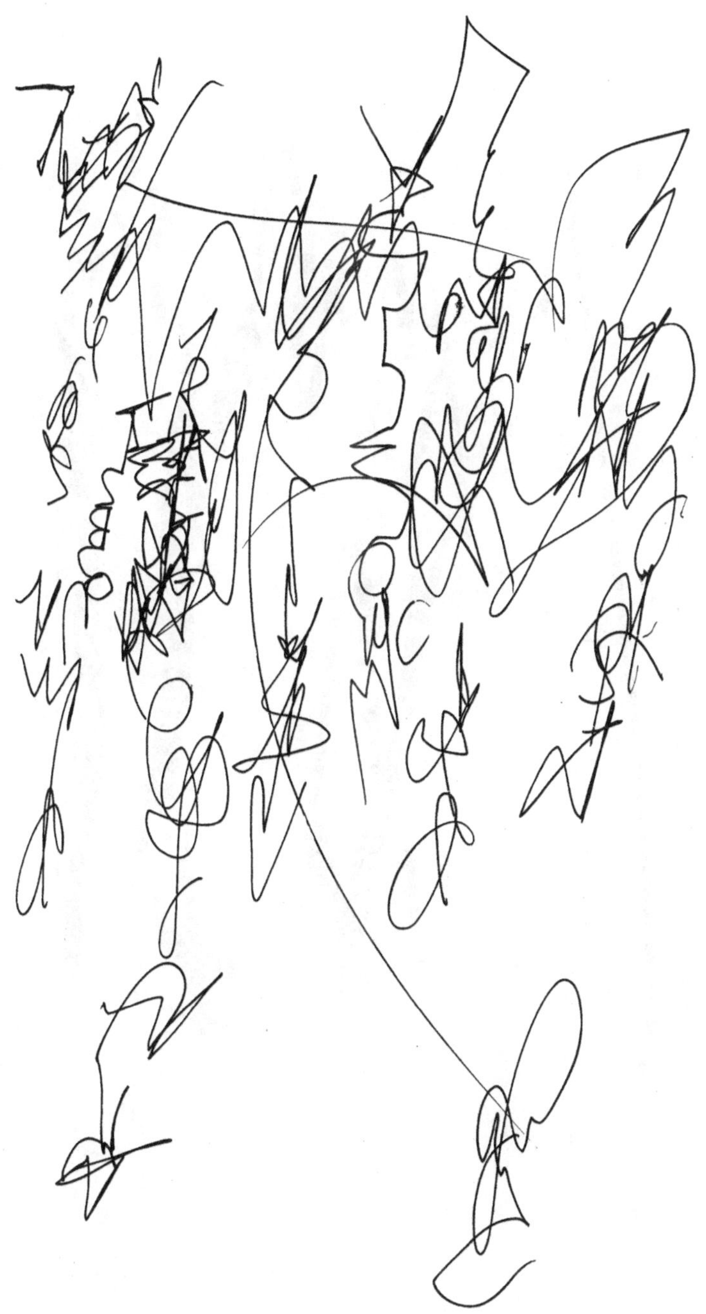

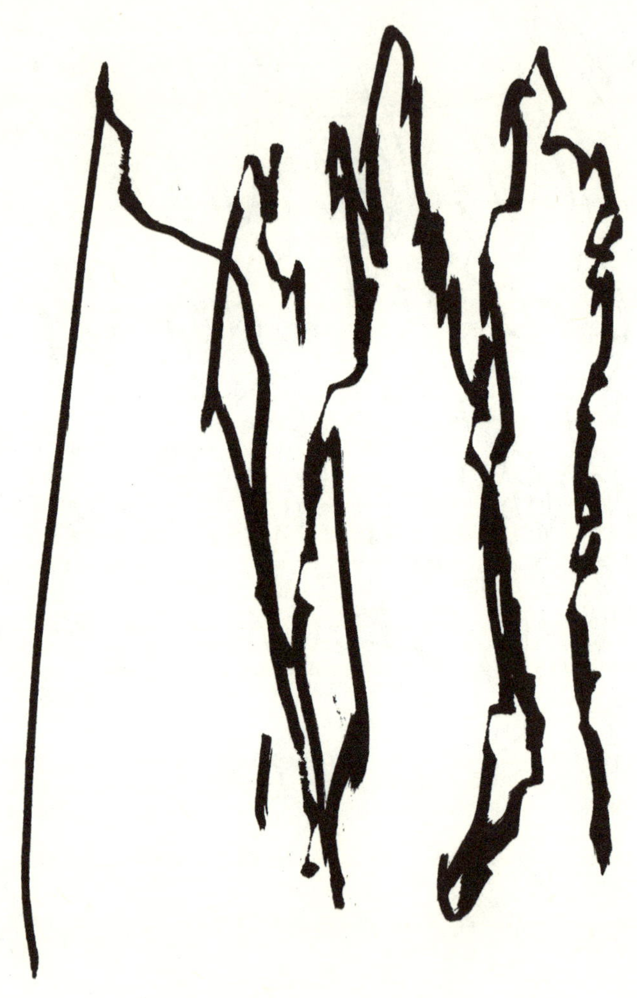

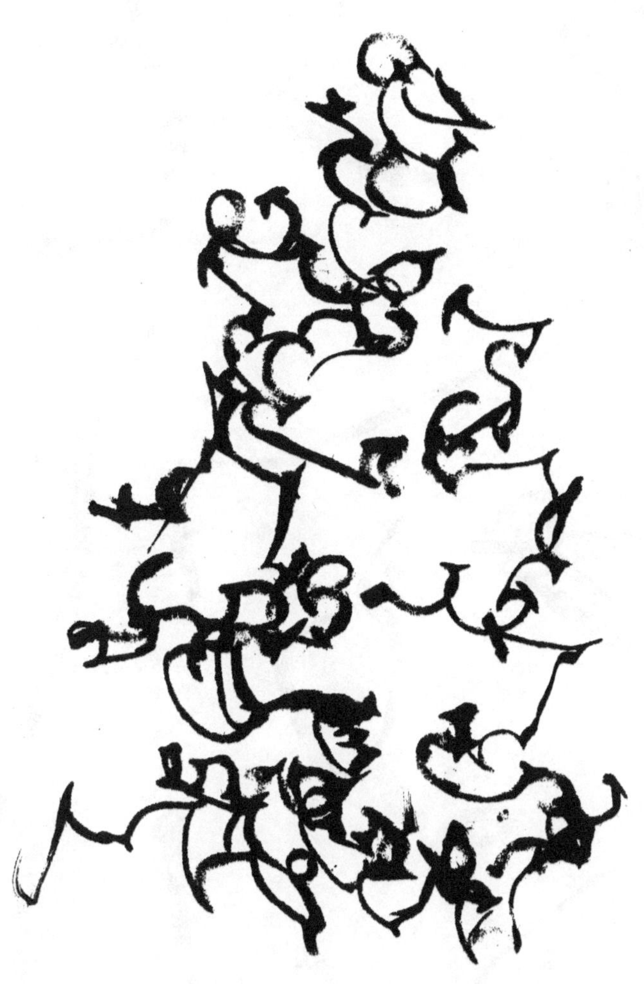

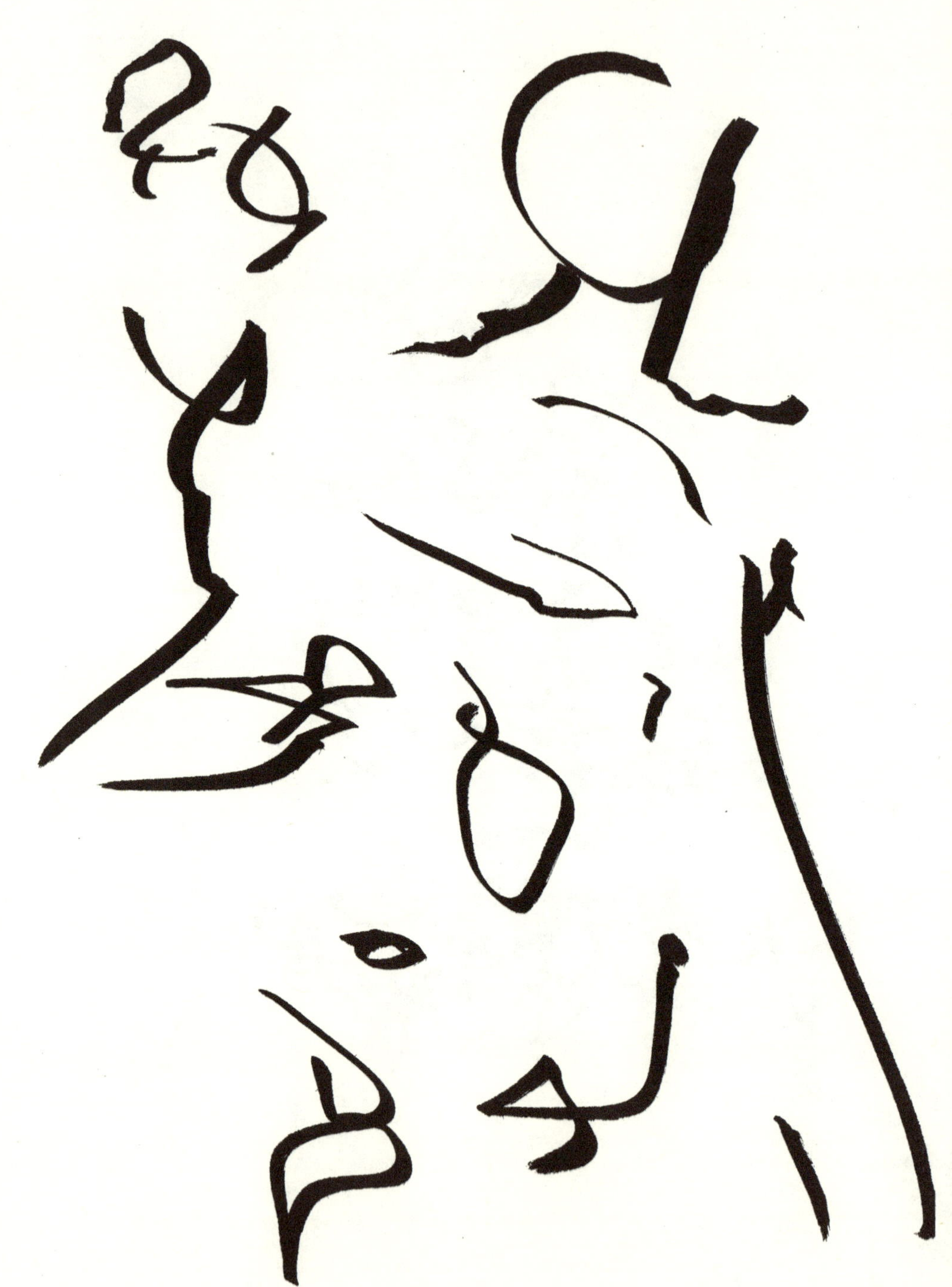

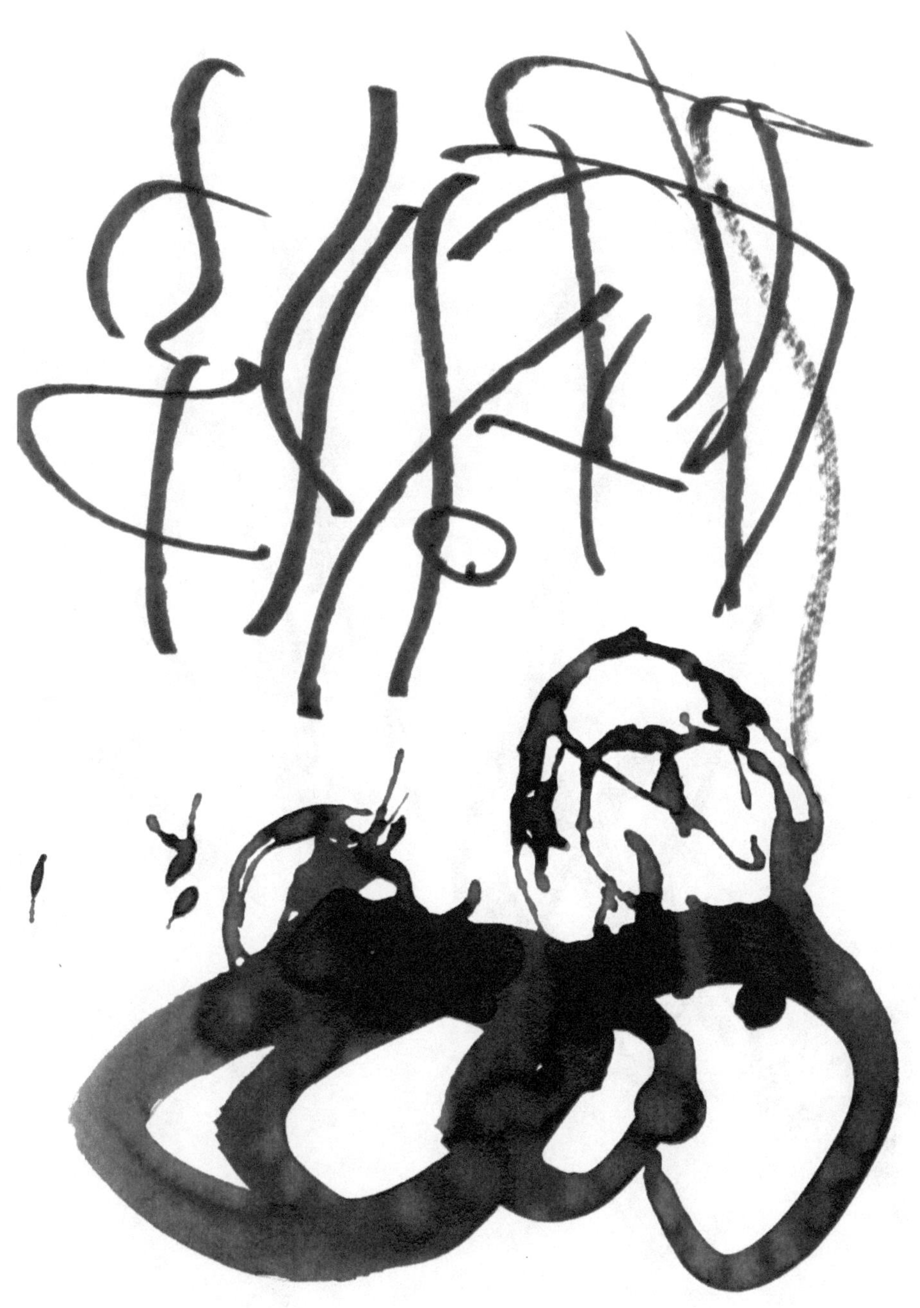

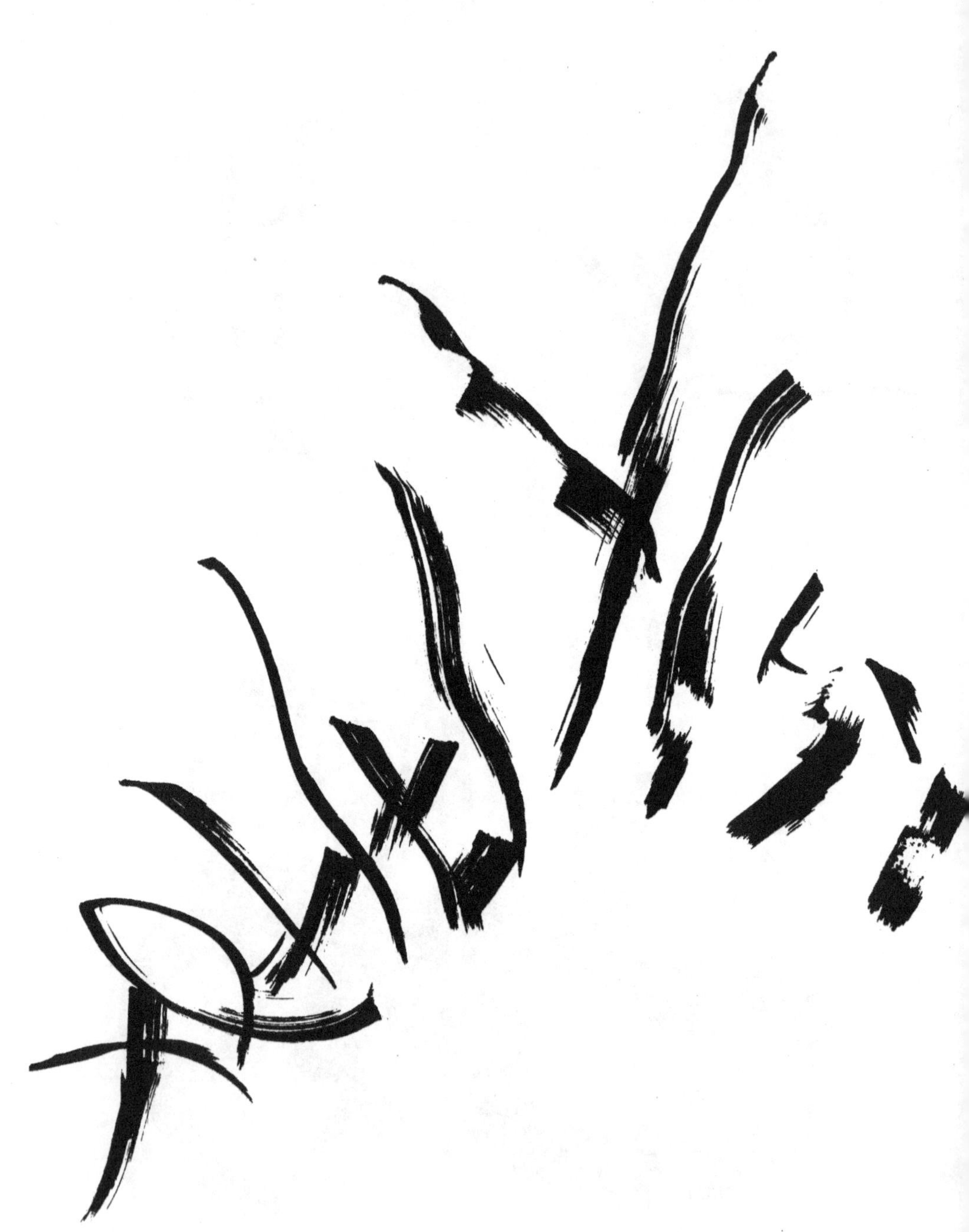

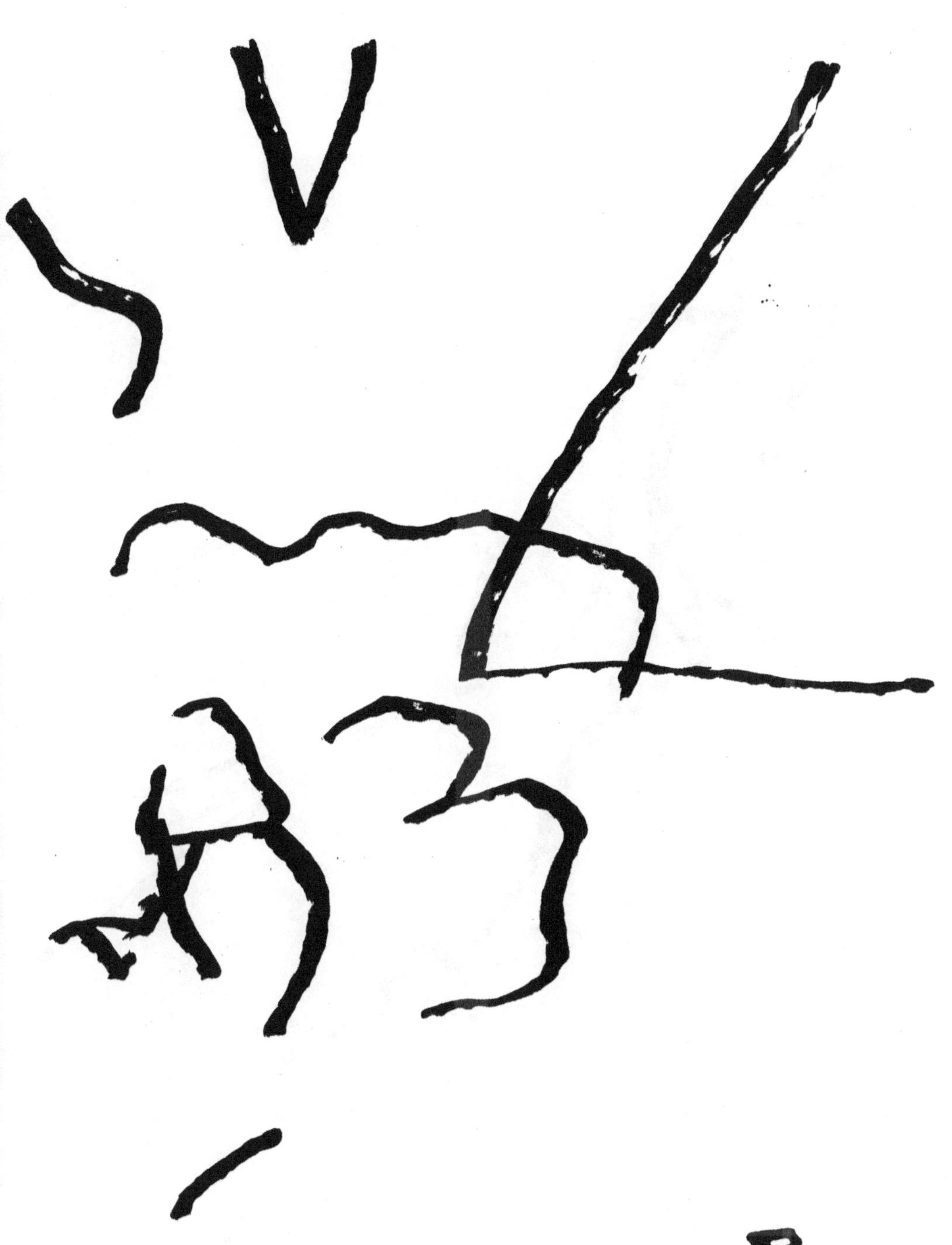

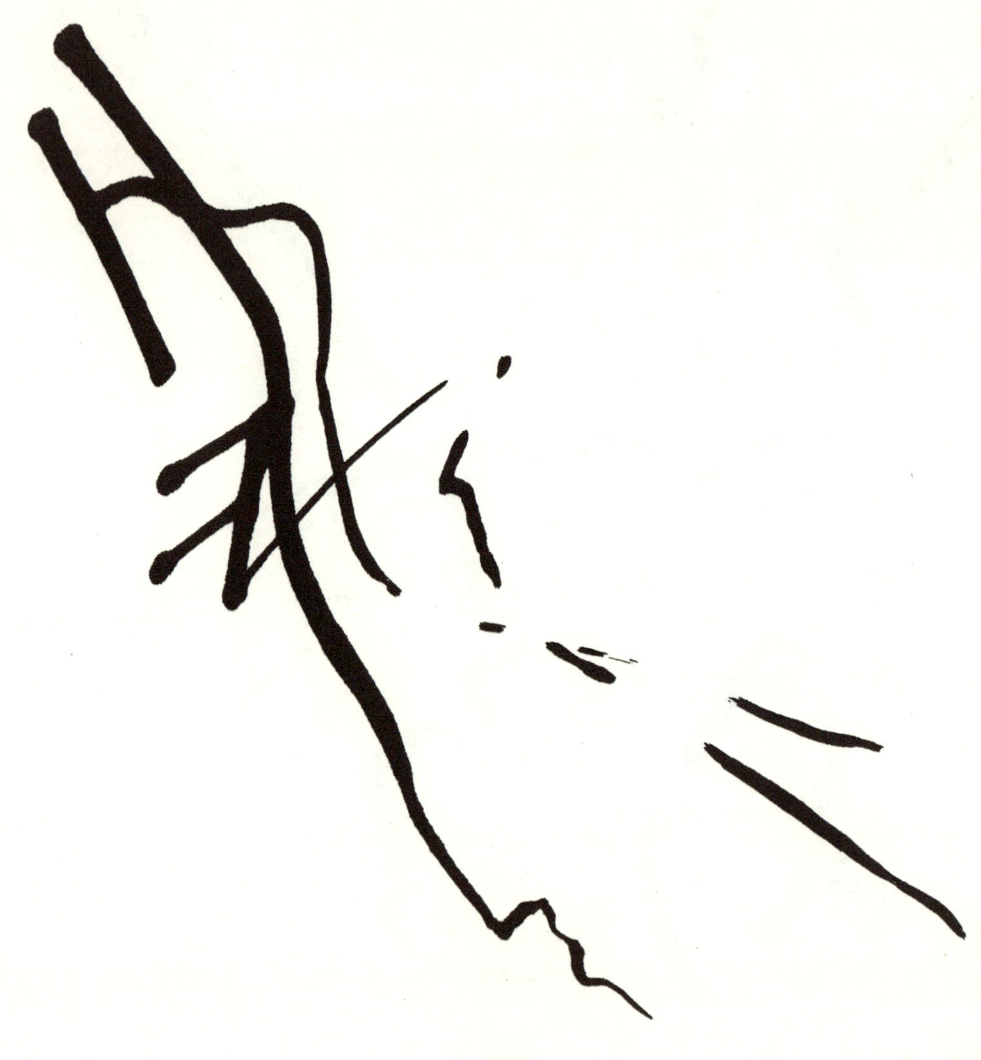

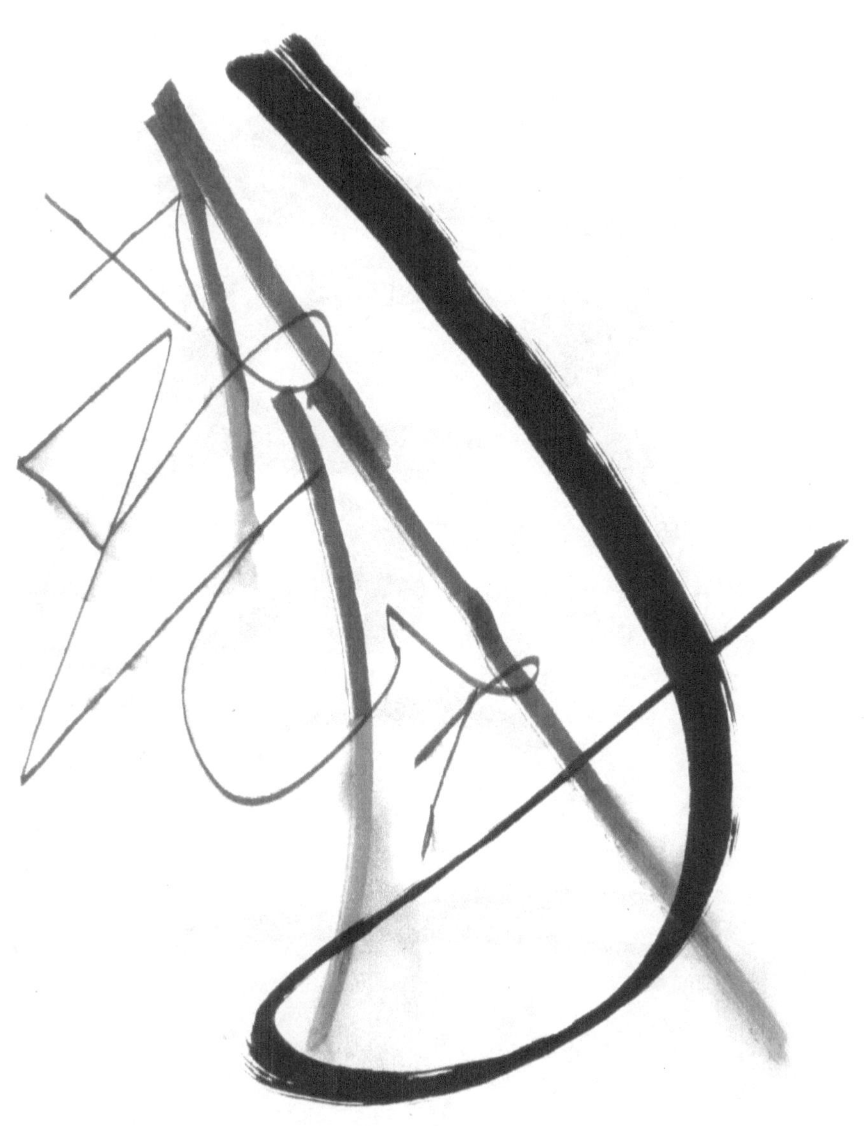

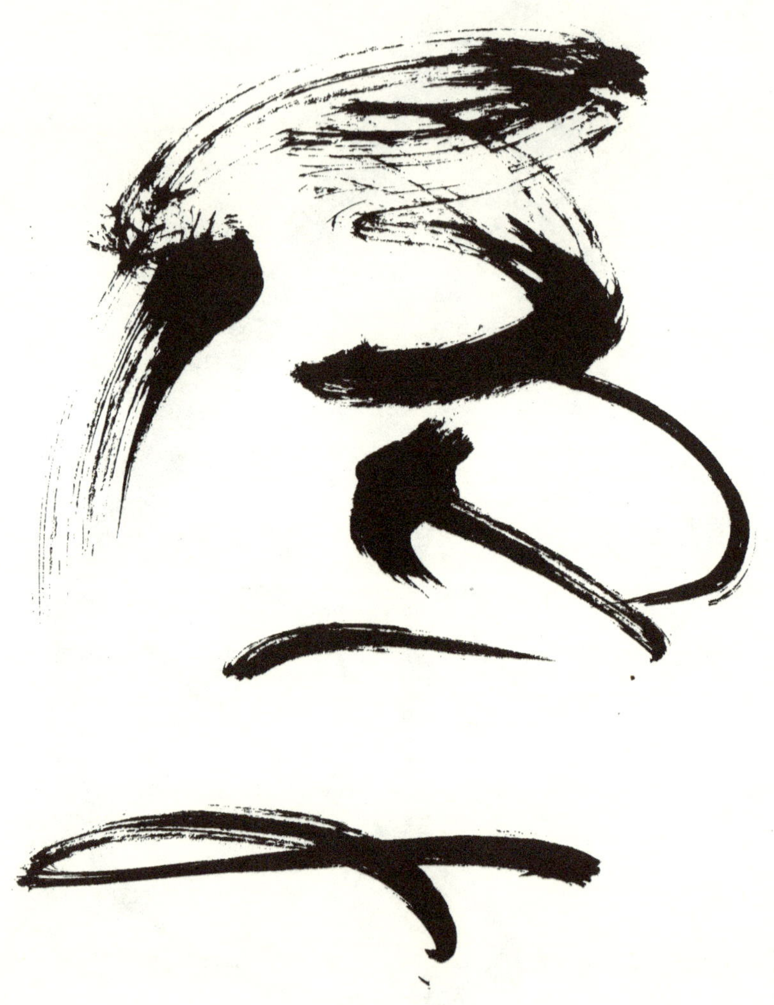

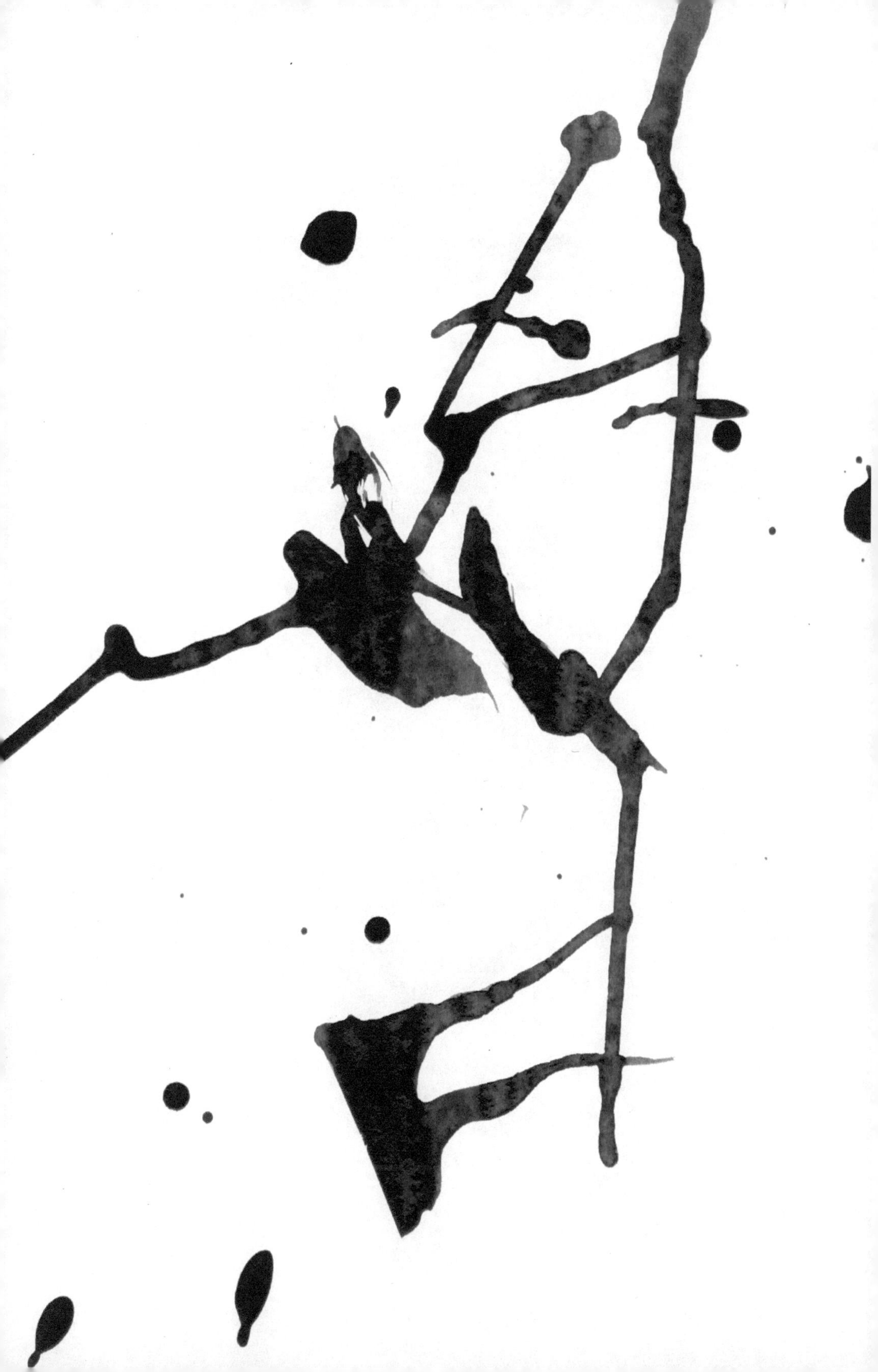

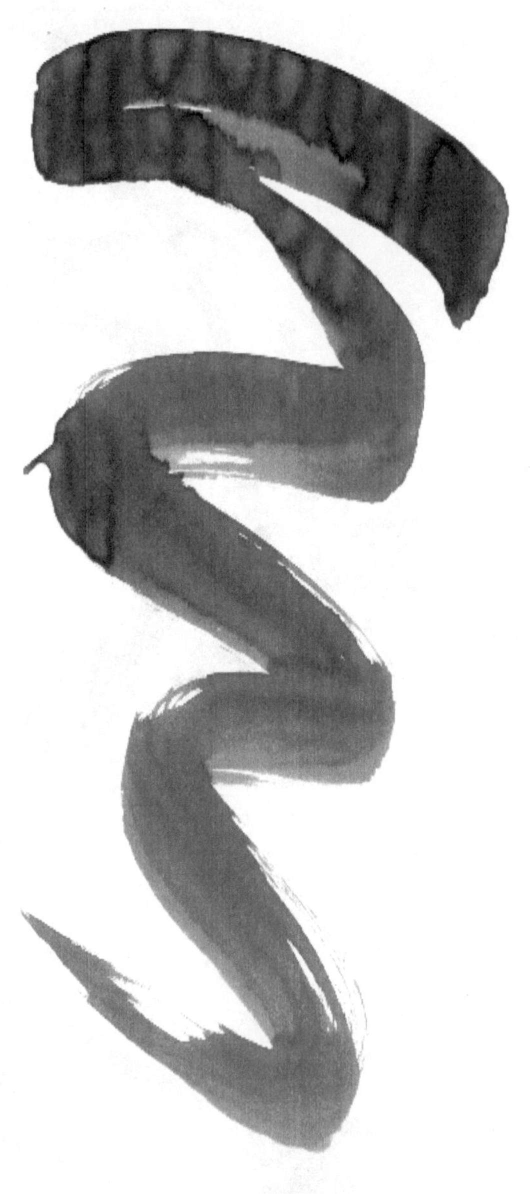

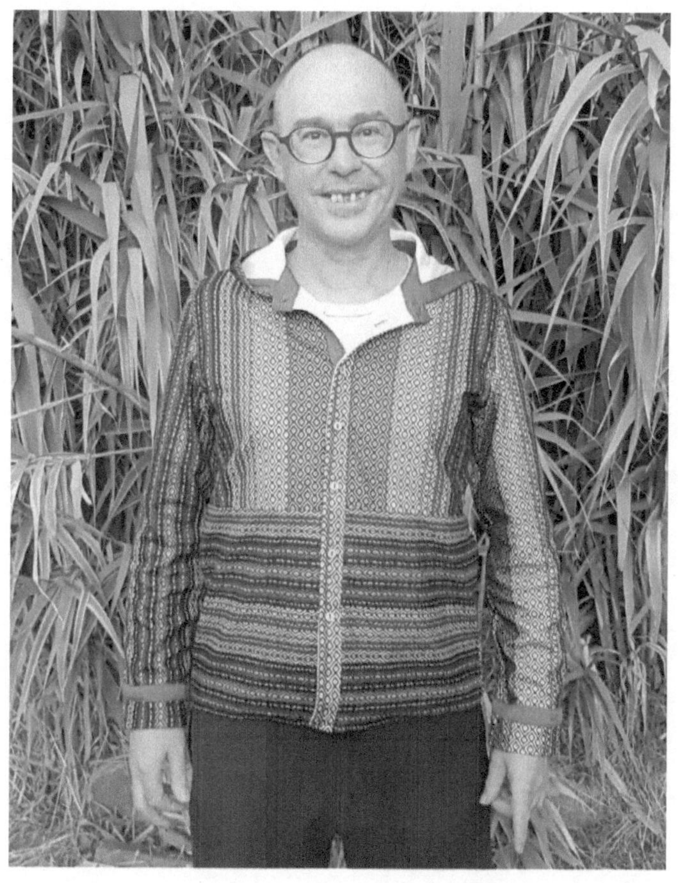

Since the late '90s, Tim Gaze has been active as a poet, writer, publisher, and performer. In particular, he has been very involved in the field of asemic writing, publishing Asemic magazine and setting up the first website, www.asemic.net. His works include the graphic novel *100 Scenes*, glitch poetry collection *noology* and sound poetry album *Shapes*. Recently, he completed a degree in linguistics, and hosts the radio show Sound Poetry etc. Dance music such as batida by the Principe Discos artists gets him going. The Adelaide Hills of Australia, in the traditional lands of the Peramangk people, is his home.

www.ingramcontent.com/pod-product-compliance
Lightning Source LLC
LaVergne TN
LVHW091133080826
845145LV00008B/2135

* 9 7 8 1 7 3 4 8 6 6 2 3 0 *